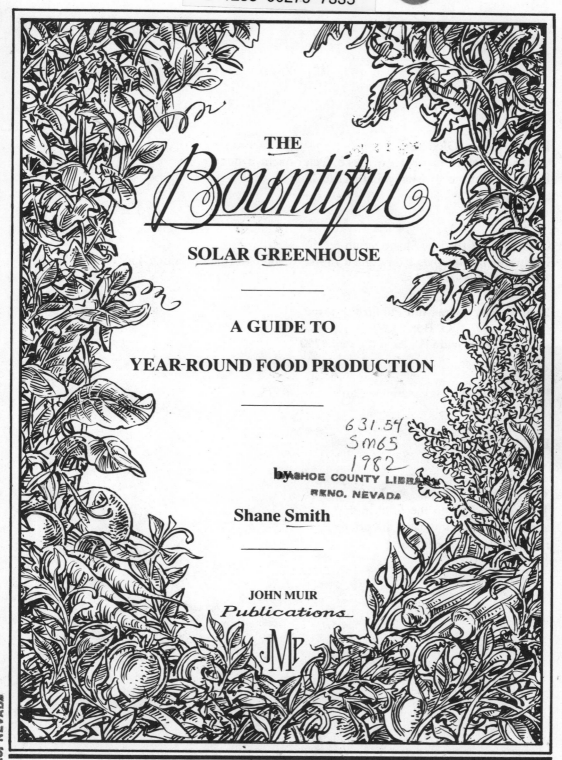

THE

Bountiful

SOLAR GREENHOUSE

A GUIDE TO

YEAR-ROUND FOOD PRODUCTION

by

Shane Smith

JOHN MUIR
Publications

JMP

Illustrations by Glen Strock
Cover, Title and Chapter Drawings by Peter Aschwanden
Herb Illustrations by Michaellallen McGuire

Copyright © 1982 by Shane Smith
Illustrations and Cover Copyright © 1982 by John Muir Publications, Inc.

Published by John Muir Publications, Inc.
              P.O. Box 613
              Santa Fe, New Mexico 87501

Library of Congress Catalogue Card No. 81-85952

ISBN   0-912528-08-7

10   9   8   7   6   5   4   3   2   1
The last number to the right in the
above sequence indicates the print-
ing history of this edition.

CONTENTS

— To my Mother and Father —

Acknowledgements

Writing a book is a hard task. It can cause you to go nuts. Fortunately there were many people who kept me afloat, encouraged, sane, optimistic, laughing, diverted, motivated, entertained, loved and writing. That's how it became real. Thanks to: The Heck-are-we-Tribe, Tom Throgmorton, Douglas Fried, Lyndsie Hunt, Gary Garber, Gale Harms, Mary Lee White, Jimmy Guacamole, Susana Merriam, Mary Wheeler, Katie Sewell, John Brown, Marnie McPhee, Bill Yanda, Portland Sun, the people at The Cheyenne Community Solar Greenhouse and Community Action of Laramie County. Also, my thanks to Paul, Stick, Peter, Glen, Ken, Michaellallen, Ada, Deborah, Lisa, Richard, Eve, Barbara, Joan, Steven at John Muir Publications. You made the potentially arduous task of putting a book together a lot of fun.

INTRODUCTION

I've known Shane Smith for a good while, and a good while is a lot different than a simple while. A good while means that the quality of the while is worth more than the quantity of the while.

The first time I met Shane was in 1978 at Ghost Ranch, a Presbyterian retreat and learning center in Northern New Mexico. For some time before our meeting I'd heard of his work at the Cheyenne Solar Greenhouse. Shane was part of a three person group from Wyoming attending a Solar Sustenance Team training session on the basics of organizing and managing a community solar greenhouse workshop. The Solar Sustenance Team had specified that each of the 25 state groups contain one person with solar design or building skills, one with community organizing or P.R. talents, and one with, at least, some gardening experience. Shane represented the latter for Wyoming and, with him, we got a great deal more than we bargained for.

The three day session was structured to spend roughly an equal amount of time on each discipline: solar design, community relations and greenhouse growing. As is typical at solar events the first two subject areas tended to get "all" the attention at the expense of the last. (After all, what's to know about a tomato . . . right?) Wrong. Shane demanded equal time for vegetables, and got it. If the solar designers went off on a tangent discussing the transmissivity of various types of glazing materials, he'd make sure they were informed about how the light coming through each affected plants. If the community organizers were examining energy imports to keep their towns warm, Shane would rigorously detail the BTUs expended to bring a head of lettuce from a seed in Southern California to a table in Maine.

"This man can make a bunch of radishes sing like the Temptations," I said to myself. The days at Ghost Ranch were packed with the excitement and intensity that only those naive enough to be totally committed to an idea or cause can endure. At night, fortified with frijoles and Cuervo Gold, smaller groups would continue, moving more into the philosophical promises of alternate energy and easily leaping over impossible chasms. Pure starlight will do that to even sane people.

At Ghost Ranch I learned what a storehouse of information and what a great teacher Shane Smith is.

Have you ever seen a truly fine teacher at work? These rare individuals have many attributes but, to me, they always have one thing in common: a sense of humor. The sense of humor only occurs when the teacher has a great deal of confidence in his physical presence and extensive knowledge of the subject matter. When these three elements combine, academic barriers fall, pretension drops and teacher and students alike are open to real learning. The learning occurs partially because the ability to enjoy a good laugh reveals the human foibles present in the academic situation: i.e., "I've got the knowledge and you don't." I don't know whether the ability to convey loads of technical information in a warm and humorous wrapping can be acquired or if it's a gift, but Shane Smith has it. I've probably heard most of the anecdotes in here two or three times but they still give me a good chuckle while they underscore pertinent facts.

I do know that Shane is one of the few lecturers I enjoy hearing over and over for there's always new and important information in what he says. There is an excitement and sense of wonder in the work he's done and it carries through in this writing. It inspires you to do something.

For instance, Shane once had my entire family running through the meadows and woods of Tennessee catching lightning bugs for the Cheyenne greenhouse. I heard him say that the little critters might help control slugs and that he needed some for experiments. I knew that Tennessee, where we were living at the time, had a much higher firefly population than Wyoming. Unfortunately for Shane, the fireflies we found moved into a new home beside my six year old son's bed and never made the trip to Cheyenne on UPS. They did light up our place for a while before we let them go. Evidently, Shane found a more reliable source than the Yandas for his supply. Yet I note that he still places them in the experimental category in this book. Perhaps, he needs more. Send all your . . .

This book is an important volume because it synthesizes three disparate types of greenhouse growing, leading the way to the most important type of greenhouse growing in the future.

Until the advent of the food and heat producing solar greenhouse in the mid-70s, greenhouse examples and technical information could be divided into three main categories. First, the elaborate and ornate structures such as the National Botanical Gardens. The climates in these houses is closely controlled and there you will find tropical plants, and exotic and rare vegetation from all over the world. The primary goals of these facilities are education and research about the plants they contain.

The second category is the commercial greenhouse which bears about as much resemblance to the first type as an apple to an orchid. The first rule in commercial greenhouses, as in any private business, is to produce the largest volume at the lowest possible cost. Commercial greenhouses are subject to the vagaries of the market place (What's in? Yellow lilies or white lilies?), as well as many other unpredictable forces. Lately, their greatest problems have been the high cost of labor and energy. Nowadays most commercial houses grow flowers or serve simply as staging areas for flowers shipped up from Central and South America. Prior to the drastic fuel price increases in the 70s, many greenhouses in the East were growing vegetables for the nearby cities. Today, as Shane explains, the majority of the nation's fresh food gets shipped from California and the South. A vast amount of technical information on growing lettuce, tomatoes and cucumbers in commercial greenhouses is available from the Agricultural Research Service. Unfortunately, very little of it has relevance to the home greenhouse grower as it is geared to mono-crop, climate controlled, chemically sustained growing. Hence, when new greenhouse gardeners seek out commercial greenhouse literature they'll find that tomatoes don't set fruit below 60°F, that they need an electric vibrator to aid in pollination or that white flies will destroy their whole operation overnight. These are all critical concerns to the commercial grower with 5 acres under glass. However, they are noteworthy but secondary concerns to the home greenhouse grower. I was once discussing the difference in priorities between commercial and home greenhouse food growing with one of the most highly respected and accredited commercial authorities in the country. "A commercial grower's idea of the perfect greenhouse tomato," he grinned, " is one that he can throw out the door, stand upon and roll all the way to a Manhattan restaurant."

The last category of existing greenhouse literature is for the hobby greenhouse. These books, and there are hundreds of them, often contain useful information on growing and propagating; but their primary emphasis is on decorative plants, not food. Also, like the two previous categories, most of the literature assumes that large amounts of conventional heating are necessary for a good environment, and that dealing with greenhouse pests is simply a matter of properly applying the right insecticide. (There are some notable exceptions, such as *Organic Gardening Under Glass* by George and Katy Abraham and *Winter Flowers in Greenhouse and Sun Heated Pit* by Kathryn Taylor and Edith Gregg.) Fortunately, the solar greenhouse books which have emerged since 1976 have consistently advised organic methods and low reliance on fossil fuels. However, the main emphasis of these solar books is on greenhouse design.

This superbly useful book is an important synthesis because it combines the most applicable information from these three greenhouse categories and the specific requirements and characteristics of a solar greenhouse. Shane Smith has the training of a professional horticulturist, a commercial grower's concern for space efficiency and low cost, and the knowledge of solar design and its constraints in the greenhouse environment. And Shane puts it together in a form that's warm, friendly and understandable. If you believe that food and energy will become even more critical problems in the later years of this century and into the 21st century, if you believe that people should have more control over their own destinies, and if you're basically an optimist and think that you can do something about it . . . then read on, you've just found an important document.

Dr. Carl Sagan in the book and TV series *Cosmos* has stated, ''Books break the shackles of time, proof that humans can work magic.''

Shane, you've worked a lot of magic here.

Bill Yanda

"The best way to do something is to do it."
—*Jose Villarreal*

PREFACE

Stop for moment, and pull from your memory your earliest thoughts of being in a greenhouse. Imagine being there again. Breathe in . . . the air is rich, humid, fragrant and full of life. It's warm on your face. It's comfortable. Compared to a grey, cold, winter day, the green plants almost glow. Walking into a greenhouse you've entered the tropics.

Greenhouses feel good to almost everyone. It's more than just stimulation of the senses, it goes deeper, further back. The tropics were the womb of human life and the greenhouse is a reminder of our origins. The tropics cradled our earliest developments; there we learned the basics of living on our planet, till tribe by tribe, humans ventured further and further from the tropics. Finally our ancestors were able to survive and flourish in adverse climates.

Here we now live in those adverse climes, protected by heated homes, sustained by frozen dinners and food processors, worried about an energy "shortage." The so-called "shortage" has caused one of the greatest lifestyle changes since World War II; and it hasn't been all bad. It's brought the beginnings of a consciousness change. Families have started riding bicycles together. The all-American backyard inventors have been resurrected; they're turning out solar collectors, food dryers and wind generators. Farmers are producing their own alcohol fuels. In response to the "shortage" and as a positive step to individually do something about meeting it, people learned about solar greenhouses. Word spread fast that solar greenhouses would not only grow food, but also heat your home. So in the barn-raising style of yesteryear, neighbors met at thousands of solar greenhouse construction workshops and built greenhouses together.

But the energy shortage also brought hardships to the economically disadvantaged. The average low income household spends more than 45% of its monthly income on energy in some form, leaving little money for housing, food, clothing and medical expenses. These people include senior citizens on fixed incomes who are often too proud to ask for assistance. And this group also includes many who are locked into the cycle of poverty—impacted by inflation, unemployment, and a sense of hopelessness. I see nothing that offers people more potential for economic independence and a feeling of well-being than the solar greenhouse.

Historically, for the most part, greenhouses have been reserved for the upper classes; but now poor and middle class people can afford to attach a greenhouse-type structure to their homes. I've seen them built of scrap for as little as $30, or fancy as can be for $30,000. The cheap and the expensive ones both produce food and heat. With the price of food and energy skyrocketing, *Organic Gardening and Farming* magazine in 1979 described it not as a case of whether you can afford a solar greenhouse, but whether people can afford *not* to have a solar greenhouse.

One common problem that greenhouse owners encounter is that growing food in the solar greenhouse is different than growing in the outside garden, and in fact, different than the traditionally heated greenhouse. Outside gardening techniques just don't apply inside the solar greenhouse, causing much frustration for their owners.

This book will answer the need for specific food production methods for a solar greenhouse. Because space within the greenhouse is limited, the major approach to greenhouse gardening may be described in one word . . . intensive. That means getting the most food production from the given space. The history of intensive gardening is married to the history of the food-producing greenhouse. Whenever people have made efforts to control the agricultural environment, intensive gardening practices followed to ensure that the control efforts did in fact result in greater productivity.

The history of food producing greenhouses actually had its beginnings in a medical prescription for an emperor, Tiberius Caesar, who ruled between 14 and 37 A.D. He was told by his doctor to eat a fresh cucumber each day, so his workers created a pit in the earth and covered it with a transparent stone such as mica, alabaster or talc. It is also speculated that manure was used in the pit for its heat producing qualities. The fresh cucumbers were supplied.

Although not much was recorded about greenhouse-type structures until the 1600s, it became a common practice to use simple techniques to (try to) control the environment around plants. They included using cloth, straw and fiber mats around and over plants to insulate them from cold nights, thus prolonging their productivity. Then, as glass technology became more accessible in Europe, lantern glass was used to cover plants on cold days and nights, much like our present use of hot caps and cloches.

In England during the 1700s, Samuel Collins wrote a treatise on the culture of cucumbers and melons, suggesting that window pane frames should be used to cover the plants in order to "force production." This same period saw use of oiled paper as a glazing cover over growing beds with the paper supported by a small portable wooden-arched frame that covered long rows of a garden. The paper was used for one season, then discarded. (The use of oiled paper is similar to our present use of plastic films; it might be interesting to work again with oiled paper as a low-cost, homemade glazing.) During the mid 1700s a wider utilization of glass as a roofing material occurred, especially throughout England and Holland. The designs of these greenhouses look amazingly similar to today's solar greenhouses. They had steeply sloped *south-facing* glass roofs, while the northern wall was a massive brick structure that often had a horizontal flue system within the brick for heat.

During the 1800s, as heating and environmental controls were better worked out with the wide use of steam, hot water and venting, the southern orientation for these two-sided glass structures was ignored. This was a step backward, as such structures were built with no particular solar orientation. These 19th century greenhouses, usually owned by royalty and the upper class, often were very elaborate. Inside they grew exotic plants and winter flowers. The lower classes, on the other hand, relied on simpler cold frame structures to extend the growing season. Into the 1900s greenhouse design changed little, with a few exceptions. The introduction of plastic-based glazings had a major impact on greenhouses, and the development of pre-fab quonset-type structures greatly changed the commercial greenhouse industry.

In the early 1970s the concept of a solar greenhouse began to take hold. It was originally developed both as an energy saving structure (as was done at the Brace Research Institute in Canada) and as a vehicle to create a contained, ecologically-balanced food producing system (as the New Alchemy Institute in New England and Jim DeKorne of New Mexico both had been developing). It was Jim DeKorne's book *The Survival Greenhouse,* published in 1975, that spurred the imagination of those who wanted a home-based wintertime producer of fresh vegetables. DeKorne, who dedicated his book to "everyone who has ever been on food stamps'', wanted to show that the pit solar greenhouse could help provide a ''technologically sophisticated life'' on the land.

In late 1976 *The Food and Heat Producing Solar Greenhouse* book by Bill Yanda and Rick Fisher gave the first convincing testimony that an attached solar greenhouse not only could grow food, but also produce excess heat which could be used by the home. Bill, along with his wife, Susan, gave a new impetus to the old barn-raising concept of community construction by organizing hundreds of unique weekend workshops where participants would build an attached solar greenhouse.

The development of the solar greenhouse has arrived at the perfect time, because our agriculture is in a fragile period indeed. Food production is centralized in the southern areas of our country where large-scale factory farming is alive and well. But in the northeast, the meat and vegetables on last night's dinner table all have traveled an average of more than 1,000 miles.

The northeast is representative of the rest of the states north of the sun belt where about 80% of the food is now imported. California alone produces approximately 25% of all table food and 40% of all vegetables consumed in the entire United States. According to some projections, by the year 2020 all that California produces will be required to feed California alone. Agriculture in the U.S., now more than ever, is totally dependent on petroleum fuels for chemical fertilizers, pesticide production, and the processing and transporting of food to our tables. Food prices are tied to the price of petroleum . . . and we know where that's headed. It now takes the equivalent of 1 gallon of gasoline to produce just 1 pound of hamburger. With current agricultural practices there is also much concern about the safety, quality and nutritional value of our food. The environmental impact of these large scale agricultural systems on the quality of our land is also in question. Historically, agriculture is the greatest ecology destoyer that we humans have ever devised—except for maybe nuclear weapons. And now, each year, we are losing about 2.5 million acres of prime farm land to another destroyer of ecologies . . . urban sprawl. With the increasing price of fuel and the loss of prime farm land we can't continue feeding ourselves without paying markedly higher food prices.

Fortunately we live in an exciting time of hope. In agriculture there is a major thrust underway to develop ecologically stable and sustainable food-producing systems. As mentioned in *Crops,* permaculture, which utilizes perennial crops and trees, has great promise in providing our food, fiber and forage in an ecologically balanced way. Biological pest control, which employs beneficial insects to control harmful ones, is already more economical and more effective than spraying synthetic poisons on an increasing number of pests. Soil conservation practices are being rediscovered. The ''system'' is approaching the realization that ecological and economic goals need not conflict, but there's still a long way to go. Correcting our fragile, intricate food system can't wait. We must begin dealing with it ourselves . . . now, at home. What is the potential here? Well, in 1944 more than 40% of our fresh vegetables were produced by home ''victory'' gardens. Now, for the first time we are capable of producing food *year round* in solar greenhouses. In these greenhouses (with proper management) we can produce ¼ to ⅓ of a pound of food per square foot of growing space per month. That's not to mention the other major benefit of a solar greenhouse . . . free heat.

Yes, it takes time and energy to have a year-round garden. But a few hours per week need not be considered work; rather, it may be experienced as a relaxing pleasure. Judging by the fact that the average American watches more than 2 hours of TV every day, it may be a welcome alternative.

I wrote this book in response to the many people who have found greenhouse gardening frustrating because it produced little food. Their main problem, as previously mentioned, was treating the solar greenhouse garden like an outside garden. It's a mistake that continually compounds itself. As the horticulturist and director of a 5,000 sq. ft. greenhouse in Cheyenne, Wyoming, I've been able to test different horticultural practices and compare the results.* The opportunity for intensive experimentation and observation would not have been possible in the confines of a smaller greenhouse. I have also applied these same garden techniques in many home greenhouses across the country for many years. Throughout the book there are references to help readers take into account their particular outside climate and its effects on their inside greenhouse food production. This book is primarily the result of experience, not speculation. Gardening is a science *and* an art; people are always developing different ways to get the same good results. The advice presented here is what I have found to work best. But because all greenhouses are different, I urge you to develop your own techniques and record-keeping systems. This should include temperatures, dates of planting, different varieties you have tried, and the results and feelings you have about them. This is essential to fine tune your operation to make it efficient for *your* unique situation.

Solar greenhouse horticulture is new and there's still much to learn and apply. *You* are a pioneer, so don't be afraid to try new things. But also benefit from the experience I'm presenting here and from the experience of other avid gardeners.

The solar greenhouse will change your life. It has the power to feed you, warm you, shelter you, make you independent, and most importantly, make you feel good. It will bring out your love, attention, creativity and patience. For now let's keep it simple—just have fun.

—*Shane Smith*
Somewhere in the Rocky Mountains, 1982

*(For more information on the Cheyenne Community Solar Greenhouse see the *Epilogue.*)

The Bountiful
Solar Greenhouse

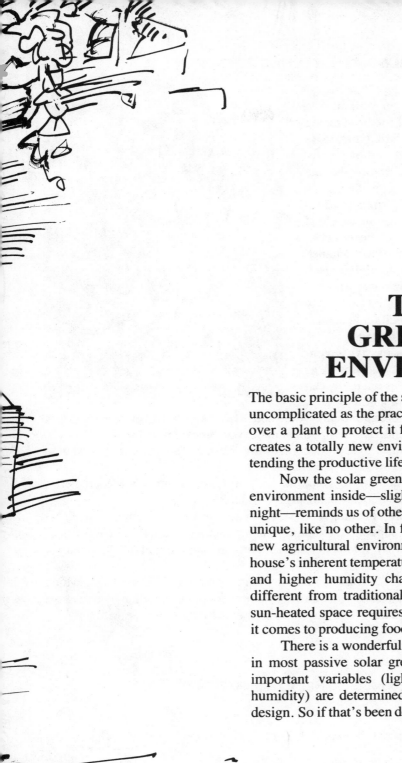

1

THE SOLAR GREENHOUSE ENVIRONMENT

The basic principle of the solar greenhouse is as old and uncomplicated as the practice of placing a glass lantern over a plant to protect it from the elements. The glass creates a totally new environment within its walls, extending the productive life of the plant.

Now the solar greenhouse is coming of age. The environment inside—slightly tropical, humid, cool at night—reminds us of other environments, but it's really unique, like no other. In fact, historically it is a totally new agricultural environment. With the solar greenhouse's inherent temperature savings, lower light levels and higher humidity characteristics, it is even very different from traditional greenhouses. As such, this sun-heated space requires special considerations when it comes to producing food.

There is a wonderful autonomous simplicity found in most passive solar greenhouses. In fact, the most important variables (light levels, temperature, and humidity) are determined by the building's structural design. So if that's been done well, all that's needed is a

certain amount of fine tuning on your part to make it an effective year round food-producing unit. Compare this to a standard greenhouse which is a glass house supplemented by a complicated array of heaters, lights, carbon dioxide generators, automatic misters, and other automated machines to create the desired environment. Despite the outside goings-on of cloud cover, temperature swings, etc., the environment in a conventional greenhouse is maintained unchanged. I personally find a special connection to the earth in a solar greenhouse, which *is affected* by the outside elements on an hourly basis. Each cloud, storm, hot spell, cold spell is part of the solar greenhouse environment.

Though the structure of a passive greenhouse determines much of what happens in it, there are still many things you, as operator, can do to make the physical environment most supportive of the biological elements that produce your food. Generally, however, you have less control over a passive solar greenhouse environment than over a conventional structure.

If you're interested in abundant food production in your protected environment—and who isn't?—you need to be aware of two kinds of plant management:

Biological management—helping to guide all life forms in the greenhouse (bacteria, fungi, insects, plants, etc.) to interact harmoniously to produce food.

Environmental management—creating a physical environment (temperature, soil, light, humidity, bed design, etc.) that supports maximum food production within the capabilities of your greenhouse. In this chapter we'll look at what's environmentally required by a plant for best production.

The basis for plant growth is the conversion of light into sugars—photosynthesis—which creates plant growth energy. But it takes a lot more than simply the plant and some light to make photosynthesis possible. Here's a list of the major requirements for photosynthesis:

1. Light
2. Carbon dioxide (CO_2)
3. Temperature (generally between $32°F$ ($0°C$) and $100°F$ ($38°C$).
4. Water

Note: if the level of any one of these environmental elements is less than optimum, the whole growing process may be slowed.

It is becoming quite common for architects to design solar greenhouses with only vertical or south facing glazing and no overhead or roof glazing. This makes a nice sunroom, but not a very good food producing sunroom. Why? Although this design is a good winter heater, it doesn't allow in enough light for year-round vegetable growth. This is especially true as the sun attains a higher angle in late spring, summer, and early fall. During this time most of the greenhouse floor is shaded. Continual shade means rough times for vegetable plants. However, greenhouses without roof glazing do permit adequate light for a few months on either side of the winter solstice. What to do if you're stuck with a non-glazed roof? Well, you can add skylights or glazing. If not, you're stuck with poor overall food yields. Still, it'll make a great sunspace to grow houseplants which don't require as much light as do vegetables. Even if you are not planning intensive vegetable production, it's nice to have the option. Food may soon be quite expensive, so I recommend installing the roof glazing.

Light

Simply put, when light hits the surface of the leaf, the energy of the sunlight combines with carbon dioxide (CO_2) in the air and water from the soil. By means of photosynthesis, these elements are converted into oxygen and sugar. The oxygen is given off into the air as a component of water vapor, while the sugar is oxidized (burned) in the plant to provide all the energy it needs for growth. The burning of the sugar in the plant, known as respiration, is the major plant activity at night.

Photosynthesis (making plant energy) and respiration (using energy) are almost opposites of each other . . . and they fit together so well.

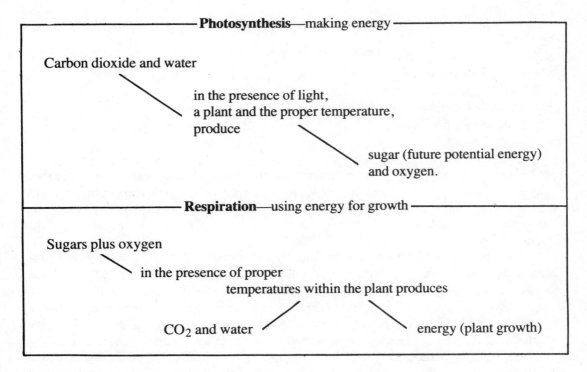

Photosynthesis—making energy

Carbon dioxide and water

in the presence of light,
a plant and the proper temperature,
produce

sugar (future potential energy)
and oxygen.

Respiration—using energy for growth

Sugars plus oxygen

in the presence of proper
temperatures within the plant produces

CO_2 and water

energy (plant growth)

Measuring Light in the Greenhouse

Plants require certain minimal quantities of light for proper growth. These quantities are commonly measured in foot-candles (fc). A foot-candle is a unit of illumination equal to the direct illumination on a surface one foot from a standardized source called an international candle. I know it's an odd definition, but it becomes easier to understand once you work with it. The main thing here is being sure your plants get enough light. Here's a rough method to figure foot candles in the greenhouse:

1. Find a 35 mm camera with a built-in light meter.
2. Set ASA at 200.
3. Set shutter speed at 1/125 of a second.
4. Aim camera at light source.
5. Dial f-stop to proper photo exposure.
6. If f-stop reads: then the amount of light is:

One foot candle

f-stop	Foot-candles (fc)
2.8	32
4	64
5.6	125
8	250
15	1000
22	2000

Vegetables need at least 1000 fc for proper growth. Usually house plants need much less.

Foot Candle Values

Light Source	Foot-candles (approximate)
Starlight	.00011
Moonlight	.02
Overcast daylight	1,000.00
Direct sun	10,000.00

Maximum photosynthesis occurs around 2300 fc for tall vegetables and 1300 fc for short bushy ones. Still, you can get acceptable vegetable growth in less than optimum light, especially when you alter other aspects of the environment. For example, you can increase the CO_2 in the atmosphere, raise a low temperature to at least 70°F (21°C), or space the plants closer together (leafy crops only).

Crops compete for light if planted too closely and nobody wants a fight in the greenhouse. When plants are crowding each other they will grow slowly; the leaves will yellow, become elongated and spindly; and the plants won't produce much food. Even when plants are not competing for space they can be short on light. Often this is due to the greenhouse design. A greenhouse with little or no glazing on the roof creates low light problems in the late spring and summer. Dark interior surfaces (except for thermal mass/storage), rather than reflecting light, can steal it from the plants. Also, shading causes low light problems. Tall plants especially will benefit from higher light intensities. For example, when you grow a bed of vining tomatoes all 6' high, you'll have a dense canopy of leaves 6'deep. It would require more than 1000 fc to penetrate the canopy to maintain proper growth because the leaves at the center would be receiving far less than the original 1000 fc. For these dense leaf canopy situations, the plants could use 2000 fc or more for optimum growth and general contentment.

Symptoms of Low Light Conditions

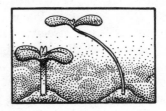

1. Elongation of stems
2. Slow growth
3. Spindly-like growth
4. Yellowing of lower leaves
5. Growth of softer, often larger leaves
6. Plants bend drastically toward light source (this is called ''phototropism'')

Types of Glazing

The history of greenhouse glazings began with thin sheets of mica, alabaster and talc laid over a hole in the earth. Before glass technology became well developed, early small coldframe season extenders utilized oil paper, much in the same way we use polyethylene today.

Now we have a wide array of choices, including glass, vinyls, fiberglass, polycarbonates, acrylics and polyethylenes. They vary in cost, ease of application and solar performance. It can be very confusing and researchers are developing additional ''new, improved'' glazings all the time. Just remember, before you buy any plastic type of glazing material, be sure it's made for use in sunlight. Many plastics break down rapidly when exposed to the sun's ultraviolet light, eventually limiting the amount of light coming into the greenhouse. Also, always look at the life expectancy guarantees before you buy. For good explanations of the many glazings and their physical differences, consult a good solar greenhouse design and construction book *before* you make your selection.

Ultraviolet Light

Light is composed of many components, illustrated on the visual level by a rainbow. Invisible to our eyes is another spectrum, and ultraviolet is an important part of it. Just about every plastic or glass glazing absorbs most of the ultraviolet rays in sunlight. This causes plastics to degrade or yellow. Researchers aren't sure to what extent ultraviolet light affects plants beneficially, but they do know that ultraviolet kills many microbial organisms. Leaf diseases caused by these organisms therefore have an easier time living in a greenhouse where the ultraviolet light is absorbed by the glazing. There is no available proof of this, but when selecting crop varieties, it might pay to look for those with resistance to leaf diseases such as powdery mildew. (See *Pests and Diseases* and *Selecting Solar Greenhouse Crops and Varieties*.)

Because greenhouse glazings absorb most of the ultraviolet light from the sun, don't expect to get a glowing bronze tan while working in a greenhouse. It's ultraviolet light that produces tans. Fiberglass, however, does let in a small amount of ultraviolet radiation and may allow mild tanning. I've noticed that people who work in any greenhouse seem to have more color in their face (though not a dark tan) and a healthier, happier look: is it the glazing or the lifestyle?

Glazing and Plant Growth

Let's look at how glazings affect plant growth. According to Colorado State University research, most glazings developed for greenhouses allow satisfactory growth. A marked difference, however, has been noted between clear glazings such as glass and those that are translucent such as fiberglass. Plants grow better under glazing materials that are **not** visibly clear. Don't get confused; it seems that translucent materials let in about as much total light as clear materials, but they diffuse the light beam as it passes through. The beam scatters over a broader area, resulting in more **even** light without sharp shadows. Because the light is being scattered, plant leaves not in the direct path of the sun receive increased lighting. Under clear glazings, any leaf not in the direct path of the sun is in a darker shadow and receives substantially less light, which means less plant growth. The diffused light is also helpful for thermal mass temperature gain as it tends to moderate steep rises and falls of air temperature. Some translucent materials such as fiberglass also tend to catch more light at steeper angles (early morning and late afternoon) than do other glazings.

Fiberglass is about the best diffuser of light; polyethylene, polycarbonates, acrylics and glass follow roughly in that order. This is not to say that fiberglass is the best compared to glass—just that it diffuses light more, which improves plant growth. The diffusion factor is only one consideration when comparing glazings. There are many other factors to consider such as cost, durability and aesthetics.

Photoperiodism

The length of time that light strikes the plant also affects its growth. This response to the length of the day or night is called *photoperiodism*. The amount of light-time can change how plants grow, when they flower and fruit, and whether or not seeds germinate or cuttings develop roots.

Usually the term photoperiod is applied to the flowering/fruiting response. In many garden books plants are listed as either long-day plants (which flower when days are long), short-day plants (which flower when days are short) and day-neutral plants (which aren't affected by the length of light or dark periods). Day-neutral plants respond to other factors such as levels of maturity and cold or warm temperatures.

Scientists have found that it is not the length of the day that triggers this photoperiod response, but the length of *uninterrupted darkness*. A long-night (or short-day) plant, for example, can be thrown off schedule if the night period is interrupted by light: this would simulate a short-night (long-day) situation. It sounds confusing, but fortunately, photoperiodism need only be taken into account when growing ornamental crops and a limited number of food crops. Most onion varieties sold in the temperate regions will bulb only with short nights (long days), though varieties have been developed for areas in the deep South with warmer winters which bulb with longer nights (shorter days). Also, strawberries are dependent on day length and generally won't produce during the winter when they are naturally dormant. A few day-neutral strawberries have been developed, though, which aren't affected by day length. These are: Aptos, Hecker and Brighton.

But fortunately, most food production is a matter of maturity response. For example, when a tomato plant grows for a certain period of time, it flowers and fruits regardless of the length of day or night.

Supplemental Lighting

Most vegetables require at least 8 hours of light per day to produce satisfactorily. If you live in a northern area with very short winter days, or if you live in a very cloudy area, supplemental lighting will increase your yields and will be worth your money.

But at what point is supplemental lighting for food production a worthwhile investment? It's a tough one to answer. Why? Because it has everything to do with the price of food and electricity—both prices varying greatly from region to region and changing almost daily . . . usually upwards. So you'll have to do a little investigation on your own.

There are a number of possible types of supplemental lighting. Most ordinary lamps can be used to grow plants, but there are differences in set-up, cost and resulting quantity of food.

Light is composed of many wavelengths that are used by plants with differing levels of efficiency. For example, scientists have found that wavelengths in red and blue spectrums are used most in the photosynthesis process, whereas plants use little green light because that's the color that leaves reflect.

Different lamps emit different colors or wavelengths. Most common incandescent bulbs emit more red wavelengths, though some incandescents are designed to give off a more blue wavelength and are called (and sold as) plant lights. Fluorescent tube lights contain special phosphors that give off energy in certan wavelengths. Most common fluorescent tubes (those

known as cool-white) emit more waves in the blue range. Many companies have developed specially "tuned" lamps to emit more blue and red wavelengths to cater to plants. These fluorescent grow lights usually cost *much* more than the standard cool-white lamps. Critical experiments have shown that maximum growth of most plants under cool-white fluorescent lights is equivalent to or better than that obtained under most of the higher priced, specially designed fluorescent grow lamps. So save yourself some money. Warm-white fluorescent mixed with cool-white is a good combination for seedling germination.

An important reminder to those who plan to grow plants under fluorescent lights: for best growth, be sure to hang the lamps very close (2'') from the top leaves and raise the lamps as the plants grow, maintaining the same distance. This is the only way to get the required 1000 fc that vegetables need. Also, always use reflectors for any supplemental lighting. You can do this simply by glueing aluminum foil onto cardboard and putting it behind and on either side of the light. For tall vegetables with a thick leaf canopy, the fluorescent lights may not be acceptable because the light doesn't penetrate very deeply. Here you may have to turn to high or low pressure sodium lamps mentioned in the following chart. For companies that supply sodium lamps, see the list at the end of this chapter.

In general, supplemental lighting is not worth the extra cost unless you live in a very low light area or desire to grow an abundance of warm season crops in the dead of winter. See *Greenhouse Food Crop Scheduling*.

GREENHOUSE LIGHTING
——— Supplemental to Natural Light ———

Type	Lamp Life (1000s of hours)	Appx. Cost/ Sq. Foot	Comments
Fluorescent			
Cool White	8-10	$3.50	Good overall growth—place 2″ above plant. Flowering may be slow especially if used as sole source of light.
Warm White	8-10	$5.00	Good for photoperiodism flowering response.
Improved Fluorescents			
Grow Lux	4-5	$5.00-$9.00	Expensive, but not much better, if any, response than the cheaper cool white lamps. Slightly better flowering response.
Agrolite	5-6	$5.00-$6.00	Same as above.
Vitalite	8-10	$5.00-$7.00	Same as above.
Incandescents			
Common	1-3	$2.00	Gives off heat. Good flowering response. Place 8″ above plant. Some stem elongation, pale growth noted.
Discharge Lamps			
Mercury Vapor	15-20	$25.00-$40.00	Poor flowering response. Spindly growth. Place 3″ above plant for every 400 watts.
High Pressure Sodium	15-20	$30.00-$45.00	Similar to improved fluorescents. Nice plant development. Expensive but lasts longer and illuminates much more area per light.
Low Pressure Sodium	12-18	$30.00-$40.00	Similar to high pressure sodium. Not as good for lettuce. 185 watts L.P. Sodium is equal to a 400 watt mercury vapor lamp due to better light efficiency.

Based on *"A Guide to the Use of Lights for Growing Plants"* By H.M. Cathey and L.E. Campbell, Beltsville Agricultural Research Center.

Distance from Lamps (inches)	Two Lamps (used 200 hours)	Four Lamps Mounted 2″ Apart	
		(used 200 hours)	(new lamps)
	fc	fc	fc
1	1,100	1,600	1,800
2	860	1,400	1,600
3	680	1,300	1,400
4	570	1,100	1,300
5	500	940	1,150
6	420	820	1,000
7	360	720	900
8	330	660	830
9	300	600	780
10	280	560	720
11	260	510	660
12	240	480	600
18	130	320	420
24	100	190	260

Illumination from standard cool-white fluorescent lamp

Source: United States Department of Agriculture *Handbook for the Home,* Yearbook of Agriculture, 1973.

Increasing Reflective Surfaces

In the solar greenhouse sufficient light may be lacking, especially toward the west and east walls (unless they've been glazed). To make matters worse, the northern part of the greenhouse is low on light during the summer when the sun angle gets high. As most solar greenhouse construction books explain, all opaque walls should be painted white or have a reflective surface. I prefer semi-gloss white because it's a little more reflective. White reflects more total foot candles than aluminized metal reflectors, though specular reflectors such as aluminum foil are acceptable. Although it is rare, they have been known to cause hot spots. This happens when the aluminum concentrates the sunlight onto a leaf, causing occasional burning. So *think white!*

To get maximum light to your plants, in addition to having white walls and roof, it's advisable to paint everything else in your greenhouse white—except, of course, thermal mass storage and plants or soil. This white paint trip would include sides of raised beds, trellising and any parts of thermal mass containers that don't receive direct sun but do receive any amount of indirect light. (Don't get carried away and paint your seedlings or gardening partner!) You might consider using light colored mulch in the darker areas of the greenhouse and light colored rock on your floors. The New Alchemy Institute placed white rock outside on the ground directly in front of the south glazing to increase light reflection into the greenhouse. This is a good idea for cloudy areas of the country.

I've had a problem with slow summer growth in the area toward my north greenhouse wall when the sun angle shadow is at its high point in June. I solved much of this summer light problem by hanging a white curtain over the black barrels that are placed against the north wall. Instead of the light being absorbed by the black barrels, it was reflected to plants. It increased plant growth adjacent to the north wall and kept the water barrels cooler—helpful for summer cooling. In late September when the light started to strike my north wall and the nights began to get cooler, I removed the white curtain in order to allow heat to collect in the water barrels again.

(See *Crop Layout* to get ideas on crop placement in low light areas.)

Carbon Dioxide (CO_2)

As I mentioned earlier, carbon dioxide in the air is essential to photosynthesis. The normal level of cabon dioxide in the air is about 300 parts per million (PPM), or three hundredths of one percent of the air we breathe. Because about 50 percent of a plant is carbon (and all of that must come from the air), you can see that plants have quite an appetite for CO_2. Much of the CO_2 normally occurring in the air comes from the burning of fossil fuels and the decomposition of organic matter, as well as from animal forms ranging from bacteria to human beings. It's partially what you're breathing out of your lungs as part of the respiration process. Besides the fact that plants always love your kind words and attention, they also like you for your body—well, at least for your high CO_2 breath.

When CO_2 is in short supply, plant growth slows. But when the supply of CO_2 increases up to and beyond 300 PPM, up to a certain point plant growth (including food yield) increases as well.

Plants use so much of the CO_2 in the air that in sealed environments like a greenhouse, the level of CO_2 may be depleted from 300 PPM to 100 PPM by noon. This can easily slow plant growth by 60 percent—not a pleasant thought. This phenomenon occurs only in winter greenhouses when there is no outside ventilation and the structure is sealed to the outside. CO_2 depletion is less in attached greenhouses where there are people, gas stoves and pets, all producing extra CO_2. Depletion is also less in greenhouses with soils high in organic matter, due to the billions of microbes breathing in that rich, black, pulsing-with-life, humus-laden soil. But depletion may still occur because solar greenhouses are very tight structures. It is almost impossible to *see* a CO_2 deficiency because the only symptom is slower growth. You won't see any telltale signs in the crop. Equipment to measure CO_2 is very expensive and hard to obtain.

CO_2 Enhancement: Mulching and Other Methods

Early greenhouse owners in Europe quickly discovered that placing a thick mulch composed of manure, peat moss, sawdust and straw around plants increased crop production. They didn't understand why. Around the early 1900s, scientific experiments proved that CO_2 was created during the decomposition of fertilizer and mulch. It was not until the later 1950s and early 1960s, however, that researchers worked with levels higher than the normal ambient (300 PPM) amounts. Enhancing CO_2 levels from a depleted greenhouse atmosphere of 100 PPM all the way to 1500 PPM resulted in significant yield increases. Since the 1960s many commercial greenhouse growers have been enhancing the CO_2 level in winter greenhouses to 1200-1500 PPM, with a yield increase of 10-30 percent. It's like fertilizing the plants through the air. It is thought that anything above 2000 PPM is wasted effort and continuous exposure to levels about 5000 PPM may be a problem to human health.

Commercial growers commonly add CO_2 from storage tanks of liquid CO_2 held under pressure, which becomes a gas when released into the air. Another common commercial method of increasing CO_2 is to burn fossil fuels such as kerosene, propane or natural gas in CO_2 generators designed specifically for this use. In Europe, many greenhouses extract CO_2 gasses from their boiler exhausts. This requires special equipment because much of fossil fuel exhaust, such as carbon monoxide, sulfer and fluorides, is poisonous to plants and humans.

Because most of us can't afford a CO_2 generator or the fuel to run one, we must look at alternatives. With the price of fuel so high, I'm sure commercial growers will soon be doing the same.

The alternatives include:

1. Decomposing organic matter (compost).
2. Raising animals in the greenhouse.
3. Burning homemade ethanol.
4. Using dry ice (frozen carbon dioxide).

Dry ice is rather troublesome and still somewhat expensive (not to mention a bit cold). Ethanol can be dangerous, being flammable, and it's especially unsafe because greenhouse structures are quite flammable. And raising animals in a greenhouse can cause offensive odors and added trouble. If cages or pens aren't kept clean, manures emit ammonia gas which, in high concentration, may cause some damage to plants.

So what about organic matter? Well, what was good for our grandparents is good for us. A compost mixture used as a thick mulch not only produces CO_2, but also heat. Compost piles can easily run at over 100° F (38° C), which can definitely help the winter greenhouse. Just one 4' x 4' compost bin at The New Alchemy Institute in Woods Hole, Massachusetts, raised the temperature of their greenhouse 2.5° F (1.4° C) and increased the CO_2 in the air by as much as 650 PPM. The Ecotope Group found that an attached, insulated compost bin with a vent system to carry air from the compost into the greenhouse raised the CO_2 levels to as high as 2000 PPM in their 32' x 12' parabolic greenhouse. Jim DeKorne, a noted solar greenhouse pioneer and author, estimates an increase up to 800 PPM. In the DeKorne greenhouse, however, this increase was due not just to compost, but also from rabbits he raised under his hydroponic beds. (For details, see *The Survival Greenhouse* by James DeKorne.) Danish growers have achieved levels of up to 5000 PPM just with the addition of a manure, peat and straw mulch, applied at a rate of 200 tons per acre.

One problem with using compost or mulch to supplement CO_2 levels in winter is that it's only a temporary solution. High levels of CO_2 will probably last 6 weeks at best. At that point, the compost must be remade or the mulch reapplied to maintain high CO_2 enrichment levels.

Because solar greenhouses are very tight structures, the possibility of CO_2 deficiencies are common. It is almost impossible to *see* a CO_2 deficiency because the only symptom is slower growth. You won't see any telltale signs in the crop. Equipment to measure CO_2 is very expensive and hard to obtain.

I recommend use of an organic mulch to bring CO_2 levels to at least 1000 PPM—if not more. This enhanced level will help compensate for lower light and lower temperatures. It has the potential of increasing yields by as much as 20 percent. You can increase the level of CO_2 above 300 PPM (the natural outside level) only when your greenhouse is tightly sealed to the outside. Please don't hesitate to ventilate to the outside if you are overheating inside. But remember, when you open up to the outside, your CO_2 level will be the same as outside, 300 PPM. When you seal back up for a cold day, the mulch will help raise CO_2 levels again. To put it simply, it would be hard to find any other single low-cost thing you could do to make such a difference in food yield.

Here's a recipe for CO_2 **Mulch Mousse**:

Ingredients

(Any combination from the two lists)

Carbonaceous	Green
straw	kitchen wastes
sawdust (avoid cedar and redwood)	green garden wastes
brown grass clippings	manures (add less the fresher it is)
brown or tan plant refuse	hair
brown or tan leaves	green grass clippings
any light tan organic matter	any green organic matter

1. Combine by volume, 1 part carbonaceous materials with 1 part green materials (see above ingredients). Both of these materials first should be ground or chopped into small pieces.

2. Mix thoroughly.

3. Lay down mixture as a mulch on all soil surface around plants. Mulch should be 3''-4'' deep.

4. Stir up mulch every 3 weeks to get top layer (that dries out) worked back under.

5. Add an extra 2'' of mulch every 2 months or whenever the previous mixture breaks down and darkens into totally decomposed compost.

Note: One drawback to the use of any mulch is that it can promote certain pests. Slugs, sowbugs and pillbugs just love to romp in mulches and unfortunately they love to eat leaves, stems and roots. If they are a problem in your greenhouse, rather than using your mulch materials as a mulch, thoroughly incorporate it into the soil so that it will degrade and produce CO_2. For control of these pests see *Pests and Diseases* .

CO_2 Ventilation

The amount of carbon dioxide supplied to the plant from the atmosphere depends upon the level of CO_2 at the leaf surface; or even more precisely, the CO_2 level at the cell surface on the leaf. In still air, a leaf can draw out most of the CO_2 at the cell surface, thus creating an envelope of CO_2 deficiency around the leaf. When there is no turbulence, CO_2 replenishment is slow around this microscopic area. But turbulent air around the leaf disperses this envelope of low CO_2 concentration, replenishing the air adjacent to the leaf with an ample supply of CO_2. Research in the Netherlands by P. Gaastra in 1963 showed the rate of photosynthesis can be increased by 40 percent with no change in atmospheric CO_2 if the wind velocity increases from 10 to 100 centimeters per second.
So it's important to keep the air in your greenhouse constantly moving around during the day (whether or not you are trying to enrich the carbon dioxide). A good idea is to get a small fan to stir up the air, even if your greenhouse is sealed to the outside. This also helps keep pests and diseases down. If you have a fan that blows warm air into your house from the greenhouse, this may be enough. You'll know if the air feels stagnant.

Humidity

Did you know that all plants have small openings in their leaves? Through these openings gases such as CO_2 and oxygen pass. Also, because plants don't utilize all the water they take up, a large amount of water vapor comes out through these openings. This water vapor, along with the vapor already in the air, causes high levels of humidity. "Relative humidity" (RH) is the term most often used to quantify the invisible water vapor in the air. It is expressed as a percentage of the maximum moisture the air can hold at a given temperature and pressure. More simply, how wet is the air? Relative humidity can be measured by a hygrometer, a relatively inexpensive instrument. By the way, as the temperature rises, the air will hold more water per unit of air than it can at a lower temperature. If the air gets saturated with water (95% RH) and the temperature drops, the dew point will be reached. The dew point occurs when the air can hold no more water as vapor and the excess is precipitated out as rain, condensation or mist.

Greenhouse Water

In a solar greenhouse that has very little air infiltration from the outside, heat is retained and relative humidity is often very high. Plants grow best at relative humidities between 45 and 60 percent. Higher humidities often may lead to more diseases. Studies show that humidity over 90 percent fosters rapid development of leaf mold and various forms of fruit and stem diseases. In general, disease problems are slight below 70 percent RH. *Disease problems are most severe if the high humidity occurs at night, so don't water during the late afternoon or evening.*

Another problem associated with high humidity is condensation. This happens when warm humid air moves along a cooler surface and the vapor is transformed by the cold into water droplets. You will see it on glazing, walls and doors, dripping from the roof like rain, giving the illusion of a little weather system cruising through the greenhouse. Condensation on

Beveled sill

glazings is a problem because the water droplets greatly reduce the amount of incoming solar energy and light. The water also drips onto sills, and if these droplets continually land on wood surfaces, you may get wood rot problems. I recommend beveling wood surfaces where the condensation lands so water just runs off. On double glazings, always try to get a tight seal between the glazings and the frame to minimize condensation between them.

Some materials can be sprayed on glazing surfaces to prevent water droplets from beading up, but their long-term effectiveness is questionable. Sun Clear, one such product, is manufactured by Solar Sunstill Inc., Satauket, NY 11733.

Basically, condensation and high relative humidity are facts of life in solar greenhouses, especially those that rarely use backup heat. Heated greenhouses will burn some of the humidity out of the air. Be sure *all* wall and wood surfaces are treated with a copper naphthenate type wood preservative to prevent mold from growing in high condensation areas. Avoid creosote or pentoxide type wood preservatives because they're toxic to plants.

I met a woman who built a beautiful free-standing greenhouse that was heated by an artesian hot spring. Sounds heavenly, doesn't it? She understood that the humidity would cause her wood to rot so she applied the common wood preservative pentachlorophenal, also known as penta. After she was well into growing, the humidity began to rise as winter came on; condensation formed on the wooden members. Eventually the penta leached into the condensation and vaporized in the air. Plant death resulted. It was a wipeout.

This poor woman was forced to strip all the surfaces—not an easy or quick task—and recoat them with with plant-safe copper naphthenate, Cuprolignium® or Cuprinol®. So when you buy lumber for the greenhouse, always ask if it has been treated and if so, *with what*. It's surprising to find how often it's been treated with penta.

Help for High Humidity Problems

There are also some things you can do to minimize problems with high relative humidities:

1. Air circulation—Circulate the air even when the greenhouse is sealed to the outside (see CO_2 ventilation earlier in this chapter). This produces more uniform temperatures which can help solve mild humidity problems.

2. Water early in the day—This will help prevent evening humidity problems which are the most severe as far as plant diseases are concerned.

3. Water only when needed—All too often people overwater in greenhouses. Excess water increases humidity problems and is not good for roots (see Watering section later in this chapter).

4. Ventilate to the outside—Whenever the outside temperature is warm enough, ventilate the moist air to the outside. This can also be done when the greenhouse is running hot, even if it is not warm outside. Not recommended if you are in, or heading into, a long cold spell.

5. Air to air heat exchangers—This fancy piece of equipment is not easy to build, and even harder to purchase. It trades warm moist air for dry cooler air. During the exchange process, the cool dry air is heated by the existing warm moist air, thus minimizing heat loss while dumping out the wet air. Plans for air to air heat exchangers were available in 1981 for $1.00 from: U Learn, Extension Division, University of Saskatchewan, Saskatoon, Saskatchewan, Canada. The title is ''An Air to Air Heat Exchanger for Residences,'' by R. W. Besant, R. J. Dumont and D. VanEe.

Low Humidity

This is a rare occurence in greenhouses, but it can happen when much outside venting is going on. Low humidity causes plants to wilt. Humidity may be increased by simply watering the floor and by using swamp cooler type air conditioners. Another way is to purchase a misting nozzle attachment for your hose to spray mist into the air. This will help cool the greenhouse while adding moisture to the air. It's beneficial to maintain higher relative humidity where you're germinating seeds and trying to root cuttings.

Temperature

Heat

Plant growth requires heat. Temperature controls the rate of water and nutrient uptake, photosynthesis, and even cell division. Each plant has different optimum temperature requirements, and different growth stages have different optimums. Seedlings often benefit from warmer temperatures where mature plants will not. For instance, many plants in the cabbage family require cool temperatures to mature properly.

We have relatively little control over minimum temperatures in unheated solar greenhouses. However, with back-up heaters, there is a higher degree of control and attached solar greenhouses can simply steal some heat from the house if temperatures are getting low. To best deal with seasonal temperature variations closely follow *Crop Scheduling*. For help in choosing the best crop and variety for the temperatures you have, see *Selecting Solar Greenhouse Crops and Varieties*.

Your greenhouse's ability to hold the heat of the day is dependent mainly upon the design of the greenhouse. Although greenhouse design is beyond the scope of this book, know that if your greenhouse is freezing your plants in winter, you need to review your solar greenhouse design. If your greenhouse freezes up, run through this checklist.

1. *Insulation*—Is the north wall and the wall against the prevailing winter wind well insulated? Is part of your roof insulated?

2. *Double glazing*—A must. Both layers should be sealed tightly to the frame, free from dirt, and should not be yellowing. Double glazing is no good if either layer is not well sealed.

3. *Thermal storage*—Is your rock, water or other storage enough? Check design/construction books for proper amounts needed for your region.

4. *Insulated foundation*—Your foundation should not be a heat sink. Is your foundation's perimeter insulated with 2″ of foam board type insulation? Insulation should extend down to at least the frost line, whether you have a foundation or not.

5. *Site*—A solar greenhouse should face within 20° of true south. There are really no two ways about it.

6. *Night curtain*—Most solar greenhouses don't use a night curtain. It's not essential, but warmer night temperatures will help increase vegetable yields. If you feel it's necessary devise night insulation for your glazing to help raise low night temperatures. Many commericially available night insulating systems are available, but they're not cheap. There's only one bad thing I can say about a night curtain. It's a costly hassle. If that is the only way you can maintain decent evening temperatures, however, a night curtain is a must. It probably becomes more essential the further north you live. Snowfall in the evening makes an excellent night curtain.

7. *Seal to outside*—Vents and doors must be weather stripped and any cracks must be caulked and checked for wear every year.

8. *Air lock*—If you use your greenhouse door to the outside with any frequency in winter, it should have an air lock. That is a small room with another door. This double-door entry prevents a blast of freezing air from entering your greenhouse every time the door to the outside opens. If you don't have an air lock entry I advise using another house entrance and sealing up the greenhouse door for the worst of the winter.

If you have properly applied each one of these basics to your solar greenhouse and your crops are still freezing, either you live in a cold, cold place, or you need to think about redesigning your greenhouse.

Weather Information

A good tool for solar greenhouse owners is a special weather radio. The federal government has set up a series of low-powered radio stations (NOAA) which play taped weather information 24 hours a day. About 80 percent of the U.S. population lives within range of one of these stations. See the NOAA weather station location list in Appendix C. The frequencies are 162.400, 162.475 or 162.500 megahertz (Mhz) depending on where you live. The station is found on a special radio band—not on AM or FM radios. In 1981, a cheap but reliable weather radio cost about $12.00. Use the weather radio or your most dependable weather forecaster to help make decisions about heating your greenhouse. For example: it's a sunny winter day and the temperature inside the greenhouse has risen to 95°F (35°C) and is still climbing. Tune in the weather radio for an up-to-date prediction for your area. If the weather is predicted to turn cold and cloudy, let your greenhouse run a little hot (but not much more than 90°F [32°C]) in winter to help charge up your storage to better handle the coming cold period. If the weather is predicted to stay clear and sunny, cool your greenhouse off to around 80°F (27°C). Vent your heat to the outside or an adjacent building and let in some fresh, dry cool air. Why cool the greenhouse only to 80°F (27°C)? Because, if the weather service predicts sun and you get hit with a storm instead, a temperature of 80°F (27°C) will not affect your heat storage or cause any problems with low night temperatures.

Remember the old saying, "Only fools believe in weather predictions." Well, I learned the hard way. It was a wonderful fall a few years back, with crystal clear warm days and cool nights. Fall's a time of year in Wyoming when we may get weather ranging from a tornado to a blizzard to a heat wave. My 88 year old friend Howard kept saying we were "gonna have a rough winter," while the clear blue skies seemed like they would never end. All the while I checked the weather radio daily in case I needed to let the greenhouse heat up in anticipation of a cold cloudy spell. The NOAA radio station kept saying "cool nights and warm sunny days." I kept venting the hot air and told myself that the yearly chore of recaulking and weather stripping could wait another day. Howard said it couldn't. "It's gonna storm tomorrow!" he said. I smiled to myself and kept working outside without a shirt, enjoying the fall sun. I checked with my trusty NOAA weather station all day. "Cool nights and sunny warm days," it repeated. In fact, they said it would be that way all week and the TV weather people agreed.

That night it clouded up.

Most of the 3′ of snow we got the next day was still on the ground in early spring. It was cloudy for 12 straight days. Howard smiled but never said, "I told you so." It was a rough winter. Caulk just doesn't go right when it's cold. Moral: don't put all your trust in scientifically calculated, satellite predicted weather forecasts. They're just tools to help . . . sometimes. The weather does what it wants no matter what we predict. Is there a Howard living near you?

Purchase a good high-low thermometer to see what the nighttime low and daytime high temperatures are in your greenhouse. Compare it to the outside highs and lows to learn how your greenhouse behaves. In 1981 a thermometer cost about $17.00. It sure takes the guesswork out of figuring your temperatures and gives you a better understanding of your environment. Mount your thermometer where direct sunlight will not strike it You may have to build a small box to mount it in. Paint the outside of the box white.

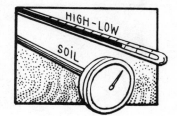

At the Cheyenne Community Solar Greenhouse, it was found that the lowest temperature usually occurred right around sunrise.

Soil Temperatures

Soil temperatures are more crucial than air temperatures. The warmth of the soil is something we're not commonly aware of because we live our days surrounded by air. Most of us, anyway.

When soil temperatures are below 45°F (7°C), roots work slowly and have a harder time taking up water and nutrients. When the air temperature begins to heat up, wilting can occur even though there is ample moisture in the *cold* soil because of slow water uptake.

Research has shown that if soil temperatures are kept around 65°F (18°C) the winter air temperature can drop $10^{\circ}F$ ($6^{\circ}C$) without any loss in yield. This is especially true with fruiting crops. Many researchers believe the great results obtained by heating the soil are due not just to the effects of temperature, but also to the effects of faster organic matter decomposition (resulting from warmer temperatures) which creates more CO_2, thus increasing the rate of photosynthesis.

There is a special thermometer with a 5'' probe that sticks into the soil for measuring soil temperatures. It's a great help in locating environmental differences. By determining where the cool areas are in your greenhouse, you can adjust your planting layout to mesh best with the environment. It's fun to observe soil temperature changes in relation to the outside weather and environment inside your greenhouse. Keep records of these soil temperatures and the air temperatures to gain a better understanding of the solar greenhouse, and to monitor the performance of your structure.

Heating the soil can be a complex proposition which, except for seedling flats, may not be worth the effort. In earlier times, people utilized the heating qualities of decomposing manure to heat cold frames. They placed an 8'' layer of raw manure about 1 ½' below the top of the soil. This manure would heat the soil that covered it for a few weeks, which might help seedlings started in containers. Planting seeds directly into soil that has heating manure in it might eventually cause overfertilization problems, especially when the roots reach the raw manure. But containers sitting on top of this heated soil do fine.

Many people have set up beds with warm water pipes hooked to active solar hot water collectors running through them. This is fine, except that it makes it difficult to work beds with a shovel. There's been some discussion about using wind-powered electrical resistance heaters running within the planting beds. I haven't heard of anyone trying it yet. Any takers? But don't get electrocuted.

Watering with warm water is one good way to keep soil temperatures warm. This is explained in the section on watering later in this chapter.

Cooling the Greenhouse

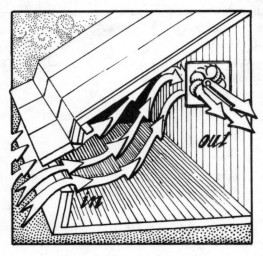

Cross-flow ventilation

In my experience, most solar greenhouse owners have more problems with overheating than with freezing. Overheating occurs when cool season crops are above $90^{\circ}F$ ($32^{\circ}C$) and warm season crops are above $100^{\circ}F$ ($38^{\circ}C$). Short periods above these temperatures are not necessarily harmful, but prolonged periods cause problems for plants. Overheating is basically due to poor greenhouse design—usually poor ventilation. Bill Yanda and Rick Fisher's book, *The Food and Heat Producing Solar Greenhouse*, has some excellent rules of thumb for ventilation. I like their recommendations because they are easy to understand and their calculations work well. Optimally, you should establish a natural crossflow of air with a high vent on one side and a low vent on the other side. These should be either at the knee wall (south) and on the roof (north); or on the west and the east. The high vent works best when placed opposite the direction of your prevailing *summer* wind and should be 15% larger than the low vent. A general rule of thumb is to have the vent area to the outside equal to at least 30 percent of the area of glazing. Please don't cut down on venting area to the outside in hopes of preventing air leakage in winter. Install the right size vents, and be sure they're insulated and built tight. Vent doors to the outside should be well constructed and made to open on *any* day of the year (especially where they say, "If you don't like the weather, just wait five minutes and it'll change.") When closed, they should be insulated, weatherstripped and sealed tight to the outside. Opening and closing of vents may be automated by using commercially available heat motors which are temperature activated pistons. Be sure to attach a safety chain so the wind won't destroy your vent door and heat motor. Again, be sure they close tightly. In the design stage, plan it so vent doors don't open into areas where you'll bump your head and/or your plant's heads.

If you live in a hot area or have a basic cooling problem, don't discount the value of an electric exhaust fan. Electric fans cost "only pennies a day" to run. A fan for summer cooling should exhaust warm air to the outside for best cooling efficiency. This will create a negative

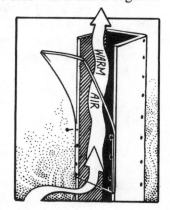

Thermal chimney

pressure so that cool air will enter through the other vent to replace the exhausted warm air. Place the exhaust fan in the high vent for best results and be sure it's blowing air *out* of the greenhouse. Try to get the air to travel across the full length of the floor before being exhausted to the outside.

Any fan will do for exhausting hot air in summer or other warm days. I have had great luck finding old fans for a few bucks at garage sales and second hand stores. Or go exhaust your pocketbook and buy spanking new ones.

If electricity is not available in your area, of if you want to attempt a totally passive cooling system, thermal chimneys may be the solution for you. Thermal chimneys are tall (often 20' high), square (about 4' by 4'), and glazed on one side. The inside of the chimney is painted black. Hot air temperatures are created within the chimney. The hot air rises fast, and much like an exhaust fan, it creates a vacuum within the greenhouse. The hot greenhouse air then moves up and out through the chimney, while cooler outside air is sucked in, ideally through low the greenhouse vent.

Another way to cool down your greenhouse is to utilize the cooling effects of evaporation. This is the same cooling we feel when wind blows across wet skin. As the water evaporates, it cools. You may purchase a mister from a garden supply store or from a seed catalog and mount it in

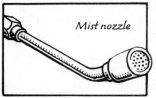

Mist nozzle

the eaves of your greenhouse. On hot days you can mist the air intermittently, either manually or automatically with an electric solenoid valve and timer. As the water droplets fall, they will evaporate, causing a substantial temperature drop. This usually works best when the outside relative humidity is below 80%. The lower the humidity, the better evaporative cooling works.

Commercial greenhouses often use an evaporative cooling system (known as a pad and fan system) which works like a big swamp cooler. At one end of the greenhouse water is dripped through a thin fibrous pad in front of a vent to the outside. An exhaust fan at the opposite end pulls outside air through the wet pad, cooling the air, and the cooled air flows across the length of the greenhouse until it is exhausted to the outside. This would be a complex system for a small greenhouse, but a simpler system described below can work using burlap and a fan. Again, all of these evaporative cooling systems rapidly begin to lose their ability to cool as the outside relative humidity rises above 70%. At 90% RH they hardly work at all.

A Homemade Burlap Swamp Cooler

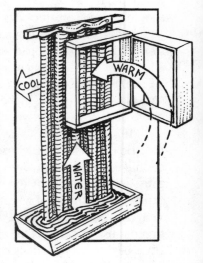

1. Cover lower vent with two or three layers of burlap, placing the lower end of the burlap in a long wide container of water that's sitting on the floor below the vent.

2. Burlap should now pull the water up (by capillary action) in front of the vent opening.

3. Turn on the exhaust fan at the opposite end of the of the greenhouse to draw air through the wet burlap, cooling the air as it passes through.

It's cheap and it works well. Just don't count on reusing the burlap bags to transport potatoes at a later date.

Some greenhouse owners have turned to using an actual swamp cooler attached to the side of the solar greenhouse, pumping cooler air into the structure. A new swamp cooler in 1981 ran about $380.

Shading to Cool

Usually shading is accomplished by directly treating the glazing surface, or by outside planting in front of the greenhouse. There are commercial greenhouse shading compounds available from commercial greenhouse suppliers. But many owners just spray on a thinned-out white latex paint diluted to the consistency of milk (70% water). There's also a new generation of paint-on shading compounds from Europe which shade the greenhouse when dry, but become clear when wet from rain or mist. This enables light to get through the shading compound when plants need it most. You're out of luck if it's cloudy but not raining. The commercial name of one such compound is Nixol® and is distributed in the United States by V & V Noordland, P.O. Box 739, Midford, NY 11763.

There are many shading compounds available on the market so check with a local commercial greenhouse or greenhouse supplier because they vary in life span and effects. Some are semi-permanent, some disintegrate and wash off after a freeze or a snow, some last only six months, while others are very hard to get off the glazing and may require scraping, a tough job and not good for the glazing. Check with a local commercial greenhouse or greenhouse supplier.

In dry areas, many people just throw wet mud onto the glass and reapply it after heavy rains wash it off. Though labor intensive, it works like a charm.

Also available are commercial shade cloths which are commonly hung inside under the glass. You can make your own by using cheese cloth, burlap or an old sheet. Hang it horizontally over the areas you want shaded. Deciduous trees, sunflowers, pole beans and grapevines planted outside in front of your greenhouse glazing create summer shade too.

Important Note: Most foodcrops grown in solar greenhouses are already short on light because of the obvious limits of the structure. When you use *any means* to shade, you are cutting down on light used by vegetable plants for photosynthesis. This can cut down on food yields unless you live in a very bright area that provides, after shading, enough foot candles (around 2000 fc—see *Measuring Light in the Greenhouse* earlier in this chapter) to grow your vegetables.

Shading in the summer won't affect growing houseplants at all if you plan, as many people do, to move your food production outside and use your greenhouse for living. But shading in winter or summer will greatly decrease the ability of your greenhouse to produce food and heat.

Earth Tunnels

Another development in cooling greenhouses is the use of earth tunnels. These are underground ducts that take in outside air. As the air travels underground, it is cooled to the temperature of the earth, which is much cooler than the hot outside air. The cool air is then ducted into the greenhouse to aid in passive cooling. For more details, consult a good passive home design book; many of the so-called "envelope homes" use this cooling method.

Water

Watering is the one thing everyone thinks he or she can do well. In reality few solar greenhouse owners do it with the correct frequency or amount. The most common problem I've encountered is overwatering (see "Overwatering Symptoms" in *Pests and Diseases*). Roots need air and overwatering fills up all the air spaces in the soil. If this goes on for very long, it hinders the plants's normal functions by causing the roots to suffocate. It seems that greenhouse owners living in dry western climates have the most problems with overwatering. Because greenhouses are water efficient compared to the outside garden, people who water their outside gardens with regular frequency may have to change their habits. There are many variables in deciding how often and how much to water. They include:

1. The amount of sunshine that plants receive. More sunshine means a need for more water.

2. The amount of outside venting. More venting also calls for more water.

3. Seedlings need a steady water supply. They should not be dripping wet, but constantly moist.

4. Clay soils need less water than do sandy soils. Get your soil tested by a county agricultural extension agent. Then try to create a good balance between sand and clay so soil is well drained but holds water reasonably well. (See *Getting to the Roots*.)

Knowing When to Water

Always check the soil before you water. Don't water out of habit! Of course, there is one obvious way to tell—look for wilting. This method, however, is the "too late" approach. There are better ways. For example:

Pots and Containers—Stick your finger into the top inch of soil; if it feels powdery dry, water it.

Beds—Dig one inch under the surface and grab a handful of soil. Form a ball out of this soil. Toss the ball from hand to hand.

If the ball	Then . . . .
is powdery dry and will not form at all	water
falls apart easily when tossed	water
falls apart but not easily	don't water just yet—check again tomorrow
doesn't fall apart	don't water yet—check in a few days
doesn't fall apart, and water is squeezed out in droplets	you got carried way and over-watered—take it easy!

When using the ball method, be aware that soils high in sand tend to fall apart more easily than other soils, so also take into account how "wet" it feels. Experience will help you fine tune this method.

Water very little or not at all on cloudy cool days. There is usally no need for it, except for seedlings. When you do water, always try to do it in the morning hours to prevent evening condensation on the leaves, which leads to disease problems. And generally, the greenhouse needs less water in winter months.

Symptoms of overwatering:

1. Bluish-green mold growth on soil surfaces.
2. Increased seedling or plant diseases and poor germination.
3. Increased number of slugs feeding on leaves (see *Pests and Diseases*).
4. Slow growth.

How to Water

The first step is to purchase a good rubber hose. Keeping it off the ground will help prevent the spread of disease. An old recycled tire rim makes an excellent storage rack. Mount the rim on a wall and wind the hose around it when not in use.

Next you'll need a nozzle. A misting nozzle is available from garden shops, seed catalogs and greenhouse supply houses and is good for starting seeds. A water breaker may be found at these same outlets and is great for general watering needs. It converts one strong stream into more gentle rain-like droplets.

You'll have to do bucket watering if you don't have plumbing. In that case, obtain a watering can that has a water breaker attachment.

Plumbing or not, try to keep water off the leaves. Water the soil, not the plants. Try to avoid mud splashing and be especially gentle with seedlings; a hard spray can bury seedlings forever and even knock down mature plants. Water thoroughly. Water as infrequently as possible, but when you do water, soak the beds well. Stop when puddles begin to form.

When watering pots and containers, stop when the water comes out the bottom. If the soil in your container has dried out, you may have to use the ''water twice'' technique. The first watering, you'll notice, will immediately run out. This is because the soil has shrunk and pulled away from the pot. The water goes right down the sides and out the bottom. This first watering causes the soil to expand and contact the sides of the pot, but the soil will have absorbed little water. Now when you do the second watering, it will soak into the center of the soil mass.

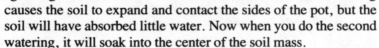

If you don't have the time or energy, there are systems you can set up to automatically water your greenhouse. These involve timers, extensive plumbing, and are usually drip irrigation systems. They're great if you're going to be away for awhile but friends may also be happy to help you out. In my opinion these automatic systems take much of the fun out of gardening and may be quite expensive (around $400 in 1981). But if you are good at tinkering and scrounging, you can devise something yourself. Automatic systems are available through greenhouse suppliers—see the yellow pages in the phone book and garden magazine ads.

Try never to let soil in beds or pots completely dry out. Besides the obvious stress that wilting causes plants, dry soil increases the concentration of fertilizer salts. Fertilizer salts cause slower growth, brown leaf margins and high soil pH. See *Getting to the Roots* for more information.

Water Quality

In rare instances, people run into water quality problems caused by pollutants or salts in the water. Generally chlorine is no problem, but fluoridation in high amounts can be harmful. (See *Pests and Diseases*.) High pH water, also known as salty or alkaline water, can be trouble, especially if your water tests out above a pH of 7.4. Your county agricultural extension agent will help you test your water; litmus paper is also available from a pharmacy. This paper turns different colors to indicate the pH of your water—the ideal pH is 6.7 - 7.2.

The quality of water varies greatly from region to region and is affected by both nature and people. It is the human factor that causes most problems because people often don't respect or maintain their water at a high quality level. Water is classified as hard and soft. Hard water is high in minerals, usually calcium or magnesium carbonates. Dishwashing and laundry soaps work best in soft (low mineral) water. People often ''soften'' hard water chemically for washing; but beware, plants don't grow well in artificially softened water. Water softeners usually raise the sodium content in the soil, which causes poor soil structure and poor drainage. They may also raise the pH of your soil out of the neutral range.

In most cities, chlorine is added to tap water to kill harmful organisms which may cause human disease. The amount of chlorine it would take to harm your plants would probably harm you as well and would not be suitable to drink. If you suspect your water is outrageously high in chlorine let it sit in a bucket overnight and most of the chlorine will disappear. (This is a trick used by goldfish lovers.)

Fluoride is also added to many towns' water supplies to help prevent tooth decay. In many parts of the country it occurs naturally in the water. Some horticultural research has shown that fluoride may cause some leaf tip burning, especially if your soil pH is below 6.5. But tip burn is also caused by high salts, high pH and overfertilization. To avoid fluoride injury, be sure your water and soil is between 6.7 and 7.3 pH. See *Getting to the Roots* and *Pests and Diseases* for more information on pH, soil and growth.

Unless you live in an area where acid rain is a problem, rain water may be a good alternative to tap water. But winter collection may pose a bit of a problem. You'll have to be creative.

With water resources in short supply, many people are turning to grey water. Grey water is "waste" water from sinks, laundry, tub and showers. As much as 80 gallons a day can be reused from a household of four. I recommend the following when using your grey water in the solar greenhouse:

1. Avoid laundry water that contains bleaches, boron (Borax), and high sodium detergents. Because most detergents contain sodium, it's usually best to forget laundry water. Be on the safe side and use only the rinse water.

2. Dilute grey water by 50% with tap water.

3. Devise a sand and gravel filter to remove lint, grease or other impurities. Even a double layer cloth bag around the end of a hose makes an adequate filter.

4. Use mild, simple soaps. Castile soaps work well.

5. Wash all food well before you eat it.

To transfer grey water to storage or to deliver it directly to your greenhouse, water may be caught in buckets from disconnected sink traps, or a more sophisticated system may be installed. You may have to set up your grey water system secretly as many areas have local ordinances against reusing water. If the quality of your water turns out to be a real problem, the only solution is locating another water source. Capturing rain water is a good place to begin.

Water Temperature

I don't like to be splashed with cold water . . . and neither do plants. It slows their growth and lowers the soil temperatures tremendously. Water is considered cold when it is below 43°F (6°C). Ideal water temperature for plants is between 65° and 80°F (18°-27°C); above 80°F (27°C) is usually too hot.

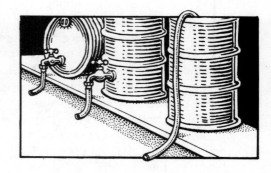

Ways to raise water temperature in your greenhouse:

1. Plumb in domestic hot water and a mixing valve; or

2. Plumb a faucet into the side of a black 55 gallon drum that sits in the sun and water plants from that barrel. For best results, place the barrel up high; or

3. Make a coil of black plastic tubing up against your north wall. Connect one end of the tubing to your house plumbing and put a valve on the other end for watering. The coil must be placed so as to receive direct winter sun. Now you have a source of solar heated water; or

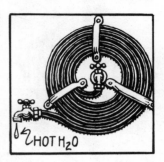

4. Buy a solar hot water heater that is made especially for solar greenhouses. Zomeworks carries the only one I've heard of. It's called Big Fin. Write to Zomeworks, P.O. Box 712, Albuquerque, NM 87103. This water will need to be mixed with cold water to provide proper temperature; or

5. European growers have done some fancy water heating by running water pipes through a compost pile. Another idea is to set a water drum in the center of your hot compost.

Besides light, atmosphere (CO_2), heat, and water, the one remaining element of the greenhouse environment is the plant itself. But before you can have a plant, you need a place to put it—and I'll discuss that in the next chapter on Interior Layout Design.

Here are some sources of high and low pressure sodium lamps:

North American Phillips Lighting Company
Bank Street
Hightstown, NJ 08520

Advance Transformer
2950 N. Western Avenue
Chicago, IL 60618

Quality Outdoor Lighting
Northbrook, IL 60062

Jefferson Electric
840 25th Avenue
Bellwood, IL 60104

Dura-test Corporation
2321 Kennedy Boulevard
North Bergen, NJ 07047

Leviton Mfg. Company
236 Greenpoint Avenue
Brooklyn NY 11

2
INTERIOR
LAYOUT DESIGN

During initial design of the greenhouse, interior layout must be given serious thought. In terms of overall food production, this is as crucial as the structure itself. Greenhouse space is always limited, so the final layout must enable you to use space efficiently. Most greenhouse owners like to devote some greenhouse space to relax and live in. But it is still important that the area devoted to food production be used efficiently to achieve the greatest food production per square foot of greenhouse space. It is also important to design interior space to be flexible for changes in cropping, increases or decreases in living space, and seasonal differences.

Some greenhouse owners are as concerned with the living space of the greenhouse as with the growing space, so food production sometimes takes a back seat to aesthetics. In trying to satisfy two sets of requirements, these folks often find themselves left with a structure that is neither functional nor aesthetically pleasing. Granted, there are some trade-offs between aesthetically pleasing living space and food production—but wonderful compromises can be made; and remember, growing food is a great way to live. Here are the factors to consider.

Sun Angles

It's always fun for me to think of sun angles and how I would design a solar greenhouse for the high mountains of Ecuador (on the equator). But in the temperate zones, the sun angle is low during the winter months because the sun never gets very high in the southern sky (northern sky if you live south of the equator). When the winter sun gets low, shading caused by interior objects may be a problem. Any tall object placed toward the southern half of a greenhouse will cause shading, so be sure barrels or raised beds are not robbing other growing space of light. In winter, light is already in short supply and vegetables need all they can get. (See light section in *The Solar Greenhouse Environment*.)

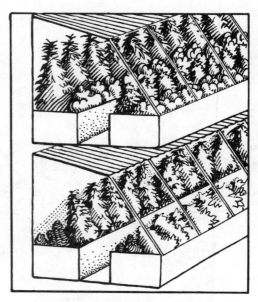

Shading at winter sun angles

Interior Surfaces

Because of the constant problem of low light levels, it's important that all light entering the greenhouse be used either for plant growth or heating (including thermal storage). The best way to achieve this is to paint all non-thermal mass surfaces white. (See *The Solar Greenhouse Environment*). If you live in a cloudy area, bringing vegetable yields up to par may mean painting over your beautiful redwood or cedar.

Traditionally, most solar greenhouses have water thermal mass storage along the north wall. But if your greenhouse is much wider than 18′ it may be wise to use some thermal mass along the south wall too. This will help create more even temperatures across the width of your greenhouse. If you do this, to minimize winter shading, thermal mass along the south face of the greenhouse should be in smaller containers that don't rise more than 1 ½′ higher than the top of the nearest growing bed. The sun side of any south wall thermal mass should be black but the north side of these mass containers should be painted white to benefit nearby plants with diffuse light reflection. Remember, thermal mass along the south side is only for solar greenhouses wider than 18′. You might also consider hanging a white curtain over north wall thermal mass in the summer to increase light along north wall beds. (See *The Solar Greenhouse Environment*).

Pit Greenhouses and Light

We get into a similar shading problem with pit greenhouses: Low winter sun angles produce a shadow across the growing beds. The deeper your greenhouse is set into the earth the more this becomes a problem. It's a trade-off between using earth-sheltering and obtaining adequate light. Again, paint everything white (except soil, thermal mass containers and plants) to minimize this problem.

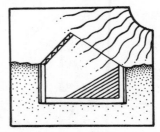

Shading at winter sun angles in a pit greenhouse

Thermal Mass

Until recently 55-gallon drums filled with water have been a common choice for greenhouse thermal mass, but now more people are looking into other storage containers. Because of the unattractive bulk of 55-gallon drums, most people are switching to more visually appealing containers such as fiberglass tanks or stacked recycled 5-gallon oil tins. Smaller containers have the advantage of more sun exposed surface area per cubic area of water. The result is more heat gain when the sun is shining, but also more, and quicker heat loss on cloudy days and at night. Small water containers are usually good for short-term heat storage (1-3 days), while larger containers are best for long-term storage (more than 3 days of cold weather). A mixture of both is generally recommended. Small containers take up less floor space and are easily moved, whereas large water containers such as 55-gallon drums are very heavy when full, so be sure they're in their final resting place before you fill them. See a greenhouse design book like Yanda and Fisher's *The Food and Heat Producing Solar Greenhouse* for sizing the amount of thermal mass needed for your climate and size greenhouse.

More and more we are seeing eutectic salt, and other phase-change thermal storage systems. They are often sold in small solar shops springing up all around. This storage takes up less space but there are questions about its life span. It's also quite expensive. Solar equipment suppliers should be able to give you more details on the eutectic salt storage products.

Raised Beds

In a greenhouse you can grow food directly in the ground, in containers, or in raised beds. A raised bed is generally a wooden sided box that is 3' - 6' long, 2½' - 4' wide and 4'' - 4' high. It is filled with a soil mix or other growing medium. A raised bed may also be built of brick, concrete or recycled material.

There are a number of ways to lay out a raised bed. The peninsular system uses space most efficiently, with the main aisle running north-south or east-west. The width of the raised bed

should be comfortable for you to reach across (about 3½' - 4') providing access from both sides. For one-sided access (such as a bed up against a wall), don't make the beds any wider than 2½'. Again, bed and aisle width really depend on what is comfortable for you. Think about the size of your wheelbarrow and the route it must take to carry soil to the beds. The old fashioned three point, one-wheel wheelbarrow has the advantage of being able to roll down narrower aisles.

Will there be lots of people coming through your greenhouse? Ground beds have the disadvantage of getting trampled as people walk through. A raised bed—even 2'' high—tends to keep most people from stepping into your garden; but it won't stop cats, dogs or curious kids. One great advantage of raised beds is that the higher they are, the less you have to bend over—and when it's comfortable to work in your greenhouse garden you'll take better care of it. Also, like any other thermal mass, a raised soil bed will store heat. Note: garden beds designed for senior citizens should be raised at least 24'' for easier access.

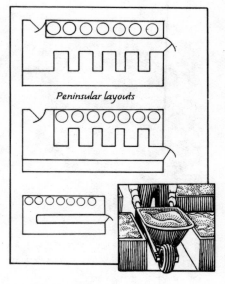
Peninsular layouts

One way to make a raised bed is to dig aisles down into the earth on the sides of the bed, rather than actually raising the bed by bringing in more dirt. This leaves the top of your raised bed at grade level. Of course this can't be done if you already have your greenhouse sitting on a concrete slab . . . unless you're good with a jack hammer.

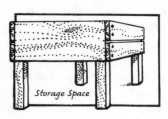
Storage Space

Raised-raised bed

Some growers prefer a *raised-raised* bed. This 1'-or-so-deep bed sits on stilts. It has the advantage of providing some storage space under the bed for pots, hose, garage sale accumulations and other junk. Because a 1' growing depth is quite limited, make sure the soil mix in this bed is not only rich but well drained. Also be sure the bed has many drainage holes in the bottom.

It's very helpful to construct a small cardboard mockup of your greenhouse to try out different design ideas. At least be sure to put your ideas on graph paper to see how things look and fit. This preplanning will make the design process easier and you'll more likely end up with something that fits your needs.

Constructing Raised Beds

Materials: A wide variety may be used to construct beds. Unless you're wealthy, try to obtain inexpensive materials. For example, scrap lumber, brick, cinder block, stone, old tires, etc., can be made into raised beds. If you use scrap wood, avoid thin plywood because it warps and separates. Also, be sure to avoid wood materials that have been treated with pentachlorophenol (''penta'') or creosote wood preservatives because they are toxic to plants. The best wood preservative I've found is copper napthenate, Cuprinol® or Cuprolignium®. Unless you're using redwood or cedar, all wood used for bed construction should be treated with this material. These products can be found at local greenhouse suppliers or lumberyards. It is also helpful to line the inside of your raised bed with plastic to make it last longer. But don't line the bottom with plastic because you want drainage all the way through.

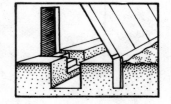
Excavated aisle

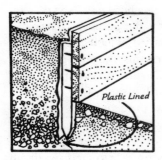

Use support stakes

Unless you have a concrete floor, you should sink support stakes on the side of the bed deep into the ground. This will anchor the bed and keep it from moving as you fill it with soil. If you're building on a concrete slab, either cross-brace or nail the bed into the concrete with special concrete nails.

Paint the outside of all raised beds semi-gloss white to increase reflection of photosynthetic light throughout the greenhouse.

A 1'' x 6'' board laid on top of the perimeter of the bed makes a nice seat for people and a good place to set pots. If you don't do this, people will tend to sit on the edge of your beds anyway . . . unless you place cactus there.

Filling the Bed

If you plan to do your growing in a soil medium (See *Getting to the Roots*) here's how to fill your raised bed. First determine whether your soil is sandy or clayey by having a soil test done by a county agricultural extension agent, or try the following "feel" method of testing. Wet a tablespoon of soil and rub it between your thumb and fingers. If it feels gritty, it's probably a

sandy soil. If it feels only slightly gritty, it is probably a mix of sand and clay. And if it feels plastic-like and smooth, it probably leans more toward clay. (If it feels really slimy, you probably grabbed a slug.) A large number of hard dirt clods may indicate a clay soil.

Always strive for a well-drained soil. Soils that are on the sandy side drain best, while clay soils hold water. In greenhouse soils it is better to rely on decomposed organic matter, not clay, to provide water-holding ability. Soils high in clay develop drainage problems, which can lead to a salt buildup and water logging—both hard on vegetable production. So keep your soil on the sandy side. If your soil is clay, add enough sand to make it drain well (up to ½ for soils very high in clay, but generally ⅓ sand). If your soil is known for its poor drainage consider using drainage tiles under the greenhouse, or at least under the beds. See a comprehensive construction manual for details.

Before filling the beds with soil on hand, have a soil test done to see if your dirt is the proper pH and not too high in salts. And for good plant growth, check on the amount of nutrients it contains. Either test it yourself with a soil test kit or ask your county agricultural extension agent for help. If your soil pH is high or low, you should add material to correct this. And if you're sure that the dirt you have on hand is absolutely awful (either sub-soil, salty or poisoned) locate another soil source and haul it in. If your soil is marginal, have patience, you'll build it up in time by taking good care of it. See *Getting to the Roots*.

Wanting to minimize heat loss to the ground, many people ask about placing foam board insulation horizontally below the entire floor. I strongly urge you to avoid it. If you have properly insulated around the perimeter of the greenhouse foundation down to frost line depth or deeper (as explained in most design books), your ground will not be a heat sink. So you gain nothing except a muddy mess and root growth problems due to poor water drainage. The earth is a good source of constant 45°F (7°C) temperatures (plus or minus 5°), which can be a great help in preventing a freeze-up in certain situations. What can happen is this: during a prolonged record cold spell (the type that freezes moustaches instantly) your thermal mass may become exhausted, leaving the earth as your only heat source. Even if the earth is only 40°F (4°C) it's still warmer than a 32°F (0°C) greenhouse, and its relative warmth would cause a positive flow of heat from ground to air and thus protect your plants from freezing.

If you feel you must pour a concrete slab (which I don't advise), rather than just a perimeter foundation, it's a good idea to insulate only around the perimeter to the frost depth and not under the whole slab. For that matter, if you have no foundation and just build on timbers or beams, still insulate the perimeter below the frost line by trenching-in a rigid foam board insulation.

Depth of Fill

For good vegetable production you should have a soil depth of about 2'. Less depth works, but tends to produce more growing problems. This doesn't mean your raised bed has to be 2' high. If your greenhouse floor is dirt, you can work the planting soil below the ground level. But if your greenhouse sits on a concrete slab, you can only go up.

Begin filling your bed with a couple of inches of sand, then add your soil. (If it is a sandy soil to begin with, you won't need to start with sand at the bottom.) Add about 2 lbs of bone meal to every 10 square feet of soil: it provides phosphorus and calcium to your soil. (See *Getting to the Roots* for alternatives.) If your soil tests low in potassium add 1 gallon of wood ash to every 10 square feet. Wood ash does have an alkalizing effect (high pH) and if that is not desired, you may want to consider granite dust for potassium. Don't use coal ash. Leave a 7'' space on top for decomposed organic matter and allow for an additional inch of clear space between the top of the soil and the top of the bed. Organic matter should be added in these quantities: 7'' deep if using decomposed compost, 4'' if using well -decomposed manures, less if chicken manure. The compost or manure should be blended throughout the entire soil depth. *Avoid raw manures!* They will burn leaf tips and throw nutrient balances out of whack. If your soil still tests out to be quite low in nitrogen, blood meal, cotton seed meal or fish emulsion are excellent fertilizers to correct the shortage.

Materials such as leaf mold (composted leaves) and peat moss are helpful too and may be added to a depth of 3'' - 4'' in addition to the depth of compost or manures. They are very low in nutrient content but do provide excellent humus, which improves the soil's tilth (water and nutrient holding ability), and they also help to keep diseases to a minimum. If your soil is very rich and contains a lot of decomposed organic matter to begin with, cut by 25% all recommendations of compost, manures, etc. Again, thoroughly mix in whatever you add to the soil.

For more in-depth information and recommendations for subsequent applications of fertilizers or organic matter after the first crop is harvested, see *Getting to the Roots*.

Seedling Space

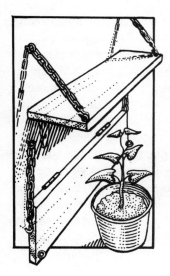

In spring people often like to utilize much of the greenhouse space for starting seedlings that will be set out later in the outside garden. Containers of seedlings may be set directly on beds when food crops aren't growing there. Or they may be placed on top of thermal mass containers. One way to increase useable space for seedlings is to build shelves. Shelves may be placed on the north, east and west walls. They may also be hinged onto the side of raised beds to swing out into an area previously used for living, or an area where aisles are wide enough—as long as there is still enough room to walk or waltz through. All shelves should be painted white. See spring seedling section in *Crops and Propagation*.

Container Food Production

Many commercial growers, as well as some small greenhouse owners, produce food in containers rather than in beds. Containers that may be used for this type of production include: 1-gallon cans, old 5-gallon paint buckets, large plastic bags filled with potting soil mix, and other recycled and commercially available planting containers. Although I have a personal preference for growing food in raised beds, containers still have a place in every food producing greenhouse because they easily utilize space that planting beds do not. This includes hanging containers to utilize air space and containers set on top of thermal mass or on the ground in aisles. Let's look at the pros and cons of using containers for all your food production.

Pros

—Cheap, easy to find recycled containers.

—Utilize unused space (barrel tops, floor space, shelves, air space).

—Eliminate problem of disease spreading from plant to plant through the soil.

—Can be moved easily around the greenhouse.

Cons

—Hard to grow big plants in containers unless the containers are very large.

—Plants in containers need more attention (water, fertilizer, more pest control).

—Fertilizing mistakes are not as easily forgiven in container soil.

Whenever you grow plants in containers be sure the soil mix is rich and well-drained and that there are holes in the bottom of the container for drainage. A common soil mix for containers is: ¼ sand, ¼ rich topsoil, ½ well-rotted manure or compost and 1 cup of bone meal per 5 gallons of mix. Perlite may be substituted for sand.

The main problem with growing plants in containers is that the plants may be too large for the container, thus creating a stress situation. So try to balance container size (root area) to the size of the plant above soil level; watch for frequent wilting and an increased susceptibility to insect problems; and stick to bush varieties of vegetables rather than large plants. Also pay more attention to the nutrient needs of the plants. Excess nitrogen as well as nitrogen deficiencies are common in container soil.

Taking to the Air

A fancy use of space in your greenhouse is rafter beds (for tall greenhouses with rafters) and high hanging pots. 1' deep beds may be rolled along on the rafters in a north-south direction so that a shadow is always cast directly on the walk path, not on a lower growing bed. This rafter bed is filled with a lightweight growing medium that will be hydroponically fed. Perlite would work nicely here. This arrangement is only for tall greenhouses with sturdy rafters—it admittedly poses quite an engineering problem. You need a way to easily get up into the rafters for regular plant maintenance.

A hanging container with a pulley is somewhat more realistic. The idea here is to pull your plant up to the peak areas of the greenhouse where the temperatures in winter are generally much warmer. You attach a long cord to the pot, then thread the cord through a pulley and anchor it down low. When you have to fertilize or water the plant, lower it to ground level, then pull the plant back to the peak area. On warm days or throughout the summer the temperatures near the roof are generally too hot for any plant to survive (often 120° F [49° C]), but in winter it works great for warm season bushy plants such as bush tomatoes or beans. Be sure your ground level layout is finished and producing food efficiently before you consider taking to the air in these wilder ways.

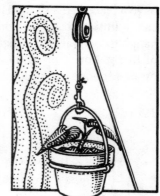

Aisles and Floors

There are a number of ways to deal with aisle and floor space. Each material has its special attributes; my favorite is brick, but let's look at how each one stacks up.

Options for Aisles

Material	Comments
Dirt	Gets muddy and may harbor disease and insects.
Wood boards	May harbor slugs and insects. Rots and is hard to clean. Bare feet may pick up splinters.
Brick	Easy to clean and pleasing to look at. Somewhat porous and drains some excess water. Expensive but easy on bare feet. Brick floor patterns are fun to play with. Some solar heat storage possibilities.
Gravel and rock	Use only pea size gravel. Drains well. Great on hot days; it can be watered down and cools the greenhouse as the water evaporates. Not so good for barefooted humans, but it's cheap. Harder to roll wheelbarrows and wheelchairs, though not impossible.
Concrete	If the whole floor is a concrete slab, plan for water drainage, preferably built in if possible. See a concrete specialist about porous concrete which is ideal for water drainage. Concrete floors are easy to clean and their white color reflects photosynthetic light to the plants. Don't paint your concrete floor black for solar heat gain because it will cause summer overheating. Concrete walkways are preferred over concrete slabs that cover the whole floor.

Wheelchair Access

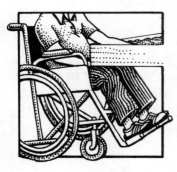

Provide 2' clearance for wheelchair access

Wheelchairs vary between 2' and 3' in width. They need a diameter of about 5½' for a turnaround. For complete access you should remove stairs into the greenhouse and replace them with ramps. Ramps for wheelchairs should not rise faster than 1' per 10' in length. For wheelchair access to growing beds it is much nicer to be able to position the chair so that it's facing a bed or growing table that has an underneath clearance (for the knees) of 2'. This provides an easy front reach from the wheelchair where the person's legs are under the bed or table rather than having to pull alongside and twist uncomfortably to the side to reach plants. Gravel flooring makes it difficult to roll wheelchairs.

Work and Leisure Space

Many folks like to set aside a small space for a work area. Here you can pot plants, start seedlings, groom house plants and do transplanting. It's a sacrifice to use precious greenhouse food production space for this activity, so you may want to use an area in your garage or workshop for this. However, if you must locate the work area inside your greenhouse, place it in one of the darker corners (the northeast or northwest). Some people have made a nice work area by setting plywood on top of a couple of their 55-gallon water drums in a corner of the greenhouse.

Many items usually found in the work space should be out of the reach of children. *Things like seeds, fertilizer and pesticides are dangerous if swallowed and should not be left out in homes or greenhouses where children live or visit.*

You'll enjoy setting aside space in your greenhouse for sitting and relaxing—unless you're in a food survival situation or use it only for commercial production. Used efficiently, the leisure space may allow enough room for two or three chairs. In this area you can still produce food in 1-gallon pots hanging overhead or 5-gallon buckets placed next to the chairs. Of course, you can always remove the furniture for more growing space if your needs dictate.

If you do plan to have a sitting area, locate it in the shadier areas of the greenhouse, the northeast or northwest corners. If a side wall is opaque, locate work areas and leisure space against this wall and to the north. If you are going to use your greenhouse socially in the

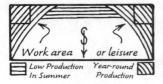

evening, include overhead lights, not for growing, but for seeing at night. It's usually nice to hook up your light to a dimmer switch for varying moods. *Keep candles and kerosene lamps away from fiberglass or plastic glazings. Greenhouses are extremely flammable!*

Solar Sauna

If you live in a sunny winter area and can afford the greenhouse space, you may want to try constructing a solar sauna. It's a great way to get over colds or to just relax. Construction involves walling off a southeast or southwest corner adjacent to the glazing and sealing it to the

rest of the greenhouse with either wood or flat fiberglass. It needs to be large enough to hold you and a few friends; 6' - 8' wide seems to be adequate (depending on the size and shape of your friends). This room should have no ventilation. During sunny winter days, it will frequently get well over 100°F (38°C). In cloudy areas, you must wait for those sunny days to get it hot. Place a few sitting benches inside and, if you want to get fancy, add a shower if you can work out the plumbing. Don't put in plants as they won't survive the heat. For a night sauna, you will have to add a heater, but be careful, *fiberglass and other plastic-based glazings are very flammable. Candles and kerosene lamps also require extreme caution.*

By keeping the door closed to prevent excess humidity, a solar sauna room can also double as a solar food dryer. However, humidity will not allow crops to dry properly and may promote mold growth, making the food dangerous to eat. So, see a good food drying book for details on how to do it.

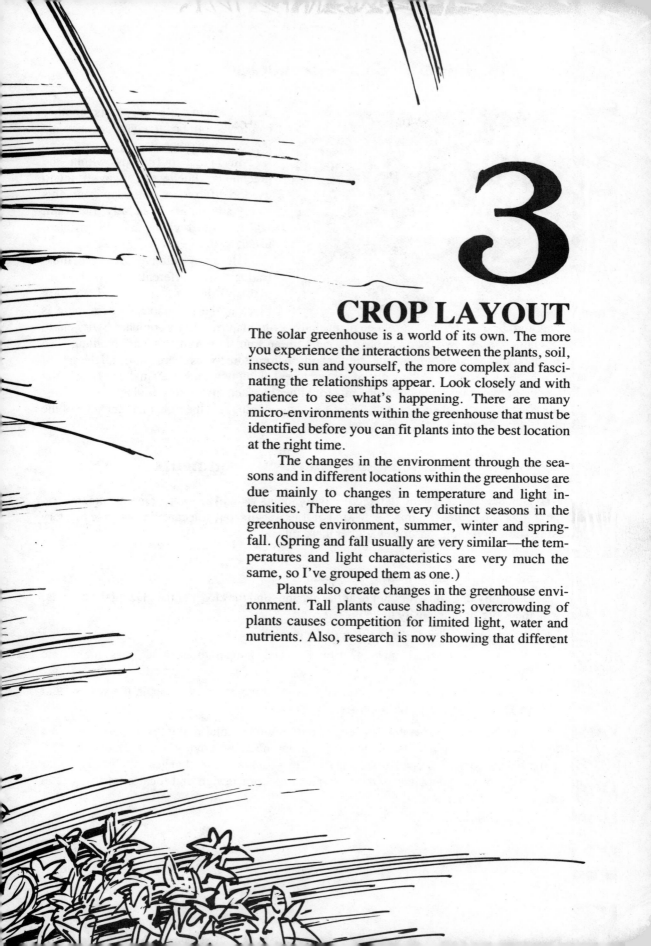

3

CROP LAYOUT

The solar greenhouse is a world of its own. The more you experience the interactions between the plants, soil, insects, sun and yourself, the more complex and fascinating the relationships appear. Look closely and with patience to see what's happening. There are many micro-environments within the greenhouse that must be identified before you can fit plants into the best location at the right time.

The changes in the environment through the seasons and in different locations within the greenhouse are due mainly to changes in temperature and light intensities. There are three very distinct seasons in the greenhouse environment, summer, winter and spring-fall. (Spring and fall usually are very similar—the temperatures and light characteristics are very much the same, so I've grouped them as one.)

Plants also create changes in the greenhouse environment. Tall plants cause shading; overcrowding of plants causes competition for limited light, water and nutrients. Also, research is now showing that different

plants growing adjacent to one another can have both positive and negative effects on each other.

In laying out crops within the greenhouse, I believe in always trying to use the differences in the environments to my advantage. Hopefully, the result will be higher yields and the efficient use of available space.

Here's a common example illustrating the different micro-environments. Think of a cool, relatively dark place in the greenhouse where there is only enough heat and light to produce plants halfway to maturity. Let's compare Swiss chard and tomatoes. Now, what do we have to eat with an immature tomato plant? Nothing. We cannot eat tomato leaves or blossoms. How about an immature Swiss chard plant half the size of a mature plant? There's still plenty of leaves to eat, although they are smaller. This is the difference between utilizing environments for either productivity or non-productivity, at least as far as our stomachs are concerned. So, it's a matter of plugging the right plant into one of the available environments at the right time.

The Seasonal Micro-environments

To isolate and understand the micro-environments we will be looking mainly at temperature and light differences. It may seem kind of tricky at first but you can eliminate the mystery by using some common sense. Remember these rules:

1. Hot air rises; cool air drops.
2. Shade has less light intensity than a sunny area.
3. On sunny days it is very hot near the glazing, and the closer to the glazing the plant is, the more light intensity there is on it.
4. On cool nights, it is colder closer to the glazing.
5. Plants near thermal mass feel more even temperatures, with less night-time fluctuations.
6. The area near a north wall thermal mass is brighter and warmer in the winter, and shadier and cooler in the summer.

Different types of vegetables have different environmental requirements, so now it's a matter of plugging the plants' needs into the appropriate micro-environments. But remember, these micro-environments change seasonally. Let's look at these changes graphically. Your greenhouse may vary depending on interior and exterior design and local climates, but in general this is what happens.

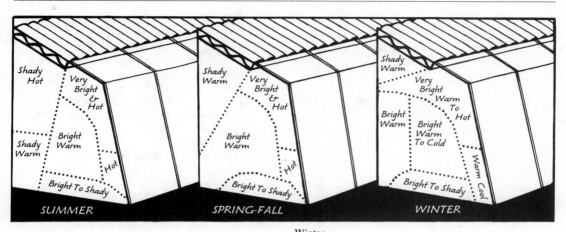

SUMMER — SPRING-FALL — WINTER

Note: Cold=below 32°F (0°C), Cool=32°-50°F (0°-10°C), Warm=50°-85°F (10°-30°C), on up.

Winter
Note: Areas adjacent to glazing become very cold at night and may have spot freezing.

Now, in order to plug into these environments we need to know what the different plants require for best growth.

Crop Light and Temperature Requirements

Crop		Light	Temperature	Comments
Beans:	Lima Bush Pole	bright - very bright	warm - hot	Will tolerate some shade. When trellised, pole beans cause shading. Seeds need 65°F (18°C) soil temperature to germinate well.
Beans:	Fava Broad	bright - very bright	cool - warm	Needs trellising which causes adjacent shading. Will not tolerate hot!
Beets		shady - bright	cool - warm	May go to seed if temperature falls below freezing.
Broccoli		shady - bright	cool - warm	Will flower fast and produce small heads if consistently warm to hot.
Brussels Sprouts		shady - bright	cool	Poor quality if consistently warm to hot. Will cause shading toward maturity.
Cabbage		bright - very bright	cool - warm	May go to seed if temperature is below freezing for a long period of time.
Cantaloupe		bright - very bright	warm - hot	Must have warm nights above 50°F (10°C). Needs trellising which causes adjacent shading.
Carrots		shady - bright	cool - warm	May go to seed if temperature is cold for a long period of time and then grown at warm temperatures.

Crop	Light	Temperature	Comments
Cauliflower	shady - bright	cold - warm	Will flower fast and produce small heads if consistently warm to hot.
Celery	shady - bright	cold - warm	Likes many months of consistent cooler temperatures. Will often go to seed by summer.
Chicory	shady - bright	cold - warm	Not good in hot areas.
Chinese Cabbage	shady - bright	cold - warm	Flowers rapidly in warm to hot conditions.
Collards	shady - bright	cold - hot	Will cause shading after a few months of growing. Well adapted to solar greenhouse environment.
Corn Salad	bright	cold - warm	Well adapted, grows low.
Cucumber	bright - very bright	warm - hot	Needs nights above 50°F (10°C). Creates much shading when trellised.
Eggplant	bright - very bright	warm - hot	Needs nights above 50°F (10°C).
Endive	bright	cool	Poor quality with hot conditions.
Garlic	shady - bright - very bright	cool - warm	Will tolerate hot and cold.
Kale	shady - bright	cold - warm	Poor quality with constant warm to hot temperatures.
Kohlrabi	bright	cold - warm	Enlarged stems (edible portion) crack with warm to hot temperatures. Flowers rapidly with warm to hot temperatures.
Leeks	bright	cool	Will go to seed if temperature is below freezing for long periods and then grown at warm temperatures.
Lettuce	shady - bright	cool - warm	Will go to seed with consistent warm to hot temperatures.
Mustard	shady - bright	cool - warm	Will go to seed with consistent warm to hot temperatures.
Okra	bright - very bright	warm to hot	Will not grow in cool temperatures. Tall varieties cause shading.
Onions	bright	cool - warm	Will not bulb in winter but are good for greens year round.

Crop	Light	Temperature	Comments
Parsley	bright	cool - warm	Plants that over-winter (grow through the winter) will go to seed in spring or summer.
Parsnip	bright	cool	Plants that over-winter may go to seed in spring.
Peas	shady - bright	cool - warm	Consistent warm to hot temperatures will reduce yield.
Pepper	bright - very bright	warm - hot	Prefers warm temperatures in young stages but will over-winter if temperature remains above 40°F (5°C). Best production above 50°F (10°C)
Radish	shady - bright	cool - warm	Consistent warm temperatures cause top growth and seed production, poor quality in warm to hot temperatures.
Rutabaga	shady - bright	cool	Poor quality with warm to hot temperatures.
Spinach	shady - bright	cool - warm	Consistent warm to hot temperatures cause rapid flowering and short production period.
Sweet Potato	shady - bright	warm - hot	Can tolerate hot temperatures well, likes long warm season.
Swiss Chard	shady - bright	cool - warm	May flower in spring if winter was cool, depends on variety.
Squash	bright - very bright	warm - hot	Requires nights about 50°F (10°C). Winter squash trellising causes shading. Summer squash is generally a low bushy plant.
Tomato	bright - very bright	warm - hot	Will tolerate short periods of hot temperatures. Vining tomatoes cause shading. Little or no production below 50°F (10°C).
Turnip	shady - bright	cool	Warm to hot temperatures will crack and produce poor quality roots.
Watermelon	bright - very bright	warm - hot	Requires nights above 50°F (10°C). Needs trellising which causes adjacent shading.

Note: Place any tropical and sub-tropical plants such as figs, oranges, lemons, etc., near the thermal mass. Coffee likes shady areas. In winter and fall place fruiting crops near thermal mass where it is consistently warm. See *Greenhouse Food Crop Scheduling* and *Crops* for further information.

Height and Distance between Plants

Crop	Distance Between Plants For Wide Bed Planting	Approximate Mature Height	Layout Broadcast = B Trellising = T Triangle = △
Beans; Fava, Broad	4''	6'	T
Beans, Bush	6''	10''	△
Beans, Pole	4''	5'- 12'+	T
Beets	4''	1'	B
Broccoli	1'- 1½'	2'- 3½'	△
Brussel Sprouts	1½'	3'- 4'	△
Cabbage	1'- 1½'	1'	△
Cantaloupe	3'- 4'	8'- 15'+	T
Carrots	1½''	1'	B
Cauliflower	1'- 1½'	2'- 3½'	△
Celery	10''	1'	△
Chives	1'	1'	△
Collards	1½'	3- 4'	△
Cucumber	2'	10- 15'	T or △ *
Eggplant	1½'- 2'	3'	△
Garlic	5''	8''- 10''	B or △
Kale	1½'	1'	△
Kohlrabi	8''	1½'	B
Lettuce	5''- 8''	8''- 10''	B or △
Onion Bulbs	5''	1'- 1½'	B
Onion Greens	2''- 3''	1'	B
Parsley	1'- 1½'	1'	△
Peas	4'- 8'	1'- 7'	T
Pepper	1½'	3'- 5'	△
Radish	1½''	6''- 8''	B
Spinach	6''- 8''	8''- 10''	B or △
Summer Squash	2½'- 4'	2'- 2½'	△
Winter Squash	4'- 5'	10'- 15'+	T
Swiss Chard	4''- 8''	1½'- 2'	B or △
Bush Tomato	1½'	2'- 4'	△
Vining Tomato	2'- 3'	6'- 12'	*
Turnip	3''- 5''	1'	B or △
Watermelon	4'	10'- 15'+	T

* = When grown in a triangle layout the plant will need either a support stake or a hanging string to grow up on. See *Crops* for further information.   + = May grow taller. The roof is the limit.

Heavy fruits such as watermelon, cantaloupe and summer squash will need something to support the fruit on the trellising. This will prevent the fruit from pulling the whole vine off the trellising as it gets big and heavy. Recycled nylon stockings or cheesecloth around the fruit tied directly to the trellising works great. For pruning detail, see Crops

Spacing and Trellising

When laying out crops it is important to space all plants at the proper distance. A general rule for fruiting and root crops is to increase spacing slightly when growing them in shady areas. For leafy crops, slightly decrease spacing in shady areas.

Certain crops grow much more efficiently when laid out in a *triangular* pattern in the bed. With a triangular layout there is usually less wasted space than with square layouts. Other efficient planting layouts include the *broadcast* method and *trellising* method. The chart on p. 60 shows where each layout is appropriate.

When seeds are broadcast, the bed is covered with plants in no particular arrangement, except that they are spaced or thinned to the proper distances. Seed either may be scattered into the bed or seedlings may be transplanted. Because most direct light enters the greenhouse at an angle to the south, always try to place shorter crops to the south and taller crops to the north or adjacent to any opaque walls. Use the following chart to see how tall each vegetable gets when mature.

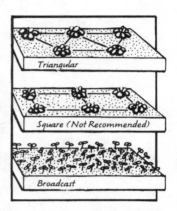

Use Triangular and Broadcast spacing for efficiency

When trellised, many crops can produce much more food per square foot. These crops include cucumbers, pole beans, peas, watermelon and cantaloupe. See chart for appropriate trellis heights. Always run trellises in a north-south direction to minimize shading of adjacent plants. Trellises may also be placed against any opaque wall or against thermal mass in summer months.

Trellises may be constructed of recycled materials such as old wood, string, fencing, chicken wire, etc. To be sturdy, support posts should be laid deep into the ground. Nail, staple or wire the materials together. Sometimes trellises can become somewhat elaborate. Trellises

made into an arch or tunnel create a new micro-environment under the arch to grow crops that like cooler temperatures and some shading. Crops that do best with arch type trellising include: cantaloupes, watermelons, pole beans, European cucumbers and winter squash. Good "under arch" crops are lettuce, chard, turnips, mustard and spinach.

Some unlikely candidates for trellising or stringing up include New Zealand spinach and summer squash. New Zealand spinach may be *gently* tied up to a trellis made of chicken wire or fencing. I've been able to train it to grow as tall as 4'. Summer squash may be wound up in a string in much the same manner as tomatoes are often trellised. This technique is explained in *Crops*.

Harvesting and Layout Choices

Some crops are harvested only once when they are mature. Examples include cabbage or carrots; once they're harvested, that's it. You need to start over again. But other crops such as Swiss chard, spinach or leaf lettuce may be harvested many times, leaving the plant in the ground to continue growing between pickings. When planting in the solar greenhouse, always consider which category each crop fits into. Then, in the easy to reach places, plant the crops that are harvested many times; and—that's right folks—in the harder to reach places, put those that are harvested only once.

Integrated Planting

In companion or integrated planting, rather than only one crop in a bed, the bed has two or more crops growing adjacent to one another. Companion planting is more like nature and less like modern farming where large acreages are filled with only one crop. Let's look at the benefits of integrated planting.

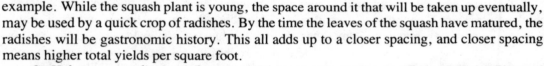

1. *Closer planting*—When two totally different plants grow next to each other they compete less than two alike plants growing side by side. Example: Growing carrots next to lettuce; the carrot has a deep root system and the lettuce has a shallow one, so there will be less competition for water and nutrients. Because both plants can tolerate some partial shading, there is no competition for light.

Another reason for closer planting is to take advantage of a slow growing plant, squash for example. While the squash plant is young, the space around it that will be taken up eventually, may be used by a quick crop of radishes. By the time the leaves of the squash have matured, the radishes will be gastronomic history. This all adds up to a closer spacing, and closer spacing means higher total yields per square foot.

2. *Helps prevent disease infestation*—Diseases are usually specific to plant families and often won't cross over to affect different families. A cabbage (or cole crop) disease, for instance, usually will not affect the tomato family. When a bed is interplanted with different crop families it is harder for a disease to spread throughout the bed. The infestation is limited and an epidemic is prevented.

3. *Helps prevent insect epidemics*—Insects prefer constant and similar stimuli from plants, such as taste, smell, etc. When a bed has many different plants growing in it, pests move

much slower in their feeding because the stimuli are being constantly altered. Also, some plants may repel certain insects and frustrate pest attacks.

4. *Symbiotic effects*—Research is beginning to confirm earlier beliefs that plants may secrete something that benefits adjacent and different plants. But secretions may also have negative effects on adjacent plants. The research generally is still sketchy and most of the information available is based on non-scientific observations or old tales. Please don't lose any sleep over any planting com-

binations you may have come up with in your greenhouse. It may be worth while to observe closely any repeated positive trends when you interplant. Your own record keeping is essential here.

The main disadvantage to integrated planting is having to harvest each planting at a different time. This makes it harder to renew the soil and replant after a harvest without disturbing other crops. Also, it's sometimes more difficult to see when a crop is ready to harvest, so you may have vegetables sneaking past their prime harvest time. An integrated bed has a wilder look to it which some enjoy, but others have trouble getting used to; especially those who prefer very organized looking gardens.

I have tried to simplify my mental attitude about gardening. A garden does *not* have to be a picture of perfect order. I often take a handful of assorted seeds including herbs, vegetables and flowers that are similarly adapted to the greenhouse, the greenhouse season and the bed location. Then I randomly sprinkle the seeds around, covering all areas of a single bed. The seeds germinate and grow in a random combination. Later I thin them out to the proper distances. This very random pattern of different plants often becomes a very productive but wild-looking bed. On the whole, however, an *organized* style of integrated planting, combining triangles, trellis or broadcast plantings, is easier to manage, especially when you are new to this.

In order to lay out a bed for companion planting, try to find plants of different families that like similar micro-environments. When possible, avoid mixing together physiologically similar crops—such as two different leaf crops. Try mixing broadcast crops with triangle layout crops, or trellis crops with broadcast crops. Interplant flowers and herbs with your vegetables. They'll not only add beauty to your garden but the flowers will provide a back-up food source for beneficial insects and will repel harmful pests; and some flowers are even edible. Be creative with interplanting; experiment and have fun.

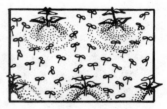

Broadcast with triangular

Basic Crop Groups

This guide will help you plan integrated crop plantings and crop rotation season-to-season. Cross-mix the *groups*.

Cole Crop—Crucifer—Cabbage Group

Broccoli	Kale
Brussel Sprouts	Kohlrabi
Cabbage	Mustards
Cauliflower	Nasturtium
Chinese Cabbage	Radish
Collards	Rutabaga
Cress	Turnip

Alliums or Onion Group

Onions
Garlic
Chives
Scallions
Leeks
Shallots

Legume Group

Beans - Soy, Bush, Garbanzo, Broad, Fava, Wax, Lima, Pole
Peas
Cowpeas

Beet Group

Swiss chard
Beets
Spinach

Carrot Group

Carrot	Anise
Parsley	Coriander - Cilantro
Fennel	Celery
Dill	Caraway

Tomato Group

Tomato	Petunia
Tobacco	Eggplant
Potato	Pepper

Cucumber Group

Cucumber	Squash—winter and
Watermelon	summer
Cantaloupe	Louffa squash
Other melons	Pumpkins

Overall, companion planting is helpful, but it probably has a smaller effect in the greenhouse than planting crops in proper locations, laying out crops to eliminate shading effects, planting crops at the proper time of year, and selecting proper varieties. It's best to consider all of these factors together when laying out a bed.

Crop Rotation

Crop rotation, an old practice, is still very important in the solar greenhouse. It keeps the soil healthy and helps to break disease cycles. Keep records of where you have planted each crop from season to season. Whenever possible try to wait about 1-2 years before planting the same crop in the same place. It also helps to avoid vegetables of the same plant group in the same place year after year. This is good preventative medicine against major disease problems. See the Basic Crop Groups chart.

Crop Maturity

Crops will generally have different maturity times than specified on packets or in catalogs. To better time your planting and harvesting in winter, allow a 20 - 30 percent longer period than listed for crops to reach maturity. For fall and spring greenhouse crops, add 10 - 15 percent more "days 'til harvest." The slightly *slower* growth in fall, spring and winter is not bad compared to zero growth outside.

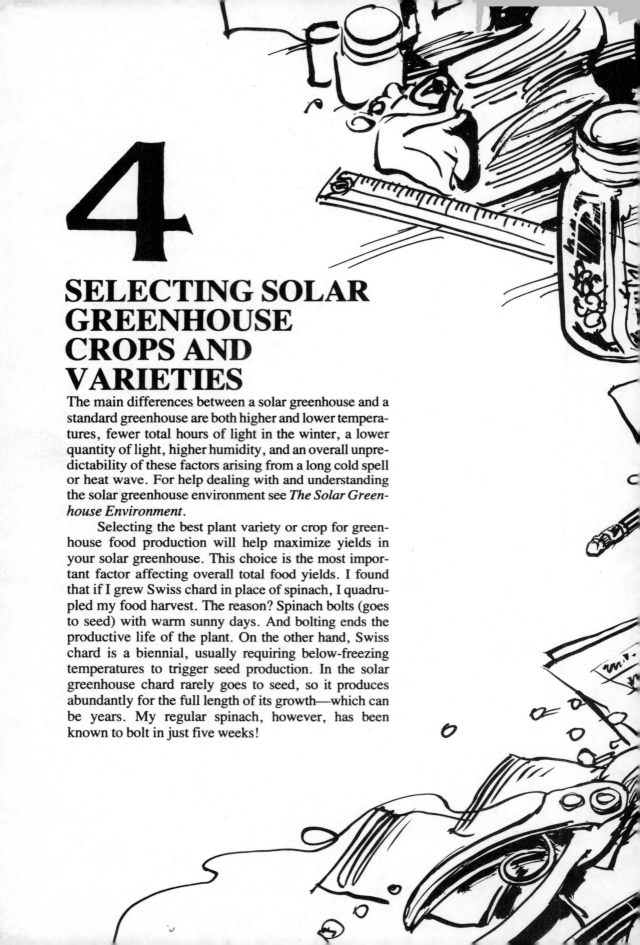

4

SELECTING SOLAR GREENHOUSE CROPS AND VARIETIES

The main differences between a solar greenhouse and a standard greenhouse are both higher and lower temperatures, fewer total hours of light in the winter, a lower quantity of light, higher humidity, and an overall unpredictability of these factors arising from a long cold spell or heat wave. For help dealing with and understanding the solar greenhouse environment see *The Solar Greenhouse Environment*.

Selecting the best plant variety or crop for greenhouse food production will help maximize yields in your solar greenhouse. This choice is the most important factor affecting overall total food yields. I found that if I grew Swiss chard in place of spinach, I quadrupled my food harvest. The reason? Spinach bolts (goes to seed) with warm sunny days. And bolting ends the productive life of the plant. On the other hand, Swiss chard is a biennial, usually requiring below-freezing temperatures to trigger seed production. In the solar greenhouse chard rarely goes to seed, so it produces abundantly for the full length of its growth—which can be years. My regular spinach, however, has been known to bolt in just five weeks!

I've also found that I can help keep diseases to a minimum by selecting a disease-resistant variety. My cantaloupe had a common disease known as powdery mildew, a leaf fungus, that was destroying my crop until I switched to resistant varieties. These varieties will occasionally show slight mildew damage, but they are now mostly healthy and vigorous plants. My yield was saved by the selection of a better variety.

If you are serious about getting the most food from your greenhouse, you must know the difference between an efficient food producing plant and one that isn't.

Plants that require much space for non-edible leaf production are often not efficient. Here are some examples. Compare cauliflower to cabbage. The whole cabbage plant is edible, every

last leaf; while the cauliflower produces many leaves but only a small edible head. (The leaves which are commonly discarded are edible, but not desirable.) Imagine two equal sized plots of land, one growing cabbage and the other cauliflower. The total pounds of food in the cabbage plot will be much greater than from the cauliflower plot. Another example: compare peas to beets. Peas require space to grow many leaves before you can harvest the small round sweet peas. Beets, on the other hand, are almost 100 percent edible. The greens, or tops, are excellent when cooked like spinach. And, of course, the roots are edible. There is little waste, With a crop of peas, the vines, leaves and roots are all thrown out or, hopefully, composted. Hence, with peas, less food per growing space is produced than with beets. So think about each plant's food efficiency. How much food does it provide in how much space?

I'm not trying to talk you out of growing peas or any other crop; peas are ambrosia in the winter greenhouse. But with the high cost of fresh food—and in emergency or survival situations—these efficiency considerations are of great importance as you plan what you want to grow.

Probably one of the most important considerations is personal taste. What good is a bushel of radishes if it doesn't get eaten? Be sure you plant only what will be consumed. Also, avoid growing food that can be stored easily or purchased cheaply. Why grow potatoes when they keep great in your root cellar and can be purchased very cheaply? Instead, get the most value out of your greenhouse by growing the more expensive and perishable crops.

In selecting a crop or plant variety well-adapted to the solar greenhouse environment, it would be nice to just review a list of varieties and crops that have been found to perform well. Such a list would be great to have, but there are some difficult problems involved. First, crop varieties are constantly changing, old ones being dropped as new varieties take their place. So there is no guarantee you will find the recommended variety over many years. Another problem is that every greenhouse has it's unique inherent characteristics. One greenhouse may be brighter, while another may be colder, smaller, hotter or more humid. Whereas one variety or crop is good for one greenhouse, it may perform poorly in another, even if they are both in the same vicinity. Eventually you will learn the unique qualities of *your* greenhouse. You will discover its personality. Throughout the book I name specific varieties and their characteristics, but it is far from a universal list. The best thing for me to do is spell out the major considerations to look at so *you* can make the proper decision for *your* greenhouse.

To begin selecting efficient plant varieties, start by subscribing to as many seed catalogues as possible. (See Appendix A for listings.) There is much to learn by comparing the descriptions of the different varieties. Not only are the catalogues educational, but they are also entertaining. Some catalogues I've found that are particularly helpful to solar greenhouse owners are: Stokes, Thompson and Morgan, Herbst Bros., Harris, Twilleys, Cameron Seeds, Porter and Son Seedsmen, and Seed Savers Exchange. While you look through the many selections available, keep the following considerations in mind.

Selection for Heat Tolerance

Whenever your greenhouse is above 85°F (30°C) in the winter or above 90°F (32°C) in the summer, it's too hot for maximum plant growth. Above these temperatures plant growth will slow, blossoms will often not set fruit, and many leafy plants as well as some root crops will go to seed, bringing an end to plant growth and a great reduction in quality. There are seed companies in the southern United States that list certain fruiting plants, such at tomatoes, that aren't damaged by the heat. For instance, Porter and Son Seedsmen of Texas list a few tomato varieties that "continue to set fruits with daytime temperatures up to 90°F" (32°C). Check out these southern catalogues if your greenhouse is commonly too hot in the spring, summer and fall months. Selection for heat tolerances is not so crucial in areas with less winter sun, or cool summers. Of course, the best way to deal with a hot greenhouse is proper venting as outlined in *The Solar Greenhouse Environment*.

But if you live in an area that receives a winter monthly average of 45% or more of possible sunshine (as listed by your local National Weather Service forecasters; also see Appendix D) you'll often experience very high winter temperatures. Here you should select varieties listed as being "heat resistant," "slow to bolt," or the like. Crops that are spoiled by going to seed include spinach, lettuce and radishes. Another solution to crops bolting is to utilize substitute crops such as New Zealand spinach or Swiss chard which are perennial and biennial greens respectively, and therefore will not bolt in one growing season.

Other plants may not bolt, but respond to overheating in other ways. For example, yields of peas drop drastically with hot daytime temperatures. However, there are certain pea varieties which are tolerant of heat as well as being cold hardy (see *Crops*), so choose wisely.

Selection for Cold Tolerance

Selection of cold hardy crops is important for solar greenhouses located in areas with much winter cloudiness or below 45% of possible winter sunshine. See Appendix D. Resistance to cold is also an important consideration for winter food production in cold frames or season extenders. In the catalogs sometimes you'll find varieties listed as "cold hardy" or "productive in cold weather." In general, many crops are quite hardy in cool temperatures (even below freezing), particularly varieties in the cabbage or cole crop groups. Other possible crops include those grown for their vegetable parts: root, petioles, leaves, stems and bulbs. A book entitled *Wintertime Gardening in the Maritime Northwest* by Binda Colebrook is an excellent guide for folks who grow food in cold greenhouse conditions, coldframes and outside in cloudy maritime climates. It's available from Tilth, Rt 2 Box 190-A, Arlington, WA 98223.

Selection for Quick Maturity

In the winter months, important limiting factors in the solar greenhouse include low temperatures, low light levels and short days. Varieties and crops that are listed as "early maturing" generally require less light and heat to reach the harvest stage. Early varieties are those listed in catalogs with the least number of "days 'til harvest." The early varieties are best planted in the fall and winter. Although you have selected an early variety, expect it to take longer to reach maturity than the catalog specifies. Catalog specifications are usually based on ideal summertime conditions, which are far from what the wintertime solar greenhouse can supply. But using early varieties in the winter often can speed the growth period a few days to a few weeks over conventional varieties.

Selection for Plant Shape and Size

When a plant grows vertically, it can provide more food per square foot of growing space. Because the growing space in a greenhouse is always limited, it is wise, whenever possible, to grow vine varieties (which can grow vertically) rather than bush varieties. With crops such as beans, peas, cucumbers, squash and melons, you are often provided with a choice of either bush growth or vining. Tomatoes offer a similar choice, but they are often listed with a different vocabulary; vine types are called "indeterminate" and bush varieties "determinate." This is because tomatoes, unlike peas, beans, melons and cucumbers don't have tendrils and so really don't "vine" per se. However, they can be trellised or supported to grow vertically, but only indeterminate tomatoes have this ability. Vines such as peas and beans will readily climb up a trellis or other support, but the vine cucumbers and tomatoes usually must be tied loosely to a support, and they must also be pruned for best production (see *Crops*).

When you set up trellising for any crop, run the trellis north-south. An east-west trellis should be set up only in areas where shading is not a problem, such as against an opaque wall or the north wall in spring, summer or fall. As the heavier fruits form on melon plants, place them in an old nylon stocking or cheesecloth tied *to* the trellis. This will prevent the weight of the growing melon from ripping down the whole vine. And the stocking will expand with the fruit as it grows. Whenever tying up plants on a support, be sure to use a soft string or cloth strip tied loosely to prevent strangulation of the plant. Does this sound complicated? It isn't. You'll get used to it, and with time your trellising can become as creative as you want it to be, with serpentine waves or extensive arches over walkways and beds—a veritable new art form.

Many plants have been developed for bush growth rather than vine growth. These bush varieties can be fit into the solar greenhouse in special places like a front knee wall bed where

Determinate & Indeterminate

there is not enough room to let the plants grow tall. When growing food in containers or pots, you'll find that bush varieties do best. Plant stress need not be a problem in containers as long as the limited room for root development provided by the container corresponds to the bush-sized top growth. Some examples include: bush beans in a hanging pot, a bush cucumber in a 3-gallon can, a Tiny Tim tomato (determinate tomato) in a 3-gallon container, and some dwarf peas in an old bucket. Play around and see

Bush by kneewall

what works. It is fun to experiment. But avoid planting large vine type plants in small containers because the imbalance of limited root space to the tall leafy part of the plant will cause periodic wilting and plant nutrition problems.

Unfortunately *summer* squash can be found *only* in bush types; but bush types can still be trained to grow vertically up a string or stake. This technique requires great gentleness and is outlined in *Crops*.

Selection for Disease Resistance

With the inherent high humidity of solar greenhouse and intensive plant and food production, diseases often can be a problem. Besides maintaining healthy plants, the easiest way to prevent plant diseases is to grow varieties that show some resistance to your particular disease problem. Catalogs list varieties that are resistant to certain diseases. Tomatoes, peas, beans, lettuce, melons and squashes are among the many crops listed. If a variety isn't listed as being disease resistant, nevertheless you may find that it out-produces a similar disease resistant variety. And even though a variety is listed as being disease resistant, the degree of "resistance" may vary a good deal. Don't be surprised if you are growing a vegetable that is listed as "resistant" to a certain disease, and still see evidence of that disease. The variety may be only more tolerant than most other varieties, or they may be totally resistant, showing no signs of the disease. That's something they don't tell you in the catalogs.

Plant maladies move fast, especially if there is a large planting of only one crop variety. Diseases can spread like an epidemic. For this reason, *never* plant just one variety of a main crop such as tomatoes or lettuce. Always grow at least two different varieties; chances are if a disease takes hold and starts to spread, it will affect one variety more than another. In growing several varieties, nature's genetic diversity will work for you. Planting a few types of tomatoes, for instance, will also enable you to observe the differences in production among them. It is a self-education process that is on-going. It results in your discovering the best possible varieties for your unique solar greenhouse, while protecting you from unforseen disease epidemics. Keep records of what varieties you plant, when and where they are planted, and what your feelings and observations are about the overall production of each. Don't be lazy about record keeping. It's not hard and will provide you with valuable information not available anywhere else.

Of course, identifying the specific disease is the first step. Check out *Pests and Diseases* for help.

Selection for Insect Pest Resistance

In a few instances there are vegetable crops that have been bred for their resistance to insect attack. Listings in garden catalogs for insect resistance are rare, but you may find that certain varieties grown in your greenhouse exhibit a greater tolerance to infestations by insects. Again, keep records. There may be other reasons for a crop's insect tolerance, so test your favorite varieties for a few seasons to see if there is some inherent ability to ward off insect infestations. It may have just been a good year for crops and a bad year for pests.

Greenhouse Varieties

There have been food crop varieties developed especially for large standard commercial food producing greenhouses. Developments have been limited mainly to cucumbers, lettuce and tomatoes—the three traditional greenhouse crops. These greenhouse varieties have been selected for high productivity under ideal conditions of light and temperatures in a totally controlled energy-intensive environment. Incorporated into these varieties were characteristics such as disease resistance, high yields, vine growth, bolt resistance (lettuce), resistance to physiological disorders (fruit cracking, blossom-end rot, etc.) and, as in the case of the European cucumber, not requiring pollination to set fruit. Often these same characteristics are also helpful in the solar greenhouse.

Such greenhouse varieties usually out-produce traditional garden varieties. Greenhouse varieties can be easily

located in the catalogs that carry them. They are usually flagged with a statement like, *"for greenhouse production,"* or *"for greenhouse forcing."* You will find that each greenhouse variety has different specific characteristics. One variety may be listed to set well under cold conditions, while another sets in hotter conditions. You'll also find much variability in the disease resistance among the greenhouse varieties. Here's where you apply what you know about your own greenhouse.

Let's say you are thinking of growing the European cucumbers (see *Crops*) and know that you run cool night temperatures and also have a problem with the powdery mildew disease. Among many choices, Stokes catalog, for instance, lists a variety that fits those criteria.

As mentioned earlier, most of the breeding work in developing greenhouse varieties has concentrated on only three crops—cucumbers, lettuce and tomatoes. This is just an indication of the potential. Imagine the possibilities of a breeding effort with *all* the possible greenhouse crops, selecting characteristics to suit the unique solar greenhouse environment.

Many of the varieties mentioned in *Crops* include the bred-for-greenhouse varieties. Take advantage of these and watch your yields increase.

Crops That Need Winter—Problems and Possibilities

Why not asparagus, rhubarb, apples, cherries, peaches, pears, apricots, currants and raspberries in your solar greenhouse? There are a couple of problems here. First, these crops are usually grown outside and the cold of winter is required for their normal growth and food production. No winter, no food production. Another problem is that these crops require an appreciable amount of space and produce for only a relatively short time. Depending on where you live, these crops may do just fine outside, and unfortunately won't do much better inside unless you live where summer frosts are common.

But there are those of us who wish we could be eating rhubarb in the dead of winter. You can sometimes fake a winter, or "force a crop" as horticulturists put it. Different crops and varieties have different "chill requirements," and these can be imitated artificially. One way to do this is to go outside in mid-winter and carefully dig up plants (you may need a pick for the frozen top soil) and transplant them inside for late winter harvests. The "half winter" treatment is usually enough to ensure proper production.

The wintertime transplanting method is, of course, much harder with an 8' peach tree; but it can be done with dwarf varieties in large containers on rollers.

These "winterphyllic" temperate crops warrant further experimentation and development. There is some good potential for growing crops such as asparagus and rhubarb in winter greenhouses. In the south, plant breeders have developed varieties of temperate fruit crops that require less chilling to produce food. Look through some southern catalogs for these special "low chill requirement" plants.

As you look through the catalogs and get a few years of growing and record keeping experience, you'll have an easier time selecting crops for your greenhouse. You will see your yields increase and come to appreciate the special thought that must go into use of your solar greenhouse. Soon it will be hard to imagine the old days of planting the same crops and varieties as you did in your outside garden. The inside garden and the outside one each require their own brand of attention.

5

PLANT PROPAGATION

In our industrial world we sometimes take for granted or never learn where things come from. Once I asked a little girl where she thought her french fries came from. She said "France." Eggs? From "the egg factory"; pineapple, from "a pine tree" and bananas came from the "store." It's a healthy thing to wonder where things come from. When it comes to plants they either grow from seeds or spores; or vegetatively from cuttings, grafting, division, or above and below ground runners.

Your ability to start plants in the solar greenhouse is the heart of the food producing cycle. If you have trouble here your whole operation is in trouble.

There are tricks you can use in the solar greenhouse for starting and establishing plants that can result in more efficiency. For example, rather than wasting precious bed space waiting for seeds to germinate, use another area for starting seedlings. Then 4-6 weeks later, transplant seedlings into a bed the same day you rip out an old crop. It's just like hitting the ground running.

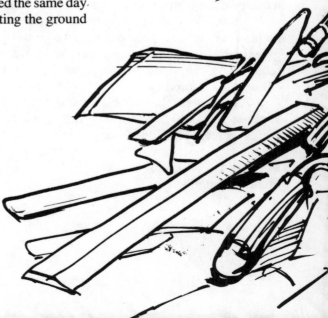

We'll also look into saving time and money by propagating clones (exact reproductions of the mother plant), also known as cuttings. Most people are quite familiar with this type of propagation for house plants. There are great benefits when the same idea is applied to vegetable crops. Cloning can shorten the time it takes to produce a new plant and will save money over buying some of the more expensive hybrid and fancy vegetable seeds.

Seed Propagation

Pollination fertilizes the egg within the plant, and the results of this sexual reproduction are seeds. Seeds are truly amazing, self-contained units. They are new genetic individuals. Within each seed is an embryonic plant and a food reserve to get the plant going until it can provide for itself. A nice little complete package.

The first step for the gardener is to obtain new, good quality seeds. Older seeds produce lower quality plants, are slower to germinate and have a lower percentage germinating and are more susceptible to disease. Generally, seeds older than two or three years begin to lose their viability, but the length of storage time varies with different crops. It's always best to store all seeds in an air-tight dry container, in a dark, cool and dry place. Temperatures as low as freezing are usually fine.

Seeds are usually bought in packets (the type you see displayed in stores in spring) or from a catalog source. I feel that a catalog gives much better descriptions of the varieties and a much wider choice. If you order from a seed catalog be sure to ask them to ship immediately, especially if your order is made in the off season (the off season is any time but late winter and early spring). Just scribble "Ship as soon as possible," on the order form. (See Appendix A for a list of seed companies.)

In choosing how much seed to buy, here's a guide to the approximate number of seeds per ounce. Count on a 60% - 80% germination rate for new seeds. The germination rate drops as seeds age.

Hybrids

One of the first choices when buying seeds is whether to grow hybrids or non-hybrids (often called open-pollinated seeds). A hybrid is defined as the result of two genetically diverse parents. But nowadays it means more. Agricultural scientists have developed what is called the F_1 hybrid. This hybrid is created by inbreeding two different parent lines for a specific number of years. During the inbreeding, each parent line is kept separate. After the period of inbreeding the two lines are finally cross-pollinated. The resulting seed is the F_1 hybrid seed. Where does the designation F_1 come from? It is the *First* generation after the inbreeding is over. Usually when you see the word "hybrid" in a catalog or packet, it's generally an F_1 hybrid.

Number of Seeds Per Ounce

Ornamentals & Herbs	Approx. No. of seeds/oz.	Vegetables	Approx. No. of seeds/oz.
Ageratum	130,000	Beans	120
Allyssum	90,000	Broccoli	10,000
Basil	20,000	Brussels Sprouts	8,500
Begonia fiberous roots & tuberous	2,000,000	Cabbage	7,500
		Canteloupe	1,000
Calendula	3,000	Carrots	15,000
Carnation	14,000	Cauliflower	10,000
Chives	22,000	Celery	70,000
Coleus	100,000	Chinese Cabbage	16,000
Cosmos	5,000	Collards	9,500
Dahlia	2,800	Cucumber	1,000
Dill	6,300	Eggplant	6,000
Feverfew	145,000	Kale	8,500
Impatiens	44,000	Kohlrabi	8,000
Marigold	10,000	Lettuce	20,000
Marjoram, Sweet	100,000	Okra	550
Morning Glory	650	Onions	9,500
Nicotiana	400,000	Peas	150
Pansy	20,000	Pepper	4,500
Parsley	19,000	Radishes	2,500
Petunias	200,000	Spinach	2,000
Phlox	14,000	Squash	250
Snapdragon	180,000	Tomatoes	10,000
Thyme	76,000	Turnips	11,000
Verbena	10,000	Watermelon	250
Viola	24,000		
Zinnia	2,500		

For a home source of regular seeds, consider saving your own. Here are some good books on the subject:

Seed Starters Handbook by Nancy Bubel from Rodale Press, 1978

Growing Garden Seeds: A Manual for Gardeners and Small Farmers, by Rob Johnson. Available from Johnny's Selected Seeds, Albion, ME 04910

Vegetable and Herb Seed Growing for the Gardener and Small Farmer by Doug Miller. Available from Abundant Life Seed Foundation, P.O. Box 772, Port Townsend, WA 98368

F_1 hybrids have distinct advantages and disadvantages. The advantages are:

1) Up to 25% higher yield.

2) Production of uniform looking plants with little deviation (an advantage for machine harvesting).

3) Greater disease resistance—this is not always true but usually more resistance is built into hybrids.

The disadvantages are:

1) High cost. They are up to four times more expensive because they take longer and are more trouble to produce.

2) They often require a more exacting horticulture. When things aren't optimum, they suffer more than traditional open-pollinated seeds.

3) You can't save your own seeds from F_1 hybrid plants. The resulting seeds from an F_1 hybrid are usually lower yielding and quite variable in their physical characteristics. You just don't know what you'll get, and you often may lose all the advantages the F_1 plant had.

Because you can't harvest and use F_1 seeds and expect decent results, F_1 growers are forced to purchase new seeds each season. Seed companies love this, especially because F_1 are more expensive, creating a higher profit. Farmers generally don't mind either, because the extra yield (also higher total profit) from F_1 seeds easily covers the higher seed expense. As a result, seed companies have become a good stable investment with high profits. Since the early 1970s most of the large seed companies have been bought by large multi-national drug and petroleum corporations. These are the same people who bring us chemical fertilizers, refined petroleum, pesticides and other agricultural products.

To give you a few examples, Burpee and O.M. Scott and Sons are owned by ITT. Harris Seeds is owned by Celanese, Ferry Morse by Purex, Northrup-King by Sandoz, and Keystone Seeds by Union Carbide. You may want to pick out seed companies with discretion. Ask who owns them.

If you want to do more reading about the effects of hybrid seeds on our agricultural system see the book *Seeds of the Earth,* by Patrick Mooney available from Tilth, Rt. 2, Box 190-A, Arlington, WA 98223.

You will have to decide if F_1 hybrid seeds are worth it. Although you can't harvest F_1 hybrid seeds for new plants, you can reproduce hybrids from cuttings as outlined later in this chapter. The best way to evaluate their worth is to compare them with non-hybrid varieties in *your* greenhouse. You'll have to do your own tests.

Germination

To germinate seeds you must create a specific environment. It may be helpful to set aside a small area within the greenhouse that has moderate temperatures and light. Good ventilation also helps. Here's a more detailed list of what's needed for good germination:

Disease-free soil and pots   Many seedling diseases cause poor germination. Therefore, use clean pots or trays. Never use old soil which has had greenhouse plants growing in it previously, unless it's been sterilized. An alternative is to use store-bought potting soil. See seedling diseases in *Pests and Diseases*.

Moisture   Germinating seedlings need constant moisture. Keep the soil moist but not dripping wet. If the soil dries out even once, it may kill germinating seedlings.

Aeration   Seeds also need air, so make sure the soil isn't constantly saturated. All containers should have holes in the bottom so excess water can drain out of the soil.

Soil temperature   See chart (page 80). In the winter many people have trouble germinating seedlings. This is due usually to cold soil conditions. Though plants vary in their temperature requirements usually seeds have trouble germinating when the soil temperature is below 50°F

(10°C). A temperature around 65-70°F (18-21°C) is optimum for most germinating seeds. Extreme high and low temperatures are harmful, so in the cold season you may have to use some source of bottom heat from electric heating cables or pads. They vary in price from $10.00 to $55.00. The pad type bottom heaters with adjustable thermostats are best, but also cost the most. Lower priced models work fine but don't last as long. If you use an electrical bottom heater, don't trust its thermostat or what the package says. Check the temperature of your soil with a thermometer. If it's high or low, make  proper adjustments. A 10°F (6°C) difference can make shambles of your seedling survival and germination. An alternative to bottom heaters is to bring your seedling trays inside the house and place them in a warm sunny window. Then, as soon as they germinate, bring them back into your greenhouse, for later transplanting.

Light   Few seeds need light to germinate. Those that do should be planted at a shallow depth in a well lit area. Lettuce is one common vegetable seed that requires some light through the soil surface. Be sure seeds receive enough light after they're up or they will become leggy. In winter you can greatly speed the development of seedlings by growing them under supplementary lights such as cool white florescent types. This may even be done in a place other than the greenhouse. Make a growth chamber by setting up an array of lights over your seedling trays. See illustration p. 23.

Depth   A general rule is to plant all seeds to a depth of 2-3 times their width. Smaller seeds have less food-energy reserves to push through to the surface so plant them at correspondingly more shallow depths. For shallow-planted seeds (smaller seeds), be extra careful that the soil surface doesn't dry out. Also, water gently.

Nutrients   Seed germination requires little if any added nutrients. In fact, nutrients such as nitrogen may cause problems. However, seedlings may benefit from *very dilute* fertilizers. It depends on how fertile your germinating medium is. See *Getting to the Roots*.

   The following is a good general soil mix for seedlings if you'd like to make it yourself rather than purchase commercial potting soil.

Seedling Soil Mix

   1 part rich top soil

   1 part sand, perlite or vermiculite

   1 part well-rotted, screened compost, peat moss, or leaf mold

   Blend well.

   If your top soil is chunky, you may want to screen it to get a better blend. The soil adds some nutrient value to the mix; the sand, perlite or vermiculite adds drainage and aeration; and the compost, vermiculite and peat moss add water holding ability, have a small nutrient value and also provide some aeration.

Planting Requirements

Crop	Planting Method	Seedling to Transplanting (weeks)	Soil Temperature for Germination °F (°C)	Comments
Beans	3	—	60-85 (15-30)	
Beans, Lima	3	—	65-85 (18-30)	
Beans, Fava	3	—	55-80 (13-27)	
Beets	3	—	50-80 (10-27)	Requires thinning
Cabbage	1	4-6	45-90 (7-32)	
Carrots	3	—	45-85 (7-30)	Requires thinning
Collards	1	4-6	45-90 (7-32)	
Cantaloupe	2	3-5	60-95 (15-35)	
Celery	1	7-10	60-70 (15-21)	
Chinese Cabbage	1	4-6	45-80 (7-27)	
Cucumber	2	3-5	60-95 (15-35)	
Eggplant	1	7-10	75-90 (24-32)	
Garlic	4	7-15	60-90 (15-32)	Bulbs, save the old seeds
Kale	1	4-6	45-85 (7-30)	
Kohlrabi	1	4-6	50-85 (10-30)	
Lettuce	1	6-9	50-80 (10-27)	Needs light to germinate
Mustard	1	4-7	50-80 (10-27)	
Okra	1	5-9	60-95 (15-35)	
Onions	4	7-15	50-90 (10-32)	Bulbs sets save time
Parsley	1	6-10	50-85 (10-30)	
Peas	3	—	40-75 (4-24)	
Pepper	1	8-11	65-95 (18-35)	
Radish	3	—	45-90 (7-32)	
Spinach	1	6-9	45-75 (7-24)	
Squash	2	3-5	70-95 (21-35)	May need dilute feeding
Swiss Chard	1	3-8	50-85 (10-30)	
Tomato	1	6-8	60-85 (15-30)	
Turnip	3	—	60-95 (15-35)	
Watermelon	2	4-6	70-95 (21-35)	

Key to Chart Planting Method:

1=transplant to save space and time
2=can be transplanted but requires special care (peat pots are recommended)
3=directly plant seed into bed
4=started from bulb or seed

Note: Vegetables that are recommended to be transplanted can also be seeded directly into the bed. But remember, transplanting saves time and space. Vegetables that are recommended to be directly seeded into beds should not be transplanted.

How to Plant Seeds

Sow the seeds into either a flat or an individual pot. A flat is a small planting tray about 2''-3'' deep. *It should have bottom holes.* Flats may be purchased from commercial greenhouse suppliers or made out of recycled materials—an old cake pan or milk carton cut in half and set on its side will work well.

Smooth it out on top. In flats, sow seeds in rows to prevent disease spread. Be sure to mark each row if there are different seeds in a flat. Leave some room between each seed depending on seed size (usually ⅓''). The flat may be watered either before seeding or after. I prefer wetting the soil in the flat before seeding because it prevents the seed from washing out later. To maintain high humidity, many people slip the flat into a clear plastic bag after seed planting. If you do this, it probably won't need watering again till the seeds germinate. But be sure to check it daily. When the seeds begin coming up, immediately take the flat out of the bag and place it in a well lit location. If the plants' leaves begin to touch each other, either thin them out or transplant into other containers or a growing bed. This prevents overcrowding, which can greatly slow growth and reduce overall yield. The best time to transplant is when plants have their first set of true leaves (the first ones with veins); look closely.

Planting sequence

Thinning Out Seedlings

If you are seeding directly into beds, be sure to thin out the plants to the specified distance (see chart in *Crop Layout*). Failure to thin out seedlings is an amazingly common problem. Some

people don't have the heart to kill a seedling as part of the thinning process—but it's sort of like destroying part of something to save it. You just have to get ruthless or they'll look like seedlings for weeks. Pinch seedlings out at the soil level rather than pulling them out because pulling may injure the roots of remaining adjacent plants. Use the following chart to determine whether you want to transplant the crop or not. When you get to thinning, refer to *Crop Layout* for a chart with spacing distances.

Transplanting

Transplanting seedlings rather than planting seeds directly into a bed frees precious bed space for production. You can plant a 4 - 10 week old seedling on the same day a bed is harvested and pulled out. This means that precious bed space isn't wasted waiting for seed germination and initial growth. Of course only crops that are recommended to be transplanted can be treated this way. And you will have to plan carefully—at least a month or two in advance—in order for this technique to be suc-

cessful. An occasional mistake might cause you to waste some seeds or seedlings, but the vast amount of time you can save makes it worth it. Try to predict when a bed will be about out of production and have to be pulled out. Always be thinking about what will go in that bed next. If the next crop you plan to grow is transplantable, get it started so it will be ready to transplant the day the bed is ready. Refer to *Greenhouse Food Crop Scheduling* for help in planning this.

There's no loss with some leafy crop seedlings even if they never get transplanted. You can let them grow in their flat and harvest the small leaves for eating. I call these "gourmet greens." They're small but good. This early munching only works with leafy crops; you don't want to eat something like tomato leaves.

Seedling with 1st leaves

But as I said before, the time to transplant is soon after plants develop their first true leaves. If you wait too long, you'll get hardened, spindly or stunted plants that seldom grow properly.

Water your seedlings before you begin transplanting. Dig deep and gently, removing one plant at a time. A sharp pencil makes an excellent transplanting tool to help ease the roots out. Get as much root as possible. Do not clean the soil off the roots. Where there are many plants' roots intertwined, place them in a bucket of water to gently separate them. To prevent damage from drying, place the plants on moist newspaper. Never pull out more than you can transplant in a few minutes because sitting out in dry air will permanently damage the roots. Discard spindly or poorly developed plants.

Gently hold the plant by the top and carefully tuck the roots into holes made in the final growing location. Keep the roots pointed downward. Plant the seedling slightly deeper than they were in the germinating containers. Don't jam roots into a hole

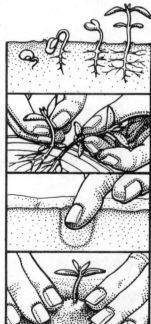

Transplanting sequence.

that is too shallow. Finally, place soil around each plant and use your fingers to gently firm it around the stem and roots. Is the plant sitting upright? Yes? Good.

After transplanting, gently water the plants again, being careful not to wash out or flatten them. And protect the seedlings from drafts or high temperatures. If you have a slug problem, you may want to put a slug trap near the seedlings. Also check for aphids; they congregate around the plant tops and under the leaves. (See *Pests and Diseases* for solutions.)

After a few weeks, application of a dilute fertilizer high in phosphorus and low in nitrogen may help seedling establishment.

Cloning Around

An alternative to starting vegetable plants from seed is to use cuttings from a mother plant and to root them the same way you do houseplants. This is actually a clone because each cutting is genetically identical to the mother plant.

There are some real advantages to cloning. First, it can save you money in seed costs. For example, look in your seed catalog at the price of European Greenhouse Forcing cucumbers. The price of one of these seeds is about 30 cents. The price of hybrid seeds is also high. When added up this can become a major expense. Starting plants from cuttings is a nice alternative to paying for F_1 hybrid seeds. With cuttings you can have your hybrid without the seed company. The money-saving potential of cuttings or cloning is amazing. You can take one existing hybrid tomato plant and create literally hundreds of plants, all with the same disease resistance and hybrid qualities of the original, as long as the mother plant is healthy.

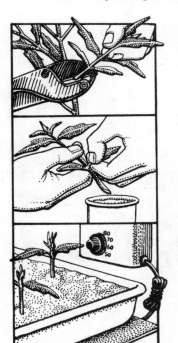

Cloning sequence

Another reason to clone is speed. The sooner your plant reaches maturity, the more food your greenhouse can produce. By using a cutting, a new plant can be ready for transplanting in 3-4 weeks. Compare this with growing from seed: up to 12 days for germination and another 6-10 weeks before it's ready to transplant. Cloning is *not* the solution to all greenhouse propagation, but it is especially effective with cucumbers, tomatoes, peppers, herbs and houseplants.

To make greenhouse cuttings, you must first prepare a cloning flat. Here's how. Simply fill a 2''-3'' deep flat with a mixture of 1 part sand and 1 part peat moss. Place it in an area that's a *constant* 70°F (21°C) (bottom electric heat cables or heating pads work well). Cooler temperatures greatly slow rooting of the cutting. There must also be some light, but the flat doesn't have to be constantly bright. An area against an east or west wall will do fine. Keep the sand/peat moss mix in the flat *constantly* wet. If it dries out often, try a mix higher in peat moss.

The first step in taking a cutting is to select a *healthy, disease-free* stock plant. If the plant is showing *any* signs of disease or poor health, *don't use it!* Find a growing tip and cut a 3'' long piece, tip and all. Preferably this tip should be from a side branch (on tomatoes and cucumbers this would be pruned anyway). Trim any large, lower leaves off the cut piece. Leave one or two leaves toward the top, but only those that are 2'' long or less.

Treat the bottom of the cut tissue with a rooting hormone. These hormones are based on naturally occurring plant substances that help trigger cells to produce roots. Rooting hormones generally come in powder formulations and are available at most gardening stores. Just dip the bottom of the cutting into the powder and shake off any excess. Vertically place the hormone-treated cutting about ¾ into the flat's peat-sand mix. Cuttings may be spaced as closely as 1'' apart.

Rooted cutting ready for transplant

If you don't like the idea of using commercial rooting hormones, you may make your own rooting compound out of purely natural ingredients like willow. Willow tea has been shown to have great root-promoting properties. To make it, steep many small willow twigs in hot water for 48 hours, then set your vegetable cuttings in this solution for 24 hours before placing them in the flat. Periodically water the flat with willow tea.

After a few weeks check your cuttings by *gently* pulling up on them. If they do move easily, test again in a week. If they don't budge, they may have roots. Extract them gently with a pencil, one by one. If they have many good roots, transplant as you would any seedling.

This same process works in starting trees or bushes. Tree cuttings are best if taken in early summer. After tree cuttings produce roots, grow them in 1-gallon cans for a year and then plant outside. These home-made trees could be the start of a nursery. Cuttings from grafted fruit trees may lose their dwarfness because it is a *combination* of grafts that causes the dwarfness.

If your cuttings are wilting and not rooting, try shorter cuttings with fewer leaves. Cuttings love high humidity, so building a clear plastic shroud around your propagation (cloning) flat to create a higher humidity may help. Or if you have a plumber friend, ask him or her to help you set up a mister that automatically mists seedlings for 30 seconds every 15 minutes. Misting systems are also commercially available.

If you have any major rot or disease problems in your propagation flat, discard all the sand/peat mix and wash the flat with very hot water and soap. Start over again with a new mix.

It will take some practice and mistakes to get the technique down. Please be patient; you'll get it. Some good non-technical texts on plant propagation are *Plant Propagation* by Philip McMillan Browse, and *Plant Propagation in Pictures* by Montague Free.

6

POLLINATION

The pollination process is comparable to conception—
the first step in creating a new individual. In nature,
flowers are pollinated by insects, bats, birds and wind.
The greenhouse usually lacks the natural pollinators
that otherwise ensure adequate fruit or seed production.
So in most greenhouse cases, humans must do the job of
pollination.

Why Plants Flower

Pollination is the primary step in a plant's reproduction cycle, the result being a seed that grows into a
new individual plant. But before pollination can take
place the plant needs to flower—that is, grow its sexual-
reproductive parts. Normally the flowering response is
triggered either by maturity (in most vegetables) or by
the length of the night (in many ornamentals). However, stress from external factors such as low nutrient
levels, too low or too high temperatures, wilting and
competition for light, water, etc.,
may sometimes in-

duce premature flowering. Also, luxuriant amounts of nitrogen and water can sometimes delay flowering; this is often true with tomatoes. The reason we're concerned about when flowering takes place is that too early or delayed flowering often results in lower food quantity.

Flower Physiology

In order to become a master pollinator inside your greenhouse, first you need to learn some simple flower physiology.

There are two major types of flowers. The first is called a complete flower. This flower contains both male and female elements. Examples are tomato, pepper and eggplant. These types of flowers are the easiest to pollinate because the male and female parts often are adjacent to each other in the same flower.

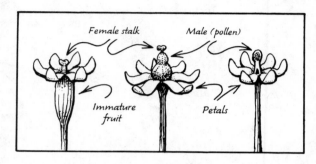

Complete & Incomplete

The other flower type is, you guessed it, an incomplete flower. In the incomplete flower the male and female parts are each in a different flower. Pollinating these flowers involves the physical transfer of the pollen from the male part in one flower to the female flower part in another.

Environmental Conditions for Pollination

Pollination is usually done most efficiently on bright days between 10:00 a.m. and 4:00 p.m., and optimally, it should take place at least once every other day. It's impossible to overdo it. Temperatures below 55°F (13°C) and above 90°F (32°C) often will damage the pollen and greatly decrease the number of fruits produced. At certain times of the year, solar greenhouses run above and below these temperatures, so adequate ventilation in summer is very helpful for good fruit set (production). In the winter you may find it wise to grow fewer fruiting crops and more leafy and root type crops that don't need pollination to produce food. (See *Greenhouse Food Crop Scheduling*.)

What and How to Pollinate

Complete Flowers

Beans   Most common garden varieties will produce a very good crop without pollination. If you find your variety is not setting fruit, try changing to a more common variety. Runner beans need pollination, and it is difficult to do, so you may want to replace them with regular pole or bush bean varieties that don't need pollination.

Okra   Okra sets pods without being pollinated and produces very beautiful flowers.

Peas   No pollination required.

Tomatoes   An easy crop to pollinate. Get a long thin stick (about 1½′ long). A ¼″ dowel will do fine. Tap the yellow blossoms gently and fruit generally will set. Tap each cluster of blossoms; don't skip any. If you suspect that any plants have a disease, pollinate these last. There are electric vibrating gadgets available to commercial growers that work fine, but so does a stick . . . and at a much lower cost. A large greenhouse full of tomatoes can be pollinated in a relatively short time. One or two light taps to each blossom cluster is sufficient.

Tapping blossom with stick

Peppers   As done with tomatoes, tapping flowers will help fruit set, but pollination will often occur by itself.

Eggplant   Eggplants are quite variable; some varieties don't seem to need pollination, while others do well with a good tap, much like tomatoes. If you are having a problem with setting fruit, try this method: find a flower that is shedding large amounts of pollen (a yellow dust will fall from flowers when tapped). Put your thumbnail under this flower and knock pollen onto your nail. Then take your pollen-laden thumbnail and touch the pollen to the tip of the female element on each blossom. (The female element is the green stalk in the center of the flower sur-

Eggplant pollination with thumb

rounded by the yellow pollen parts.) Apply more pollen to your nail after pollinating about five or six flowers, and repeat the process on all your blossoms.

Incomplete Flowers

Squash   First locate the male flower—it will have a thin stalk leading up to the flower base. Within the flowers, you will find a shorter stalk tipped with yellow powder (pollen). The female flower is easy to recognize; it has a little immature squash behind the flower at the point where the petals are attached. The pollen must be transferred to the tip of the structure within the female flower. If pollen is not transferred to the female element, the immature fruit located behind the petals will never grow, and eventually it will begin to rot while

Male blossom pollinating female with immature fruit

still attached to the plant. To get the best pollen and fruit set, pollinate the flowers as soon as they open the first time. There are a number of ways to transfer the pollen. Use a small paint brush, a used match, or the whole male flower. The last method is the easiest and the best. I call it the 'male flower stalk method.' Here's how it's done: pluck the male flower where it's attached to the plant, then strip all the yellow petals off the stalk. You'll be left with a stalk tipped with the yellow pollen. Holding the bottom of the stalk, touch the pollen on the stalk's end to the female element in the center of the female flower. You can pollinate 2 or 3 female squash flowers with one male pollen stalk. Also, you can sometimes use pollen from one type of squash to pollinate another type, such as yellow squash to pollinate zucchini. Within days you'll know if your pollination has worked. If it didn't work, you'll notice that the fruit will begin to rot from the blossom end. Pluck it off and discard it.

Rotted Squash tip

There is the occasional problem of not having enough male flowers to pollinate your females. There's not a whole lot you can do, but you may attempt to use another squash variety that has some male flowers, or you may try to refrigerate the male when they are in abundance for use at a later time. To do this, place the male flowers in a plastic bag and refrigerate them—don't freeze them. To a point, the longer the flowers are in the cold, the longer the pollen will be viable. The maximum storage time is approximately 3 weeks, but this may vary greatly.

Many cultures eat the squash's male pollen stalk. Here's how: break the stalk at the point where it turns from green to light yellow. Dip the whole yellow portion (including pollen) into a batter and deep fry it. It's considered a great delicacy. Here's another thing to try. At the point in the stalk where you've broken it, look for a bowl-like indentation containing a small amount of clear liquid. This liquid is the nectar. Taste it and see why bees are into pollinating.

Cucumbers   Europeans have developed a cucumber specifically for greenhouse culture known as European Forcing Cucumbers. They don't need to be pollinated at all and yield many long, sweet, thin-skinned seedless cucumbers. Although the seed is somewhat expensive, the high yields and less work involved make it a good choice for the solar greenhouse, especially during the warmer months. For more information on growing this type of cucumber, see *Crops*.

But if you are growing *regular* garden variety cucumbers in your greenhouse, they *will* need pollinating to set fruit. To tell what sex your flower is, look for a small immature cucumber behind the yellow petals of the female flowers. It's similar to a squash plant. The male flower lacks immature fruit and is just a flower on a thin stem. Tweezers are a great aid when working with these small flowers. The procedure is essentially the same as with squash except that the cucumber flowers are much, much smaller. This makes it harder, though not impossible to do. The task may require some time and energy, so you might want to stick with the high yielding European cucumbers.

Melons   Melons and cantaloupe are pollinated like squash, but like the cucumber, they have much smaller flowers. Look for the small, often fuzzy, immature melon or cantaloupe behind the female flower. The male flower won't have one. As with squash, transfer the pollen to the center of the female flower either by using a small paint brush or the male flower stalk method. The fruits will not set if they are not pollinated. Unfortunately, there aren't any varieties available yet that will produce without pollination. Maybe someday.

Artificial Fruit Set

Synthetic chemical hormones are also available in spray form that, when applied to blossoms, will cause the fruit to grow without pollination. However, there have been reports of lower quality fruit (soft, misshapen fruit with poor color and poor storage characteristics). In view of the quality risks and the always-present questions associated with using any synthetic chemical on food, use of fruit setting chemicals should not replace regular pollination of blossoms. However, these chemical sprays may help to set fruit during adverse temperature conditions.

Trouble-Shooting Problems

Problem	*Possible Cause*
Poor fruit set	Temperatures above 90 °F (32 °C) or below 60 °F (15 °C). Sudden cold or cool temperatures. Very dry air.
Blossom drop	High temperature. Low humidity. Low soil moisture. Nearby incomplete combustion fumes, generally from a heater.
Misshapen fruit	Incomplete pollination (not enough pollen to female element). Also due to cold nights below 55 °F (13 °C).
Cracked fruit	Alternating high and low temperatures. Some varieties are listed as "crack resistant," so try them next time. Usually not due to pollination.
Low numbers of blossoms	Too much nitrogen.
Fruit rotting (incomplete flowering plants)	No pollination, or pollen that was used wasn't viable.
Immature fruit shriveled (cucumbers only)	Either they weren't pollinated (regular cucumbers only) or the plant had too many mature cucumbers present on the vine (common with European cucumbers). Keep the vines picked or production will be slowed.

7

SOLAR GREENHOUSE FOOD CROP SCHEDULING

Almost any common vegetable can be grown in an unheated, well-built and well-designed solar greenhouse at any time of the year in most areas of the United States. Among crops, however, there is a drastic difference in productivity and health: the difference being between a plant that just barely survives and one that is abundantly productive. Along with selection of plant variety and crop layout, scheduling is a major key to high food yields in a passive solar greenhouse.

Although planting of crops occurs throughout the year, I've split the year into two primary growing seasons: summer and winter. The summer greenhouse season is from March to October and winter is from October to March. It is the transition months and weeks around October and March when much of your planting occurs.

In the winter season characterized by short days, low light intensities and cool temperatures, leafy and root crops—also known as "cool season crops"—are most productive. Peas, cauliflower, broccoli and broad or fava beans and a few other crops, though not leafy and root crops, also do well in the winter season.

Fruiting crops usually fit best into the summer season, characterized by longer days, more light and warm-to-hot temperatures. Non-fruiting crops that also do well in the summer are collards, New Zealand spinach, Swiss chard and a few other minor crops.

For the best value from your growing space, it makes sense to stick to vegetables that are more valuable and perishable. Also, plants that can be harvested many times (for example, Swiss chard and leaf lettuce) are a better choice for high yields than ones that are harvested only once (cauliflower or head lettuce, for example). But remember, plant only what you know will get eaten.

Although not efficient winter producers, if you want to grow fruiting crops in the winter, plant them in the warmer areas of the greenhouse (as indicated by the chart in *Crop Layout*). The warmer your greenhouse is, up to 85°F (30°C) days and 65°F (18°C) nights, with a minimum of 50°F (10°C) the better your fruiting crops will grow. If you plan to actively heat your greenhouse to raise its winter temperatures for fruiting crops, please be sure that you're getting your money's worth. Remember, it takes energy and money to heat. It also takes away from the concept of a *passive* greenhouse, which is one of the solar greenhouse's best features.

If you let it run at its natural temperature, it will provide *surplus* heat to your home at no extra cost. Is the trouble, time, money and energy worth a few more red tomatoes? Maybe, maybe not. The same space, unheated, will provide impressive yields of greens, herbs and roots with no extra trouble. Although it's always nice to have a few tomato and pepper plants through the winter, to devote a lot of space to out-of-season fruits greatly reduces overall greenhouse yields. Experiment and see for yourself. Remember, think efficient food production.

If you plan to try cool season crops (usually grown in winter) in your summer greenhouse, plant them—you guessed it—in the cooler areas of your greenhouse (as indicated in *Crop Layout*). It would be much more efficient, however, to grow these leafy and root crops outside in summer.

Spring and Fall Planting

The spring season in the greenhouse can be used to start seedlings for your outside garden. This will greatly increase outside productivity. (See Spring Transplants in *Crops*.) Spring and early fall months are also a good time to sneak in some quick maturing crops such as summer squash, bush beans, Chinese cabbage, radishes and kohlrabi.

With the exception of many herbs, some flowers and Swiss chard, digging up outside garden plants in the fall for greenhouse production is usually not worthwhile. Remember, the criteria for selecting greenhouse food crops are usually *entirely different* than for selecting plants for outside production. (See *Selecting Solar Greenhouse Crops and Varieties*.) Also, the shock of transplanting can set plants back, and often they never return to productivitiy. Usually you will do better to anticipate the changing seasons and start most of your winter greenhouse plants from seed.

With the exceptions of chamomile, basil and dill, most common herbs transplant well into the greenhouse. Flowers that transplant into the greenhouse with good results include: petunias pansies, allyssum and some daisies. Outside snapdragons survive but don't flower very well, so grow only ''greenhouse'' snapdragons in your greenhouse.

Starting Winter Crops

The biggest crop scheduling trick is getting your winter, cool season crops started on time. It's very important to get their root systems established *before* the cool nights and short days set in around November. If you wait until winter arrives to start your cool season crops, you won't see any significant production until late winter. So plant the winter crop early—September through October.

Getting your greenhouse converted to primarily cool season crops is not an easy task. Often the plantings of warm season fruiting crops will still be vibrant and healthy well through November and even into early December. But soon the yield drops drastically and then it's too late to start seeding cool season crops and expect decent growth. A bit of a dilemma. To convert the fall greenhouse for winter, you may need to cultivate a ruthless attitude that will enable you to rip out beautiful cantaloupe or tomato plants to make room for winter crops. But first do your pulling up of the fruiting beds that have the lowest production, or those that are having disease or insect problems in their old age. If you plan to leave a few fruiting plants for winter—which I recommend—try to leave the ones near the thermal mass (north wall area) where it is warmer in the winter. At the same time, don't allow massive plantings to cover up large portions of the thermal mass. This would prevent direct solar gain for heat storage.

Summer—What to do with your Greenhouse

Often people aren't quite sure how to use their summer greenhouse. For people who live in northern areas with a short growing season, the summer greenhouse provides a place to grow crops that are hard to grow outside. Plants such as cucumber, tomato, cantaloupe, melons and winter squash, which have barely come into production outside when the first frost attacks, will produce abundantly for many months in the solar greenhouse. Even people in longer growing season areas can benefit from the longer productivity of warm season food crops inside the solar greenhouse. The summer greenhouse also offers an opportunity to maintain perennial/perpetual crops, many of which are exotic in nature. Those include artichokes, fig trees, citrus, etc., or the more common New Zealand spinach and herbs.

On the other hand, you may decide to let the greenhouse rest during the summer and concentrate your energies on outside food production. This may open your greenhouse space to houseplants and ornamental crops, or for use as a living and storage area. If you do, you may want to consider shading the glass during the summer for the benefit of those living inside. (See Shading in *The Solar Greenhouse Environment*.) But don't get *too* used to this extra space. Remember, come winter, this is your food producing greenhouse.

Year-round Crop Scheduling Charts

Following are two general crop schedules for use in 100% unheated solar greenhouses. If you add extra heat and/or lights, you can extend the summer warm season crops into both sides of winter.

The crops are listed only during the months in which they will have the *highest* productivity. Most crops will live beyond the time periods listed here. As mentioned earlier, you can grow cool season crops in summer or summer crops in winter, but it often means a drop in quantity and quality of food. Keep your own records and fine-tune your planting schedule each year. The first schedule is for areas with sunny winters, the second for areas with cloudy winters. The letter **P** designates a possible month to **plant** the crop. The letter **M** indicates the crop may be growing toward **maturity**. The letter **H** indicates the crop may be **harvested,** if mature at this time. Remember, this is only a general guide. There are so many variables involved in gardening that it's hard to get real specific. An especially hard winter may result in lower overall productivity. For best results, study *Crop Layout* and *Crops* . Also see *Plant Propagation* for information on which plants to transplant and which to seed directly into beds.

Sunny Winter Schedule

(Receives a winter monthly average of 45% or more of possible sunshine as listed by your closest National Weather Service, or see *Possible Sunshine* chart in Appendix D.))

Month

CROP	J	F	M	A	M	J	J	A	S	O	N	D
Beans—Broad, Fava	PMH	PMH	PMH	PMH	H	H			P	PM	PM	MH
Beans—Bush		P	PM	PMH	PMH	PMH	PMH	PMH	PMH	MH	H	
Beans—Pole			P	PM	PM	PMH	PMH	PMH	MH	MH	H	
Beans—Lima				P	PM	PM	PMH	PMH	MH	MH	H	
Beets	PMH	PMH	MH	MH	H	H		P	PM	PMH	PMH	PMH
Broccoli	PMH	MH	H						P	PM	PMH	PMH
Brussels Sprouts	MH	H							P	PM	M	M
Cabbage	PMH	MH	MH	H				P	PM	PMH	PMH	PMH
Cantaloupe			P	PM	PM	PMH	MH	MH	MH	H	H	
Carrots		PMH	PMH	PMH	PMH	PMH	PMH	PMH	PMH	PMH	PMH	PMH
Cauliflower	MH	MH	H						P	PM	PMH	MH
Celery	MH	H							P	M	M	MH
Chinese Cabbage	MH	MH	H						P	PM	PMH	MH
Collards	PMH	PMH	PMH	MH	MH	MH		P	PM	PMH	PMH	PMH
Corn Salad	PMH	PMH	MH	H					P	PM	MH	MH
Cucumber			P	PM	PM	PMH	PMH	MH	MH	MH	H	
Eggplant			P	PM	PM	PM	MH	MH	MH	MH	H	
Endive	MH	H	H						P	PM	PMH	PMH
Garlic	PMH	PMH	PMH	PMH	PMH	PMH	PMH	PMH	PMH	PMH	PMH	PMH
Kale	PMH	MH	MH	H					P	PMH	PMH	PMH
Kohlrabi	PMH	PMH	PMH	MH	MH	H		P	PM	PMH	PMH	PMH
Lettuce	PMH	PMH	PMH	MH	H			P	PMH	PMH	PMH	PMH
Mustards	PMH	MH	MH	H				P	PMH	PMH	PMH	PMH
Okra				P	PM	PM	PMH	MH	MH	H		
Onions, for Bulbs		P	PM	PM	PMH	MH	MH	MH	H	H	H	
Onions, Green	PMH	PMH	PMH	PMH	PMH	PMH	PMH	PMH	PMH	PMH	PMH	PMH
Parsley	PMH	PMH	PMH	PMH	PMH	PMH	PMH	PMH	PMH	PMH	PMH	PMH
Peas	MH	MH	MH	H				P	PM	PMH	PMH	MH
Pepper			P	PM	PM	PMH	PMH	MH	MH	MH	H	
Radish	PMH	PMH	PMH	PMH				PMH	PMH	PMH	PMH	PMH
Rutabaga	MH	MH	H						P	PM	MH	MH
Spinach	PMH	PMH	MH	MH	H			P	PMH	PMH	PMH	MH
New Zealand Spinach	PMH	PMH	PMH	PMH	PMH	PMH	PMH	PMH	PMH	PMH	PMH	PMH
Summer Squash		P	PM	PMH	PMH	PMH	PMH	PMH	PMH	PMH	MH	H
Winter Squash		P	PM	PM	PMH	MH	MH	MH	H	H		
Swiss Chard	PMH	PMH	PMH	PMH	PMH	PMH	PMH	PMH	PMH	PMH	PMH	PMH
Tomato		P	PM	PMH	PMH	PMH	PMH	PMH	MH	MH	MH	H
Turnip	PMH	PMH	MH	H	H			P	PMH	PMH	PMH	PMH
Watermelon			P	PM	PM	MH	MH	MH	H	H		
Spring Outside Transplants*	PM	PM	PM	PM	M							

*See specific schedule in Crops.

Cloudy Winter Schedule

(Receives a winter monthly average of less than 45% possible sunshine as listed by your closest National Weather Service, or see *Possible Sunshine* chart in Appendix D.)

Month

CROP	J	F	M	A	M	J	J	A	S	O	N	D
Beans—Broad, Fava	MH	MH	MH	MH	H			P	PM	PMH	PMH	MH
Beans—Bush		P	PM	PMH	PMH	PMH	PMH	PMH	PMH	MH	H	
Beans—Pole				P	PM	PMH	PMH	MH	MH	H	H	
Beans—Lima				P	PM	PMH	PMH	MH	MH	H		
Beets	PMH	PMH	PMH	MH	H			P	PMH	PMH	PMH	PMH
Broccoli	MH	MH	MH	H				P	PM	PMH	MH	MH
Brussels Sprouts	MH	MH	MH	H				P	PM	PM	M	MH
Cabbage	MH	MH	PMH	MH	H	H		P	PM	PMH	PMH	MH
Cantaloupe				P	PM	PM	MH	MH	MH	MH	H	
Carrots	PMH	PMH	PMH	PMH	PMH	PMH	PMH	PMH	PMH	PMH	PMH	PMH
Cauliflower	PMH	MH	MH	MH				P	PM	PMH	MH	MH
Celery	PMH	MH	MH	MH	H			P	PM	PMH	PMH	MH
Chinese Cabbage	MH	PMH	PMH	MH	H			P	PMH	PMH	PMH	MH
Collards	MH	MH	MH	MH	MH			P	PMH	PMH	PMH	MH
Corn Salad	MH	PMH	PMH	MH	H			P	PM	PMH	PMH	MH
Cucumber			P	PM	PM	PMH	PMH	MH	MH	MH	H	
Eggplant					P	PM	PMH	MH	MH	H		
Endive	PMH	MH	MH	H				P	PMH	PMH	PMH	MH
Garlic	MH	MH	PMH	PMH	PMH	PMH	PMH	PMH	PMH	PMH	MH	MH
Kale	PMH	PMH	MH	MH	H			P	PMH	PMH	PMH	PMH
Kohlrabi	MH	MH	PMH	PMH	MH	H		P	PMH	PMH	PMH	MH
Lettuce	PMH	PMH	PMH	PMH	MH	H		P	PMH	PMH	PMH	MH
Mustards	MH	PMH	PMH	MH	MH	H		P	PMH	PMH	PMH	MH
Okra					P	PM	PM	PMH	MH	MH	H	
Onions, for Bulbs		P	PM	PM	M	M	MH	MH	MH	H	H	
Onions, Green	PMH	PMH	PMH	PMH	PMH	PMH	PMH	PMH	PMH	PMH	PMH	PMH
Parsley	PMH	PMH	PMH	PMH	PMH	PMH	PMH	PMH	PMH	PMH	PMH	PMH
Peas	MH	PMH	PMH	MH	H		P	PM	PMH	PMH	PMH	MH
Pepper					P	PM	PMH	PMH	MH	MH	H	H
Radish	PMH	PMH	PMH	PMH	PMH	H		P	PMH	PMH	PMH	PMH
Rutabaga	MH	MH						P	PM	MH	MH	
Spinach	PMH	PMH	PMH	PMH	MH	H		P	PMH	PMH	PMH	MH
New Zealand Spinach	MH	MH	PMH	PMH	PMH	PMH	PMH	PMH	PMH	PMH	PMH	MH
Summer Squash				P	PM	PMH	PMH	PMH	PMH	MH	MH	H
Winter Squash				P	PM	PM	PMH	PMH	MH	MH	H	
Swiss Chard	PMH	PMH	PMH	PMH	PMH	PMH	PMH	PMH	PMH	PMH	PMH	MH
Tomato			P	PM	PMH	PMH	PMH	PMH	MH	MH	H	
Turnip	PMH	PMH	PMH	PMH	MH	H		P	PMH	PMH	PMH	MH
Watermelon				P	PM	PM	MH	MH	MH	MH	H	
Outside Spring Transplants*	PM	PM	PM	PM	PM	M						

See specific schedule in Crops.

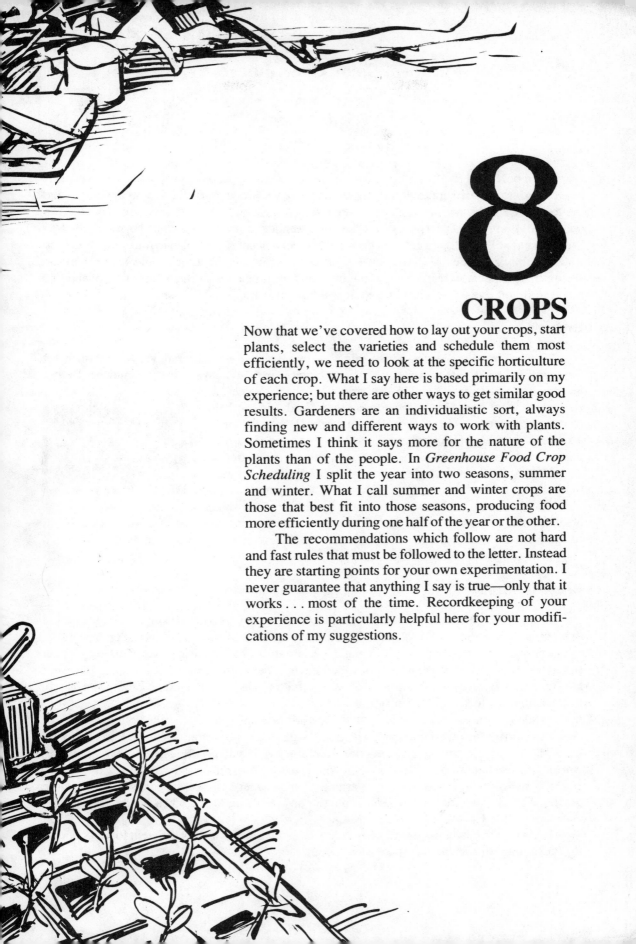

8

CROPS

Now that we've covered how to lay out your crops, start plants, select the varieties and schedule them most efficiently, we need to look at the specific horticulture of each crop. What I say here is based primarily on my experience; but there are other ways to get similar good results. Gardeners are an individualistic sort, always finding new and different ways to work with plants. Sometimes I think it says more for the nature of the plants than of the people. In *Greenhouse Food Crop Scheduling* I split the year into two seasons, summer and winter. What I call summer and winter crops are those that best fit into those seasons, producing food more efficiently during one half of the year or the other.

The recommendations which follow are not hard and fast rules that must be followed to the letter. Instead they are starting points for your own experimentation. I never guarantee that anything I say is true—only that it works . . . most of the time. Recordkeeping of your experience is particularly helpful here for your modifications of my suggestions.

Winter Crops

Beets

Each beet seed really has up to five seeds inside. A big problem people have with beets is overcrowding. So be sure to thin them, or they'll never produce. Because both the greens and the roots are edible, you can eat your thinnings. If you eat both the roots and greens in salads or cooked like spinach, beets can be efficient greenhouse producers. Just the roots? Not so efficient but still good. Try golden beets, they're very sweet. If you plan to transplant beets, do it while they're under 1½'' tall. Also, beets may go to seed after a cold snap or in the springtime, especially if it was a cold winter in your greenhouse. Beets like slightly alkaline soils, so if you live in an acid soil area, try adding some lime or wood ash.

Broccoli

To prevent your crop from maturing all at once, plant a few different varieties at different times in cool bright areas. Broccoli usually matures in 60-80 days in the greenhouse. Before purchasing seeds, read catalog descriptions closely. Some varieties produce more side sprouts than others, and this can help prolong production. After you cut the main head, let it grow for an additional harvest of side sprouts. On the other hand, you may prefer one large head instead. So choose an appropriate variety.

Broccoli plants transplant fine when they're seedlings— that's the good news. However, broccoli grown in sunny winter climates may turn into flowers very rapidly and produce small heads—that's the bad news. It prefers to mature in constant cool conditions. Because the bulk of the plant is usually discarded, it isn't a very efficient greenhouse food producer. But it's a tasty crop for fresh winter eating.

Brussels Sprouts

In the solar greenhouse, brussels sprouts are slow growers, often taking 130 days or more to reach maturity. So it's best to start them in early fall. If they mature in a warm environment, as in late spring, the taste may be bitter and the sprouts may form loose heads. This crop is best suited for those living in a cloudy cool winter environment. Space the plants 2' apart. They get tall when they mature (about 3') so be careful of shading. Brussels sprouts are easily transplanted while in the seedling stage.

When the sprouts (cabbage-like buds) are just beginning to form, pinch out the center or growing point at the top of the plant. This encourages the upper sprouts to form. Remove lower leaves and leaf stems as the plants mature. Hopefully, you will have finished the harvest before warm spring weather arrives. If not, they will develop a hot, bitter taste.

Growing Brussels sprouts is similar to growing cabbage, so see the next section for more details. The hybrid varieties are very productive and reach maturity a bit earlier. A good hybrid variety is "Jade Cross."

Because the leaves are usually discarded, Brussels sprouts are not efficient food producers for the amount of greenhouse space they require.

Cabbage

There is a wide selection of varieties to choose from. Cabbage falls within three main categories: early season, mid-season and late season. Usually the early and mid-season types provide better total yields in the solar greenhouse, while the late season varieties keep better and weigh more, but are later to mature. You can also select the savoy leaf types which have wrinkled bubbly-type leaves. They taste very good and are hardy, but they tend to harbor more insects in the wrinkles, especially aphids.

Cabbage transplants well in the seedling stage. Give each cabbage at least 10'' - 12'' of space. Don't cultivate too deeply, as they're shallow rooted. If your greenhouse gets very cold (32° F, 0° C or below) and then warms up again, your cabbage may begin to flower. This is

because cabbage is a biennial and the cold has fooled it into thinking it is two years old. Happy (last) Birthday. Pull it up; it won't produce now.

Cabbage needs a rich soil and sun. It can grow in shadier areas, but growth will be slower. Besides being a good winter crop, it's also a good crop to grow between the winter and summer seasons. It's an efficient crop for solar greenhouse production because almost all parts of the plant are edible.

Rotate areas where cabbage is planted to help prevent the disease clubfoot (a fungus causing lumps on the roots), yellowing, and low yields. Clubfoot is more common in acidic soil areas. If you have problems with cabbage yellowing, switch to a disease-resistant variety.

Carrots

When I think of carrots in the solar greenhouse I have a wonderful memory of a cold cloudy winter day. My first solar greenhouse carrots were just about ready. I was giving a tour to a class of beautiful 4 year-old Head Start kids. They were smiley and awed by my plants growing in the dead of winter. They were full of questions and were very loving children. I had two on my shoulders, a few on each arm and one sitting on each foot. I managed to drag myself and the children over to my carrot bed and hollered: "What's this plant?" "Onions!" one shouted. "Dandelion." another said. A shy one, shaking her head no, quietly mumbled, "I don't know." "Well look," I said as I shook a few kids off, moving toward a carrot top. "Iiiiitttssss aaaa . . . " They were all eyes as I pulled it up. "CARROT!!," they yelled and screamed in unison. It was as if I were a magician . . . presto: a carrot. I wondered how long it would have been before they learned where carrots came from if they never had seen my greenhouse carrots.

A year-round supply of home grown carrots will add a spark to food that nothing else can provide. There is just no comparison between home-grown and store-bought carrots.

Carrots will fit into any empty place in your growing beds and can be planted any time of the year. However, unusually hot weather can sometimes cause a strange flavor and fibrous texture. High amounts of manure in the soil will promote oddly shaped carrots for you modern sculpture lovers. Winter carrots in the greenhouse will take longer to produce than outside carrots, but the harvest is well worth the wait. Some winter carrots may go to seed if you grow them through spring.

Carrots grow best if directly seeded into the bed, as they don't transplant well. Plant a few carrot seeds in any area that has some open space. Just barely cover the seeds with soil and *keep the soil moist* till the seeds germinate. If your soil gets crusty on top, lightly cultivate and try interplanting with radishes to break it up. Carrots prefer sandy soil; in heavy clay soils you may have better luck with the smaller varieties. I've had the best yields with standard long varieties. One, known as Nantes Frubund, available from Thompson and Morgan, was developed to grow under colder winter conditions. Stokes offers Coreless Amsterdam which is popular in Holland greenhouses. Many varieties have been developed with good disease resistance.

The hardest part about growing carrots is thinning them out so they're *at least* 1'' apart. If they are not thinned, they won't produce. Put on your "ruthless gardener" hat; get out there and thin!

Cauliflower

Cauliflower grows much the same as cabbage and broccoli and is subject to the same pests and diseases. It takes about 50 - 70 days to mature. Tie up the leaves around the head as it is forming to prevent browning of the white curd.

Healthy cauliflower

Buttoned-up head from prolonged hot weather

It is not a very efficient food producer in the solar greenhouse, as much of the plant is usually discarded and the center white curd is relatively lower in vitamins than cauliflower's cabbage-type relatives. Purple headed varieties, however, contain more vitamins.

Prolonged hot weather can cause the head to flower rapidly and can also make the head button up (produce small heads). In the winter this is more common in high sun areas. So in sunny winter climates, cauliflower may not be the best choice for the solar greenhouse. Sorry for the pan review, mon cauliflower.

Celery

This crop is best grown where winters are long, cloudy and the greenhouse is cool. Where this is not the case, quality may be lacking. Warm temperatures make celery stringy and will trigger early flowering, ending its productive life. But a plant or two is always worth a try. Seed germination is slow (3-4 weeks), and then it needs about 125 consistently *cool* days to reach maturity. Celery likes a relatively wet, rich soil. Due to its exacting requirements and slow growth, it is not an easy or efficient crop for the solar greenhouse.

Chard - Swiss Chard

Chard is a very close relative of beets. I can't say enough good things about this vegetable. But I'll try. It seems to have been put on the earth specifically for solar greenhouses. It tolerates both high and low temperatures very well. The whole plant is edible and grows rapidly, and often for a few years. It can be harvested many, many times. Incredible, eh?

Swiss chard comes in three main types: red-veined, white-veined and green-veined. White-veined seems to be the most productive in the greenhouse. But the others do well too.

As with beets, there are many seeds contained within each ''seed,'' so be sure to thin when they come up. Space your plants 6''- 8'' apart. You can eat all your thinnings.

Harvest by breaking off the outer leaves when they are 8''-10'' in size. Don't leave the leaf-stem (petiole) attached as it will rot on the plant and harbor disease. Get it right down to the base. This leaf-stem is edible (though sometimes stringy), and may be cooked like asparagus. Chard can be eaten raw in salads or cooked like spinach. It's good both ways.

Chard is an excellent tasting, nutritious crop in the winter greenhouse, but it may have a slightly bitter taste when grown as a summer crop. It can be fooled into flowering by a period of very cool days (temperatures around freezing) because it is a biennial like cabbage. If your chard flowers, pull it up and start again. The white-ribbed varieties seem to be slower to flower than other varieties. I've had some produce non-stop for three years. (See photo of old chard plant.)

Chard can produce for several years

Consider growing chard in place of spinach. It can be harvested many more times and is much less apt to go to seed. Spinach is short-lived and quick to flower. By growing chard instead, you'll find your space is many times more productive.

Rhubarb chard is red-veined and very colorful (good for Christmas). Grow it the same as you would white or green-veined chard and see which one you prefer. You can do some interesting designs in your growing beds by alternating red and white chard in a row. Unlike true rhubarb whose leaves are poisonous, rhubarb chard or red chard's leaves are totally edible. Be sure your children understand the difference.

Chinese Cabbage

Chinese cabbage is an efficient food producer for areas with cool, cloudy winters. It will bolt (go to seed) very rapidly when grown in areas with a lot of winter sun. There are a few varieties that are more bolt-resistant and better suited for those areas. Stokes' summertime variety is one.

Chinese cabbage is very fast growing, transplants well in the seedling stage, and will usually mature in 40 - 60 days. The variety ''Michihli'' is narrow and tall, but doesn't keep as well as the other ''Wong Bok'' types. The non-heading varieties are great for multiple harvests; keep picking the oldest leaves.

I have found that my Chinese cabbage gets attacked by aphids and slugs where adjacent crops are pest-free. So keep your watchful eyes out for 'em.

Chives

Chives are a very efficient greenhouse food producer because they survive year-round. Because you only harvest the green tops, the root system is never disturbed and the plant grows back rapidly after each harvest. That is very different from onions which must first be started from seeds or bulbs and don't even have good bulb development in the short days of winter.

However, I have found that chives grow slowly in winter. I have been able to stimulate winter growth by cutting the chives to a height of 1'' and then fertilizing them. It brings up winter production by a substantial amount. Chives grow well in 5-gallon buckets or raised beds. Chives can be started from seed or from transplants obtained from outside gardens. Place them in a sunny spot that has rich soil. Be sure not to overwater—it will slow the growth and make them more susceptible to diseases. Harvest chives by cutting the slender tubular leaves at the base. I like to dice up the leaves, store them in a plastic bag in the freezer and then sprinkle them on all kinds of food and salads for a great mild onion flavor. Every greenhouse should have at least one clump of chives.

Collards

This is another crop, much like Swiss chard, that seems to be especially suited to the solar greenhouse. It's a relative of the cabbage and looks like a non-heading cabbage. It can produce over a long period of time and tolerates warm temperatures, cold temperatures and partial shading quite well. Each plant needs about 1½ square feet of growing space. Harvest only the lower leaves. After 3 - 4 months it can get tall—as much as 4' high, which is good production for the amount of space it takes up. But then, it may begin to shade other nearby crops, so keep this in mind when laying out your beds.

Collards are usually cooked much like cabbage, but check out some southern soul food recipes for great dishes with ham and beans. Mmmm. Give it a try, it's good.

Corn Salad

This small plant, used as a fresh green, is popular in Europe. Although it isn't super productive, it will grow year-round in the coldest of solar greenhouses. The seeds are large and seedlings transplant well. The plant fits into small spaces and grows close to the ground compared to similar greens. It's great if you need a gourmet green for dinner guests.

Cress - Curly Cress

Cress is a small pungent green that's often used as a garnish. It's similar in taste to watercress, but is much easier to grow. It's quick to mature and can be harvested 20 days after you plant it. Eat it before it goes to seed. For a continuous supply, you'll have to do successive plantings.

Edible Chrysanthemums

Some people know this plant as Chop-suey greens. It has a wonderful sweet, mild, nut-like flavor that is unique among salad greens. All the leaves are edible. It's a good winter producer and grows to a height of about 4'. Each plant needs about 2' of space when mature. Leaves may be constantly harvested. Always pick the older, lower leaves first. In spring it will provide you with a beautiful crop of yellow, daisy-like flowers that are a nice addition to a flower arrangement. It's a beautiful, dual-purpose winter plant. Aphids, however, may be attracted to it, so be on guard.

Fava Beans - Broad Beans

Fava beans are cold hardy beans. They are the only beans that will produce well in your winter greenhouse. They are very different from common garden beans and grow upright on one thick stem. They make good use of vertical space, growing up to 5' tall, and may need a little support with stakes and string to remain upright. For survival situations they are valuable because they are one of the few winter greenhouse crops that's high in protein. The protein content is similar to soybeans, but they contain less oil. Hot weather may spoil their flavor. To induce early and larger crops, you can pinch off the tops when plants bloom. Seed may be obtained from Johnny's Selected Seeds, Stokes, Thompson & Morgan, William Dam Seeds, and Vermont Bean Seed Company. The wonderful scent of their bloom in the afternoon is reason enough to grow it.

However, fava beans should be eaten with some caution. Some people are genetically unable to properly digest favas. Within 24 hours of eating, symptoms including vomiting, diarrhea and dizziness may occur. Fortunately, fatalities are rare and recovery is usually quick. The most susceptible genetic groups include people (and their descendants) of Mediterranean countries, also natives of Egypt, Iraq and Iran, along with some Chinese people and Blacks. Check with an allergist if in doubt. Those folks not listed above should enjoy fava beans with no problems.

Kale

Like collards, kale is a member of the cabbage family and is grown for its leaves and stems. It's not nearly as heat tolerant, however, as collards. The flavor of kale improves as the weather gets colder and is best after going through a few light frosts. Because frost in the solar greenhouse is usually rare, it will be hard to get the best quality. So the flavor may be too pungent for some. It may be better grown outside or in a cold frame.

Kale is a very nutritious and hardy plant that can be harvested much like collards. Leaves should be harvested before they become old, tough and woody. Ornamental kale, grown mainly for looks, is a very colorful plant and rivals the beauty of many flowers. It is found in the flower section of seed catalogs. It's most beautiful in the dead of winter.

Kohlrabi

This crop is like an above-ground turnip, but I think it tastes better than a turnip. It grows relatively fast in the winter solar greenhouse (70 days) and may be planted close together (6'' apart).There are both purple and green varieties. And there is a new hybrid variety called "Grand Duke" (available in a number of catalogs) which can tolerate wide temperature fluctuations better than other varieties. Alternating hot and cold temperatures can cause the bulb of the kolhrabi to crack. While the purple variety is less apt to crack, it grows slightly slower. Cracking can be a real problem in warmer greenhouses.

Lettuce

Lettuce, one of the oldest greenhouse food crops, is also one of the most popular. It is the king (or queen—nobody knows for sure) of the salad greens, and is very productive in the solar greenhouse.

The temperature requirements fit well into the winter season of greenhouse gardening. The crop is productive even at low temperatures and low light conditions (as low as 400 foot-candles). Warm temperatures and longer daylight hours may cause the leaf tips to brown.

Lettuce prefers a rich, well-drained soil. When planting seeds, don't bury them too deep; to trigger germination they need to see a little light shining through. Lettuce prefers slightly acid soil; optimum is 6.8 pH. Keep the soil moist until the seedlings emerge. Lettuce transplants well. The root system is shallow, so be careful if you are cultivating. Space the plants about 4''- 5'' apart. When you water, try not to splash soil up on the leaves.

The key to good greenhouse lettuce production is understanding not only its growing requirements, but also the variety differences. There are four basic types to choose from: leaf lettuce, head or iceberg, Boston or butterhead (forming a loose head), and cos or romaine (an upright semi-heading lettuce). Leaf and loose-head lettuce are the earliest maturing varieties and the best choice for the greenhouse. In the winter solar greenhouse, you can expect a crop in 50 - 80 days depending on your temperature and light conditions. The iceberg head and cos types of lettuce usually take longer—up to 150 days till their harvest.

Even within one single lettuce type there is a great difference in growing characteristics. These include the time it takes before bolting occurs, resistance to an assortment of diseases, the likelihood of the tips burning, etc. For more information on bolting see Chapter 4, *Selection for heat tolerance*. Many of these characteristics are listed in seed catalogs. It is these characteristics that greenhouse growers select to get maximum lettuce production. Some varieties, usually the leaf and butterhead types, have been specifically developed for greenhouse production.

Most leaf lettuce types for greenhouse production are selections from the original Grand Rapids variety, first developed in 1890. Many selections have been made from the Grand Rapids variety since then. Stokes offers three different Grand Rapids types for greenhouse production. Burpee Seeds offers one called Greenheart. Another variety that they sell, Green Ice, does well in the solar greenhouse. Waldmans Green, a darker green Grand Rapids cousin, is available from many catalogs. Most seed companies sell Grand Rapids types. Grand Rapids is a good substitute for head lettuce lovers because it is crispy, much like head lettuce, but more nutritious and productive.

Other varieties of *leaf* lettuce include Black Seeded Simpson, Oakleaf and Ruby. Their leaves are a little softer and may be prone to some bottom rot. Oakleaf is amazingly slow to bolt and produces for a long period. Give it a try and see how it does in your greenhouse. Ruby is crisper than Oakleaf and is reddish in color, but it goes to seed quicker. Your taste buds will be the final judge.

Butterhead types are more popular in European greenhouses than in the United States. They form a loose head and have softer, thicker leaves than the crispier Grand Rapids types.

They're more perishable. Common garden butterhead varieties include Bibb, Buttercrunch and White Boston. Two European catalogs Rijk Zwann and Bruinsma carry many varieties of butterhead types specifically for greenhouses. Good greenhouse growing characteristics have been incorporated into these varieties including slowness to bolt, shorter growing period (a few are even earlier than the Grand Rapids types), upright growing habit (leaves up off the ground for less rot) and resistance to some diseases. Stokes catalog carries two European butterhead types for greenhouse production. The European greenhouse lettuce varieties would be the best choice for the serious butterhead lettuce grower.

There is one cos lettuce variety that is a good choice for the solar greenhouse. Crisp Mint sold by Thompson and Morgan grows upright and is very resistant to bolting. It's slower growing than Grand Rapids, but its slow bolting characteristics enable you to harvest it for a longer period of time. It also resists bottom rotting.

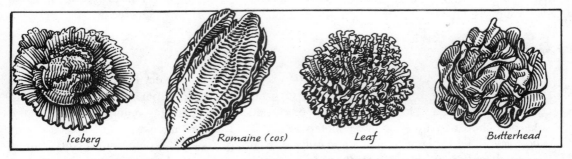

Iceberg   Romaine (cos)   Leaf   Butterhead

Iceberg or head lettuce can be grown in the winter greenhouse just fine, but it will be the slowest producer (almost twice as long as leaf types) and also the *lowest* in nutritional value of all lettuce types. How come this is our favorite, America? Leaf lettuce has up to five times the vitamins that Iceberg has. If you want to grow head lettuce, select the varieties that are listed as slow to bolt. The European catalogs Rijk Zwann and Bruinsma, carry a few head or Iceberg lettuce varieties for greenhouse production. But I think you would be better off to learn to like leaf lettuce.

Harvesting lettuce can be done in one cut (harvesting the whole plant); or better yet, you can get two or three cuttings off the plant before it gets bitter or bolts. To do this, be sure to cut only the larger older leaves, leaving the young center leaves to continue growing. Clean off old, dead or broken leaves from the soil surface. If you don't they'll begin to rot and the rot may spread to the underside of the lettuce plants. This bottom rot can be very destructive.

In the wintertime, you can keep lettuce disease to a minimum by providing good ventilation. On a sunny day, if the greenhouse is warm enough, open a vent to the outside for a few minutes. Use a small fan to prevent air stagnation during the day. Lettuce is a heavy feeder, and it tolerates a high amount of nitrogen fertilization. That causes very fast growth, but may also increase your crop's susceptibility to more diseases.

To insure continuous production during the winter greenhouse season, it's a good idea to always have a few lettuce seedlings started for later transplanting to fill in empty areas after harvesting other crops.

Lettuce is very productive and no wintertime greenhouse should be without it. Start studying seed catalogs now. Those fresh picked wintertime salads are such a luxury.

Mustard

Mustard is a productive green for winter growing. It is related to the cabbage family and is very nutritious. There are many varieties to choose from, some with curled leaves, others with smooth leaves. Both do well in the solar greenhouse. The flavor can vary much among varieties, some being milder flavored than others.

In the winter greenhouse, you can get up to 2 - 3 plantings because mustard takes only 6 - 8 weeks to mature. Select varieties that are slow to bolt, especially if your area catches much winter sun. Mustard may taste strong and may sometimes bolt prematurely if it is grown in a warm environment. However, in cloudy winter areas it is a prolific producer. Harvesting can be prolonged by cutting only older larger leaves, leaving the center to continue its growth. Eat it in salads or cook it like spinach.

Onions

Onions are almost as old as civilization, originating in ancient Egypt. Onions can be grown for bunching (onion greens), or for their bulbs. For bulb production, they need fairly cool temperatures and longer days. This pretty much limits growing onions for bulbs in the solar greenhouse to mid- and late-winter planting. The solar greenhouse is a good place to start onion seedlings for later transplanting outside in spring. As long as onion bulbs (sets) can be bought cheaply in the store, it might be best to utilize your limited greenhouse space for other crops. You can use outside space for bulb production and store them in a cellar for winter eating.

Growing onion greens is practical all year long and easy to do in the solar greenhouse. They can be produced from onion sets or from seeds. Onions for greens may be planted much closer together than for bulbing—2'' spacing will do fine. The greens can be pulled up entirely or cut at the soil for multiple harvests. When the plants begin to form flower buds, the plant should be pulled up and consumed. Many varieties of onions have been developed for use as onion greens, also known as bunching onions, including Evergreen, Beltsville, Hardy White, and White Sweet Spanish.

Another type of onion called Multiplier or top set will work well for both onion greens and bulbs. During midsummer, the Multiplier produces bulblets at the top of the flowering stalk. These can be planted like onion sets for growing winter greens. By fall, the Multiplier onion produces 3 - 4 bulbs in the ground, which can be harvested and replanted like the top sets winter greens.

Because any type of green onion takes up relatively little space and can add so much flavor to winter food, I highly recommend them for your greenhouse. (See Chives.)

Parsley

Parsley was originally put on plates to sweeten your breath at the end of a meal, but now it is usually used by Americans as a garnish to make food look pretty. All of us who have washed dishes for a living can vouch that most of it gets thrown away. It's almost a sin. Try eating it instead. It tastes good, really! It's great in salads, and is full of vitamins, especially vitamins A, C and iron.

Parsley is a biennial and will often go to seed in late spring and summer. It is relatively productive in the winter greenhouse, and there is always some room for one or two parsley plants in any bed. Parsley can take up to 4 weeks to germinate. Soaking the seed overnight before planting will help it along. Warm soil temperatures (above 70° F, 21° C) will slow seed germination, so keep it at around 60° F (16° C) while germinating. It does best in a sunny place, and can be brought in from the outside in fall but will go to seed in spring, thus ending its productive life. It transplants easily, especially in the seedling stage.

There are two primary varieties, curled leaf and the flat Italian parsley. Both do fine in the solar greenhouse, but I've found it easier to get people to try eating the curled leaf parsley. Stokes Seed Company now offers a curled variety known as Unicurl. Instead of the leaves curling out, they curl in. This variety will trap less dirt, making the foliage easier to wash. If older leaves turn yellow, the plant is in need of some nitrogen. Many people (including me) are allergic to parsley if it's going to seed (often in spring) even though first-year parsley won't bother them. In my greenhouse I graze on parlsey almost like a cow.

Peas

Whenever I've tried to get people to record greenhouse food yields by weight, I've noticed that it's rare to see any record of a pea harvest, even though peas are a common and productive crop in the winter greenhouse. The problem is that peas don't make it to the scales. They usually get eaten first. Maybe I should weigh people before and after they work around the peas.

Peas are one of the best wintertime treats that a solar greenhouse can provide. They make good use of vertical space, provide protein, and are sweet as candy. But in sunny winter areas, they're a little harder to grow. Using a bacterial innoculant powder to coat pea and bean seeds before planting will help peas capture nitrogen from the air. It is available through seed catalogs. This innoculant is not generally needed in soils that peas have been grown in before.

There is a great choice of pea varieties, and I urge you to experiment with a few different ones each year. Pea varieties have been bred for many different characteristics including: vining growth, bush growth, disease resistance, edible pods, earliness, and hot weather tolerance. Most pea varieties produce fine in cool weather. In the solar greenhouse, to make efficient use of vertical space, you will usually want varieties that grow tall ($2'$ - $5'$). Disease resistance is also important, especially against powdery mildew. Heat tolerance is another important characteristic, particularly in winter climates with lots of sun. If your peas are maturing in hot temperatures (above 80° F, 27° C), you'll probably get heavy vine growth, but few flowers, and hence few peas. Check out the heat tolerant varieties if this is your situation.

Here is a run-down of peas that have shown some adaptability to the solar greenhouse environment. I have selected them either for their disease resistance, ability to grow tall, or ability to produce in warm weather. These include:

Wando: This is not a new kitchen appliance. Available in most catalogs, it's noted for its ability to withstand warm temperatures. Wando peas grow up to 4' high in 60 - 80 days in the solar greenhouse.

Green Arrow: Available in most catalogs, it has good resistance to the following diseases: fusarium wilt, downy mildew and leaf curl virus. It grows 2'-3' tall and takes 60 - 80 days to mature in the solar greenhouse.

Gloriosa: Available through Thompson and Morgan. It has good ability to withstand warm temperatures, grows 4'- 5' tall and matures in approximately 80 days. Yields well in the solar greenhouse and shows some tolerance to powdery mildew.

Sugar Snap: Available in most catalogs, both peas and pods are edible. Grows 5'- 6' high. Needs a well-lit place and approximately 80 days to mature in the solar greenhouse. It is susceptible to powdery mildew disease, but the great taste makes it worth a try.

Oregon Sugarpod: Grows 3'- 4' high. Somewhat tolerant of warm weather. Approximately 70 days to harvest in the solar greenhouse.

Grenadier: Available from Burpee, it shows some resistance to powdery mildew, a rare and important characteristic.

Dwarf Grey Sugar: Available in many catalogs, I've found this edible pod variety to be heat tolerant. It grows to about 3' tall and does best when trellised, though some catalogs suggest it's not necessary. It takes about 70 days to reach maturity.

All of the above varieties should be trellised. Chicken wire works very well, or use what you have on hand. When deciding where to plant peas, be mindful of the shadows the vines will cast on adjacent plants. I have found it best to run trellises on a north-south axis to prevent a full-day shadow. Even a short length of trellis running 3 feet long can produce many peas. Peas also do well in a 5-gallon container with a teepee type trellis. Some dwarf varieties may come in handy in areas where you want to grow peas but don't want shading on other crops.

I plant two rows of peas for each trellis, one row on each side. A 2'' spacing between seeds works fine. You may initially have to help the peas get started up the trellis. Pea vines are very fragile and frequently get damaged during harvesting. To prevent this, pick the peas with two hands instead of ripping them off with one hand. Keep the vines well picked to prolong harvest. It seems you get slightly more total food from the edible podded peas than from the basic pea varieties. Give peas a chance.

Potato

Potatoes are not a good choice for the solar greenhouse because they can be purchased very cheaply in the store at any season, and can be stored year-round in root cellars. It's better to utilize limited greenhouse space for more valuable and perishable crops. If you do grow potatoes in your greenhouse, you can prevent many potential disease problems by planting only USDA certified seed (certified free of disease). Many people grow potatoes in large containers such as garbage cans. It is also common to grow potatoes in a light compost/soil mixture. This mixture allows you to *lift* up the compost and harvest the potatoes while the plant continues to grow, harvesting them as you need them. Too much light on potato tubers causes skins to turn green, and such potatoes can be slightly poisonous. So keep harvested tubers in the dark.

Radish

Radishes are fast producers when given the right environment. Basically they are easy to grow, so many folks plant more than they can eat.

Radishes like cool temperatures and moist, friable (not compacted) soil. Most varieties do well in the winter season. Radishes will be ready for harvest in about 4 weeks. The closer they're grown to the winter solstice the longer they'll take to mature due to the lack of light. Winter radish varieties are slower growing (8 - 12 weeks), much larger and longer-keeping than regular varieties. Try different varieties to find the degree of pungency you like.

A common problem with radishes is production of leaf growth with little or no root development. This can be caused by a number of factors, such as prolonged warm temperatures (above 70° F, 21° C), failure to thin the seedlings (thin to at least 1'' apart), too much manure or nitrogen in the soil, growing them too dry (radishes like moist soil), and growing in very shady areas.

Radishes are a great crop to interplant. Put a few seeds in any empty place you have; they're a good filler. Because the seed germinates fast, it's best just to seed them directly into the bed rather than transplant seedlings.

Salsify

This plant is also know as the vegetable oyster. The root is cooked and used just like an oyster. Salsify will grow fine in the solar greenhouse, but it needs 150 days to reach maturity. Don't transplant it as that will destroy tap root development, which is what you're growing it for. Sandy soil is its favorite. Try just a few plants at first to see how they do, and whether they pass your taste tests. Salsify grows fine into the warmer months. It is not an efficient food producer due to the long growth period before harvesting, but it doesn't need much space.

Spinach

Spinach has low heat tolerance and bolts very quickly. In high winter sun areas, you are lucky to get much of a harvest before it flowers. But in cooler winter climates with less sun, spinach is a good producer, though not quite as good as lettuce.

Select varieties that are slow to bolt; they'll produce more over a longer period of time, and you may get several harvests. To prolong the harvest period, pick only larger, older leaves, and let the smaller leaves continue to grow.

Varieties that seem resistant to bolting include Bloomsdale Long Standing and America, both being generally available. Melody, a common spinach variety available in many catalogs, is grown for its disease resistance to downy mildew, mosaic virus and blue mold. Winter Bloomsdale is resistant to blight disease. Spinach transplants fine in the seedling stage and likes a light soil that is somewhat moist. Space them 6'' apart. The best harvest and quality can be obtained when grown in temperatures below 60° F (16° C).

Consider the much higher yielding spinach alternatives such as Swiss chard and New Zealand spinach before planting a lot of standard spinach.

New Zealand Spinach

This thick-leaved spinach alternative has one great advantage over spinach: it's a perennial that doesn't die after it flowers. One plant can produce for many years. Also, the leaves still taste fine during flowering. It spreads out over a bed, and it grows slightly slower than spinach with cool temperatures, but it's productive over a much longer period, even during the hot weather of summer.

You can make efficient use of space by tying it to a north-south trellis. The vines are very delicate and break easily, so tie it up gently. By growing it vertically, it will yield much more per square foot. New Zealand spinach can also be trained to hang off the edge of a raised bed, thereby making aisle space productive. It likes a rich soil. Seedlings transplant easily into beds. I have interplanted it under taller plants with good success.

Turnips

Turnips grow fine in the solar greenhouse, but they also grow very well outside and keep nicely in a root cellar. Still, it's nice to eat a fresh turnip in the dead of winter. They take about 8 weeks to reach harvest unless you like them smaller. You can eat turnip greens like cabbage or spinach. There are varieties developed to just produce greens.

Grow turnips like radishes, but give them more space (about 3''- 4''). Because the seed germinates fast, it's best to seed them directly into the bed rather than transplant the seedlings. Because they grow fast and both tops and roots are edible, they're an efficient food producer.

Watercress

This crop likes water, so plant it near the faucet and water it every day. Never let the soil dry out. If you can find it growing in the wild, transplant it carefully into the greenhouse. It can also be started from cuttings (see *Plant Propagation*). It likes to grow in a lot of organic matter. Don't let the plant flower; cut the flower buds off as soon as they appear. It takes 70 - 80 days to reach maturity from seeds, and slightly less from cuttings. Mix it in your salad to add a peppery snap. The taste of watercress may get to be too strong as warm weather appears.

Summer Crops

Beans

Fresh beans in early May? Yes, in the solar greenhouse you can have a crop that early if you plant in March. You may even be able to push the harvest earlier.

There are two major types of beans: vines, such as pole beans, and bush or dwarf types. The vines utilize vertical space when trellised and can grow up to 25' high if conditions are right. The problem is finding a tall enough basketball player to pick them. Vining beans yield over a longer period than bush beans, but take about 10-20 days longer to reach maturity. The bush or dwarf beans need no trellising, as they reach only 12'' high. You will get more total

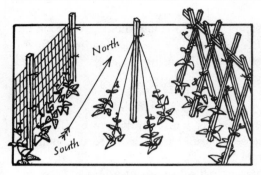

Three ways of supporting bean vines

yield and use space more efficiently with vining beans, but the bush types grow well in containers and do especially well when planted toward the south end of beds where little shading occurs. There is always a place for some bush beans in your greenhouse.

Vining beans provide good summer shade when grown over the front of your greenhouse mass and may prevent excess heat gain in water or rock storage media. The cooler temperatures of your shaded mass may help keep the summer greenhouse air cooler. Wherever you are growing vining or pole beans, make a trellis for the plants to climb. Plant one seed every 4'' along the trellis. To prevent shading problems among plants, think about where your summer shadows fall before you plant the pole beans. Running trellises along a north-south axis will eliminate problem shadows in most greenhouses.

Bean seeds need a soil temperature of at least 60° F (15° C) for best germination. Lower temperatures often cause the seed to rot in the soil. A crusty soil surface also can cause problems to emerging seedlings. A mulch will prevent this crustiness. Applying a legume innoculant (available in most seed catalogs) to the soil will utilize the ability of microbes to provide beans with nitrogen from the air. But this only works on beans, peas and other legumes. There are a few rare bean varieties that need an insect pollinator in order to produce beans. If you end up with such a variety, there won't be beans produced after flowering. If this happens, switch to another common variety. But in general most pole and bush beans set fruit without pollination. Scarlet Runner beans are an exception and are not recommended.

Beans are susceptible to a number of diseases, so here are a few precautionary tips:

- Use disease-free seed from a reputable seed company.
- Don't work among your bean leaves if they are wet. This spreads disease.
- Don't soak seeds before planting. One diseased seed will contaminate the whole batch.
- Each season rotate beans with other crops.

If a disease occurs, find out what it is with the help of your county agricultural extension agent. Then look through the seed catalogs for a bean variety that may have some resistance to the disease. Plant it next season.

In the solar greenhouse, be sure not to let your temperatures get much above 95° F (35° C). Such high temperatures will cause beans to have lower yields because the plant may drop flower blossoms. Blossom drop will also occur when you over or under-water the plants.

You can get up to three crops of beans in the summer season. I have found Kentucky Wonder to be a good pole bean. The asparagus bean, which makes foot-long beans and is cooked like asparagus, has done well in solar greenhouses, but it grows quite tall. A great catalog to look into is printed by The Vermont Bean Seed Company. They have the most extensive selection of bean and pea varieties to choose from.

For greenhouses in the north country, think about trying some longer season beans that are usually hard to grow in your outside garden. Garbanzo beans, also known as chick-peas, and lima beans require at least 100 warm days to produce. There are some bush limas, however, that are somewhat quicker. Garbanzo beans like sandy, drier soils and their leaves look like locust tree leaves. Garbanzos are good eating; when cooked they have a great nutty flavor. Have you ever tried hummus made from garbanzos? It's a delicious dip.

Cantaloupe and Muskmelon

Northern gardeners who live in short-season areas will go wild over the new experience of abundant home-grown cantaloupes in the solar greenhouse. I have even seen cantaloupe production be the prime motivator in the building of a solar greenhouse!

There are some cantaloupe varieties that are tolerant to the diseases fusarium and powdery mildew. Powdery mildew can be a big problem in solar greenhouses, and when this is the case, mildew tolerant varieties will really help production. I've also had particularly good luck in getting quick production with some of the earlier varieties. So in general, you should first try to find varieties with either tolerance or resistance to mildew, and then choose the quickest maturing among them. It's wise to test a few varieties each year. My very favorite is Israeli Cantaloupe (PMR), available from Porter and Son Seedsmen.

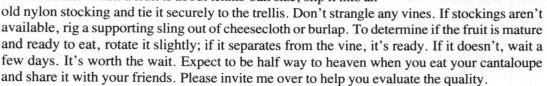

I've found it's best to build a sturdy 5' or higher trellis. Grow one plant every 3' along the length of the trellis. It might be a good idea to plant a few seeds in each spot and later thin to one hardy plant. To minimize shading problems, run the trellis north-south.

Cantaloupes like a rich soil that's full of decomposed organic matter and on the wet side. Be sure the soil is friable (not compacted) or on the sandy side. When flowers begin to appear, start your pollinating procedure to ensure fruit set (see *Pollination*). Remember, no pollination, no fruit.

As the fruits begin to develop on the vines, they will need support. The fruits can get so heavy they will rip the whole vine off the trellis. When a fruit is about tennis-ball size, slip it into an old nylon stocking and tie it securely to the trellis. Don't strangle any vines. If stockings aren't available, rig a supporting sling out of cheesecloth or burlap. To determine if the fruit is mature and ready to eat, rotate it slightly; if it separates from the vine, it's ready. If it doesn't, wait a few days. It's worth the wait. Expect to be half way to heaven when you eat your cantaloupe and share it with your friends. Please invite me over to help you evaluate the quality.

Cucumbers

Cucumbers are probably one of the most productive summer season crops you can grow. For best greenhouse production, grow the European seedless cucumbers, also known as greenhouse forcing cucumbers. Their fruit resembles the burpless cucumber, growing up to 20'' long. They are very high yielding, thin skinned, seedless (parthenocarpic) very sweet and without bitterness. The nicest thing about them for the greenhouse grower is that they don't need pollination and will freely and continuously set fruit.

The European cucumber is for fresh eating only and won't pickle very well because of its thin skin. If you plan to grow any traditional cucumbers, they *will* need pollination. This isn't easy to do with the tiny cucumber flowers, but it can be done (see *Pollination*).

Many American seed catalogs now carry the European cucumber seeds, which are more expensive than most other seeds. However, the greater yields make the price worth the investment. There *is* one way around the high cost of hybrid seed—see "cloning around" in *Plant Propagation* for a further explanation. Stokes and Herbst seed catalogues sell a very nice selection of different European cucumber varieties. Also, two seed catalogues from Holland, Bruinsma and Rijk Zwaan, each carry an extensive selection of cucumber seed for the greenhouse.

Don't try growing both regular and European cucumbers in the same greenhouse, especially if there are any pollinating insects around. If the European cucumber plants receive any pollen, they will likely grow misshappen, odd-tasting, bitter fruits with seeds. Yuk!

When selecting a European cucumber variety, read about the characteristics of each and try to grow the one best suited to your particular environment. Some will tolerate higher temperatures better, while others are more tolerant of lower temperatures. Other characteristics you can choose from include: darker fruit color, shorter or longer fruits, longer shelf life, and tolerance to some diseases. Toska is a good variety for beginners because it is forgiving of pruning mistakes. Most varieties have only female flowers but a few also have some male flowers. Male flowers don't produce fruit, and pollination only causes production of seeds and lower quality fruit. For these reasons, male flowers should be pruned off. (See *Pollination* to identify the male flower.) If seeds do form in your European cucumbers—not common—don't bother planting them. They will not grow into European cucumber plants because such seeds rarely breed true.

Because the seed is so costly, don't waste even one. Here is the best method I know for starting European cucumbers: plant one seed into a peat pot with a soil mix rich in organic matter. New potting soil is best. Maintain a soil temperature of at least 75° F (24° C) for best germination and keep the pots in a well-lit place after germination. Make sure the pots are moist at all times, but not soggy. Never allow them to get dry. If you plant two seeds in one pot and both come up, usually one plant must be sacrificed unless you're a pro at untangling roots without doing damage. For this reason (and the high cost of seeds) it's best to plant only one European seed per pot.

When the seedling has 4-5 leaves, it can be transplanted. Poke a hole in the bottom of the peat pot to ensure quick root development after transplanting. It's best to transplant into moist soil. Cucumbers need at least 2' of soil depth that is well drained, very high in decomposed organic matter and a pH of 6.5-7.0. Space plants about 2' - 3' apart. Cucumbers enjoy high amounts of nitrogen in the soil but not high amounts of salt. If salt damage occurs (indicated by leaf tips browning), leach out the salt with a few heavy applications of water.

Although cucumbers have a high water requirement, excessive watering may leach out many of the needed nutrients from the root zone. A mulch, however, will help conserve water in the soil, prevent excessive soil temperature fluctuation, and help prevent loss of nutrients. A feeding of nitrogen when the plants are 5' tall is helpful (see *Getting To the Roots* for sources of nitrogen).

Cucumbers prefer air temperatures of 70° -90° F (21° -32° C) with optimum growth at 85° F (30° C). Wide temperature fluctuations can adversely affect flavor. High temperatures can also cause misshapen fruit.

Cucumbers also like high levels of light, so growing in the shade will greatly reduce yields. If you are watering with cold water, try to warm it up to 60° F (15° C), if possible because colder water slows growth. As with most crops, morning watering is best. Avoid getting the plants wet when watering. Ventilation will help prevent excess humidity levels, so make sure there is good air flow around the leaves during the day.

The European cucumber can be grown up a trellis but is most productive when grown up a suspended cord or twine hanging from the ceiling. As the plant grows, the main stems are loosely wound around the twine. Prevent any bending or pinching of the main stems. If needed, plastic clips, available from many seed catalogs, may be used to attach the vines to the twine. Anchor the twine to the base of the plant by tying a loose knot that *will not slip* or strangle the stem. Twine may also be anchored to a small stake in the ground near the plant.

To train the plant for the best yields and use of space, prune side shoots, or laterals. There are a number of ways this can be done (see illustrations). One is to cut off any side shoots or suckers at the first 4 leaf axils. The next 8-10 shoots should be cut down to one leaf each, allowing only 1 or 2 fruits to form here. The remainder of the shoots should be trimmed to 2 leaves each. Plants are usually trained to 7' (it's hard to pick them any taller), at which point you can train the leader back toward the ground, winding it down an adjacent twine. You may want to pinch the leader at 7' and then select 2 shoots at the top to train back toward the ground.

These plants are so eager to produce fruit that they'll often start setting cucumbers at just a few feet tall. For a taller, more mature, healthy plant, prune all fruit occurring within 20'' of the ground before it develops because these early fruits can drain or stunt the plant.

For best production, you must keep the fruit well picked. If too many fruit are sitting on the vine at the same time, all the new fruits forming will begin to shrivel and die just after flowering. That's *not* what you're after. The more you pick, the more you get.

In Japan and Europe people are experimenting with the grafting of European cucumbers onto rootstocks of a gourd, usually *Cucurbita ficifolia*. This has been found to greatly increase yields and improve disease resistance. The grafted plants begin producing fruit earlier and can tolerate a lower soil temperature. The only drawback noted so far is a possibility of the transmission of a virus disease while grafting. Keep your eye on news of this experiment for future solar greenhouse cucumber production.

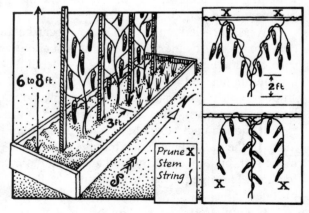

European cuke pruning

Because European seedless cucumbers have thin skins, moisture is rapidly lost from the fruits. So to prevent wilting, it's best to wrap the fruits in a plastic bag and place them in the refrigerator as soon as they are harvested. They're so sweet; no wonder this is the only type of cucumber that Europeans eat.

Eggplant

Eggplant does well in the summer season. The seeds need warm soil temperatures to germinate (75°-85°F) (24°-30°C) and each plant needs about 1½ square feet of growing space. Eggplants like a rich soil with a high level of moisture. To ensure good fruit formation, practice pollination (see *Pollination*). Some varieties need pollination more than others. The types that grow long, thinner fruit such as Ichiban, need less pollination; they'll often set fruit without any pollination at all, or like tomatoes, with just a tap to the flowers with a stick. When it comes time to harvest, do it before the fruits lose their glossy appearance.

Eggplants are in the tomato family and are susceptible to many of the same diseases. So they aren't a good rotation to follow a tomato or pepper crop. Grow one plant for every two people you are feeding . . . unless you're addicted to eggplant.

Husk Tomato - Ground Cherry - Strawberry Tomato

The husk tomato is a close relative to the true tomato. A lower growing plant, it produces a unique tasting and very sweet fruit within a leafy husk. Each plant should be 1½'- 2' away from other plants. Grow them much like true tomatoes. Requiring about 70 days to harvest, the fruits are ripe when they turn gold, but because husk tomatoes don't utilize vertical space very well, your vertical space can probably be better utilized with a more productive crop. They are used for fresh eating, sweetened as a desert or made into taco sauce.

Jerusalem Artichoke - Sun Choke

This is a sunflower that produces potato-like tubers. It has no relationship to the true artichoke. It grows about 6'- 8' tall. Although the plant will grow and produce in your greenhouse, it is not an efficient food producer for the amount of space it requires. When planted outside of the greenhouse adjacent to the glass, it can shade the front of the greenhouse and thereby moderate summer temperatures.

Luffa - Vegetable Sponge

Luffa, in the squash family, will grow abundant vines up just about anything. It needs at least 100 warm days to reach maturity in the greenhouse. The flowers need pollination to set fruit; follow the procedure for squash. When the fruits are immature (5''- 6'' long) they may be eaten like summer squash. But if you let the fruits mature, they should be dried, peeled and used as bathing sponges. The luffa likes high temperatures. They aren't a good choice for smaller greenhouses because they require so much space. I have seen them grow to the top of a 15' high trellis. You may want to start them early in a peat pot in a warm place in the greenhouse for later transplanting into your summer garden.

Mushrooms

Grocery store mushrooms are possible, but difficult to grow in dark areas of the solar greenhouse because they require *very* exacting conditions which are generally hard to control. For this reason I don't recommend planting mushrooms in your greenhouse. Chances are slim that you'll have anything to harvest. But it is common to see mushrooms (not the cultivated types) popping up all over. I've had edible mushrooms come up in some growing beds in the greenhouse where none were planted, but before eating them, I first had a local expert tell me they were closely related to the cultivated mushroom *Agoricus campestris* and assure me they were OK to eat. In 5 square feet we harvested more than 20 pounds from under the broccoli. They were good eating.

If you have wild mushrooms come up spontaneously, *don't eat* them until you've had an expert positively identify them. I've seen wild poisonous mushrooms growing in beds where people had planted edible mushrooms. It can get a little scary. Better safe than sick or dead.

If you are interested in growing wild, edible mushrooms, a book on the subject, *Growing Wild Mushrooms* by Bob Harris, is published by Wingbow Press. It covers a wide variety of mushrooms and gives directions for culturing and cultivating them. If you want to try growing the grocery store type, follow the instructions that come with the spawn (available from many seed catalogs).

Okra

Although okra is hard to grow in short-season areas, it usually does fine in the summer greenhouse season. It will be new to many northern gardeners, except those who were raised in the South where it enjoys great popularity. This relative of cotton and hibiscus is often used in soups or it is sliced and fried. I enjoy it pickled with hot peppers.

Okra varieties differ considerably. Height can vary from 5'-10'. Pod size varies in length and width. Varieties also differ greatly in pod shape and color, leaf shape, and flowers. I haven't had a chance to test all the many varieties, but what I've grown have produced well. It seems that the taller plant varieties produce more total yield, but the dwarf varieties (which grow 4'-5' tall) also do nicely in the greenhouse.

Before planting, be sure your soil is not too rich in nitrogen. An excess will cause heavy leaf production at the expense of flower and pod production. Overwatering may also cause this problem. Seed germination will be faster if the seed is soaked overnight. Okra likes a sunny place and warm temperatures and should be spaced about 1' apart. It transplants fine in the seedling stage and does well interplanted with other crops.

The immature pods, which are what you harvest, begin to develop after flowering. The okra flower is one of the most beautiful of all vegetable flowers. It needs no hand pollination to set harvestable pods. Harvest begins about 70 days after planting. Production will slow greatly with the cooler temperatures of fall.

Peppers

Peppers, in the same family as eggplants, tomatoes and tobacco, grow best in full sun and warm temperatures. They like a moderately rich, well-drained soil. Each plant needs approximately 4 square feet unless the variety you have is a smaller, dwarf type. Being a relative of the tomato, the pepper, unfortunately, is susceptible to many of the same diseases as the tomato.

Cayenne and bell peppers can grow as high as 4' and often benefit from staking. This will prevent the plant from falling over, will promote vertical growth, and will increase your yields per square foot. As with staking any plant, use a piece of soft cloth to loosely tie up the plant and prevent stem damage.

Pepper seeds can take as long as 9 weeks to germinate. For best germination and seedling growth, place them in a warm (at least 65°F [18°C]) sunny place. However, hot summer temperatures above 100°F (38°C) can damage pollen and prevent fruit set. Also temperatures below 60°F (16°C) will greatly slow fruit production. High levels of nitrogen in the soil can cause luxuriant leaf growth at the expense of fruit production, so be alert if you suspect this problem. Although peppers do best in warm temperatures, I have found that they actually overwinter better than a tomato and will even produce a few fruits in the dead of winter.

There is a wide variety of peppers to choose from including: bell peppers, which produce sweet large fruits; cayenne peppers which are usually slim, pointed fruits ranging in hotness; pimiento peppers that are sweet, slightly pointed peppers used for canning and stuffing; tabasco, that are usually hot peppers, slim or tapered; and celestial peppers that are hot fruits, produced upright, up to 2'' long, and often used as ornamentals. Bruinsma Seed Company from Holland offers a few bell pepper varieties developed for the greenhouse environment. They are somewhat disease tolerant and grow taller than standard varieties. As most peppers mature, they change color from green to purplish to red. Peppers benefit from high soil moisture levels until fruits begin to mature. At that point, cut back on water somewhat.

Squash - Summer squash

Summer squash includes zucchini, patty pan, gold, yellow squash, etc. It is known as summer squash because the fruits are harvested immature in the summer and usually eaten fresh. Winter squash, on the other hand, is allowed to mature and can be stored into the winter.

Most available summer squashes are bush varieties. There is a wide range of varieties; some grow more compact, some are more open. I have found the straight neck and crook neck yellow squash very prolific producers, but it's hard to keep on top of their needed pollination.

Summer squash yields abundantly in the warm solar greenhouse, but when temperatures consistently drop below 55°F (13°C), it lives but doesn't produce much. Seed may be started in peat pots and transplanted as bed space becomes available. It may also be planted directly into the bed.

Squash likes soil rich in well-decomposed organic matter. Each plant will need at least 9 square feet by the time it's ready to produce. (While it is still small you can often sneak a few radishes into the area the mature squash will soon occupy.) It can also be grown in 5-gallon containers in a very rich soil mix, one plant per container. Plant squash in a warm place that receives plenty of light. After the plant has started fruit production, it will benefit greatly from a soil feeding such as manure tea. However, if the plant shows any signs of salt damage, avoid this practice. Though most summer squash are classified as a ''bushy plant,'' I've had luck making them grow up a thick, suspended string. After the

stem is about 2' long, I lift the tip of the plant so the whole stem is vertical. (Be very gentle now, the stem cracks easily.) Now wind the string (with a little slack) down through the squash, and *loosely* tie it to the base of the plant or anchor it to a ground stake. By growing them vertically you can use space very efficiently.

A relatively new variety of summer squash known as Gold Rush (a golden type of zucchini), is very resistant to environmental stresses of all sorts including overwatering, underwatering, heat and cold. And it is also tolerant to powdery mildew. Gold Rush is available from most seed catalog companies.

Any summer squash you grow will need pollination, so be sure to read *Pollination* for details. If you see any varieties that are listed as being predominantly female flowering, pass them by because you will need male flowers to pollinate all the female fruits. During cooler periods a much lower percentage of male flowers is produced, making it difficult to pollinate.

On the leaves of many zucchini squash you may see small, angular, whitish-colored splotches. This is not a disease, but a common characteristic of summer squash. Don't confuse it with powdery mildew, a white powder-like disease found in random, round splotches. See *Pests and Diseases*.

Harvest most summer squash when they are relatively small (8'' long for zucchinis). This is when they're the sweetest. And the more you pick, the more they'll produce.

Winter squash

Winter squash includes many of the well known "storage" squashes such as butternut, buttercup, hubbard, pumpkin, acorn and spaghetti squash. They are considered mature when thumbnail pressure doesn't mark the skin. If stored properly (50°F [10°C]), they will keep for many months. These squashes usually grow vine-like, but some bush varieties are available. All non-bush varieties should have a trellis to grow on.

If you are trellising winter squash, place one plant every 12 square feet. If you have to tie up the vines, as usual use soft pieces of cloth to avoid strangulation of the stems. These vining varieties can really spread, so you may have to prune back some of the vines to prevent the conquest of your sunspace. Bush varieties are more restrained in their growth and may be grown in 5-gallon containers.

Winter squash is a heavy feeder and benefits from soils rich in decomposed organic matter. It requires pollination to set fruit, and needs 100-150 warm days before fruit is produced. Greenhouses enable people living in the very short season areas to produce the long season winter squash where they can't get the squash to mature properly outside.

You can also eat your winter squash before it matures, like summer squash. This will increase your total yields, as the more you pick from it, the more squash your plant will offer you. Immature squash won't keep long so use it within a few days. For best quality, store it in the refrigerator.

Northern gardeners may also use the greenhouse to start winter squash inside for outside transplanting. Whenever transplanting any squash, use larger peat pots that can be planted directly into the ground—their roots are sensitive to naked transplanting.

Tomatoes

As in outside gardens, tomatoes are probably the most popular greenhouse crop. I think it's because tomatoes bought at the store are often low in quality and high in cost. It is hard to beat a home grown vine-ripened, sweet flavorful tomato. Anything else is a poor substitute. Outside garden tomato production techniques will work in the greenhouse, but using methods specifically developed for the greenhouse will give you even better yields, less problems with pests and diseases, and most important—better quality tomatoes. The advantage of a solar greenhouse crop is that you can produce tomatoes earlier and for a longer period; and they'll usually be bigger than those grown outside. Because tomatoes are so perishable, they are often very expensive to purchase. The greenhouse provides a great alternative.

There's such a wide range of characteristics in the many tomato varieties available that choosing the best ones can make a large difference in fruit yields, quality and overall growing success. Tomato varieties have "bush" growing characteristics (called "determinate") or "vining" characteristics (called "indeterminate"). The indeterminate tomato has a growing tip that's capable of growing indefinitely. The determinate tomato, on the other hand, will eventually produce a flower cluster which "tops off" the growing point, producing a low, bushy plant. The determinate tomato commonly is used on large acreages with mechanical harvesting and by home gardeners who like smaller and more manageable plants and early production. In the greenhouse the bush tomato is best grown in containers. Vining tomatoes can be trained to grow vertically, and will have higher total yields, especially in raised beds, so they're best for maximum greenhouse production. In the catalogs, you'll find many other characteristics to choose from besides bush and vine. These include tolerance of warmer and cooler temperatures, resistance to cracking, fruit size, earliness, coloring and disease tolerance.

Tomatoes are a warm season crop and grow best at temperatures between 65°F and 80°F (18°-27°C). Growth slows greatly at temperatures above 95°F (35°C) and below 50°F (10°C). It isn't hard to keep a tomato plant alive down to 32°F (0°C), but it won't grow and may look sickly due to the great stress it's under. Along with warm temperatures, you must have full sun striking the plant for much of the day; so leave the shady sections of your solar greenhouse for other crops.

Tomatoes do best in a well-drained soil. And be sure there is plenty of decomposed organic matter in the soil. It is important to keep phosphorus levels high, especially for fruit and flower formation. Bone meal is an excellent source as it provides not only phosphorus but also calcium, which helps prevent the tomato disorder called blossom end rot. Do a soil test to see exactly what your soil needs. Tomatoes are sensitive to a buildup of soluble salts, so if you use chemical fertilizers, avoid those that contain any chlorine or sodium, or high amounts of raw manures. Tomatoes need pollination in order to properly set fruit. Please turn to *Pollination* for further instructions.

To prevent the spread of disease, be sure to wash your hands with soap before handling any tomato seed or plant. Seed can be sown into a peat pot or flat. In flats, don't sow seeds too close together; crowded plants are more susceptible to disease. One seed every 1½'' is usually adequate. In peat pots sow 2 seeds per pot and pinch out one if both germinate. Be sure to pinch because pulling out seedlings injures the remaining plant's roots. Germination is best at 75°-85°F (24°-30°C). After germination, seedlings need full sunlight to prevent stem elonga- tion. The usual soil temperature for growing seedlings is 65°F (18°C). It has been found, however, that seedlings exposed to "cold treatment" produce as much as 25% more total fruit. But to do the cold treatment you need good control of temperatures. Here's the procedure for cold treatment of tomato seedlings.

After the first true leaves emerge, reduce the soil temperature to 52°-56°F (11°-13°C) for 10 days (sunny conditions) or 3 weeks (cloudy conditions). Try to maintain optimum light during the cold treatment period to prevent stem elongation. A cool bright corner of the floor in your solar greenhouse or a cool south-facing house or garage window may provide the cooler temperatures and light. Check it with your thermometer. The "cold treatment" is an easy way to increase your yield.

Tobacco, a relative of tomatoes, is a carrier of the disease called tobacco mosaic virus, which smokers can spread when working with tomato plants. Milk helps prevent transmission of virus diseases, so spray the seedlings with skim milk before transplanting. After the spray dries, the plants will be protected from viruses for about 12 hours. Again, always wash your hands with soap before transplanting. Transplanting tomatoes is a job best reserved for non-smokers.

Tomatoes need less water than cucumbers but should not be so dry or hot to become wilted. Be sure to water at regular intervals as irregular watering will promote blossom end rot. Mulches help to lessen any type of water stress and will buffer widely fluctuating soil temperatures and help prevent this rot. See *Pests and Diseases* for more information on both blossom end rot and tobacco mosaic virus.

Space each tomato plant at least 2' apart. Tighter spacing increases the incidence of disease. In areas of many cloudy days, it might help to space your plants wider to provide optimum light penetration. And I've found that tomatoes receive the most light when rows are planted north-south.

To best utilize greenhouse space, prune or train your plants. Greenhouse tomatoes can grow as high as 10' plus, and if prop- erly trained can yield all the way up the vine. Pruning should be done only to "greenhouse variety" tomatoes or those listed as indeterminate or vining. Never prune bush or determinate vari- eties. As with transplanting and seed sowing, before pruning is begun wash your hands with soap to prevent the spread of disease.

Plants should be trained to one or two main stems. This involves pinching out side growing points, or suckers (see illus- tration). These side shoots are found directly *above* a main leaf at the crotch where the leaf stem (known as the petiole) attaches to the main stem. If these are not pruned early, they will enlarge rapidly and soon be hard to distinguish from the main stem. Begin pruning as soon as the first side shoots appear, and do it at least every 5 days. After plants are 8'-10' tall, prune the tip of the main stem to hasten development of the last fruits. Many people prefer growing tomatoes with two growing points per plant in a V-shape. To do this, follow the above procedure but early on let one sucker survive pruning at about 1' and become a second main stem. Keep this second stem pruned as you did in the single stem method (see illustration). Space plants at about 3′ apart using this system. To prevent spreading disease, always prune any plants suspected of disease last. You don't want to spread it with your fingers.

To support the plant as it grows, attach it to a long sturdy pole buried 2′ deep in the soil, 5″ from the seedling. As the plant gets taller, tie the stem to the pole with a soft strip of cloth. Tying it too tight will strangle the plant and prevent it from growing any taller. Another slightly better method that's commonly used is to hang some plastic twine or soft thick string from the ceiling directly above the plant. Tie the end of the twine (not a slip knot) to the base of the plant, leaving slack in the loop (see illustration). Then, as the plant grows, begin to wrap the plant around the string. Begin with some slack in the length of the string as it will be taken up when the plant gets tall. You can also anchor the string to a small stake in the ground rather than to the plant, which will prevent strangulation of the stem. Outside gardeners have popularized growing to-matoes in round wire cages. This method, though not quite as efficient as the training methods outlined above works in the greenhouse and is simpler for novices. In the greenhouse, how-ever, make your wire cage taller (about 6′ high) and about 2′ in diameter.

Stringing tomatoes

Don't remove leaves covering the fruits. They prevent the sun from heating the fruit, which would cause cracking. Ventila-tion is very important in controlling tomato diseases. Sometimes it helps to cut off some of the lower leaves of a tall tomato plant to get better air circulation under and through the plant. Keep at least 5½′ of vertical leaf area on the plant and, except for suckers, never prune leaves above any blossoms or forming fruit. Don't get too carried away with pruning; remember, each leaf is producing energy and sugar for the plant and for fruit formation.

Sweet 100 is one of the few cherry tomatoes that grows indeterminately. It bears large clusters of fruit like grapes. The Sweet 100 fruits are as sweet as candy, rich in vitamin C, and seem to be quite cold-tolerant.

I'm sure you'll want to test your greenhouse's winter tomato production ability. I suggest that you try to overwinter a few of your tall healthy full tomato plants, as well as starting some of the early, cold-tolerant varieties found in northern seed catalogs. Often these early varieties are determinate or bush plants and should not be pruned as pruning will only lower their yield. Some good winter bush tomato varieties are Sub-Artics and Scotia.

The most common difference among tomato varieties, especially those developed for greenhouse culture, is the response to diseases. Though many varieties have some tolerance or resistance to many of the common diseases, unfortunately there is no such thing as a 100% resistant variety. At best, one variety may have tolerance or some resistance to 4 separate diseases. There is ongoing development of tomato varieties with resistance to multiple diseases, and each year new ones are available. In order to select a variety with resistance to your plant's particular disease, first you must get positive identification of the disease. Then consult the catalogs. Help can be obtained from a local plant disease clinic, usually located through your nearest state land grant college or county agricultural extension agent. For further help in controlling plant diseases, turn to *Pests and Diseases*.

Watermelon

Growing watermelons is much the same as growing cantaloupes, though I've found that cantaloupes generally yield more in the greenhouse. So cantaloupes are preferred, but if you just *must* grow a watermelon, start the seeds in a warm, bright location. Be sure your greenhouse maintains night temperatures well above $50^{\circ}F$ ($10^{\circ}C$) before you start your plants in spring. Because they don't transplant very well, start them in peat pots. When transplanted into the bed, give each plant 8 square feet. While plants are young, you can intercrop with some

other plants such as carrots or chard. But as soon as they start producing vines, they need all of their allocated space. Watermelons like well-drained, sandy soil, high in decomposed organic matter.

Like cantaloupes, watermelons should be trellised and pollinated (see *Pollination*). It is best to run trellises north-south. Also, like cantaloupes, the fruits need a sling so the trellis directly supports the weight of the fruit (see the Cantaloupe section of this chapter).

About the hardest thing about growing watermelons is knowing when they're ripe. You can read all the garden books you want, talk to all the old experts, thump it, look for when the tendrils turn brown near the fruit, count the days, etc., and still pick your one prize watermelon too early or too late. I've concluded that knowing when a watermelon is ripe is a God-given gift reserved for the chosen few with the best watermelon karma. For this reason, I always grow the smaller icebox watermelons. They produce more fruits per vine, which gives the unblessed grower a better chance of catching a ripe melon. The smaller fruits are also easier to support on the trellis.

Flowers for the Food Greenhouse

Growing flowers in the food producing solar greenhouse is often thought to be a waste of space, but don't believe it. Flowers are wonderful, especially in the dead of winter. Besides being beautiful and real pleasure producers, they can also contribute to your overall food growing efforts.

Flowers provide a back-up food source for many beneficial insects. When predators or parasites can't locate any insects to feed on, they will often obtain food from the nectar and pollen within flowers. So the presence of these flowers may prevent the starvation of a beneficial insect.

Many believe that marigolds secrete a substance into the soil that inhibits the establishment of nematodes, a small destructive root worm that weakens plants and nasturtiums may be grown as a "trap crop." When nasturtiums age, they begin to be very attractive to aphids. This attraction will draw them off other plants and onto the nasturtium. When many aphids are seen on the nasturtium, destroy the large aphid population by pulling up the nasturtium (don't shake the aphids off!) or by spraying the plant with a botanical pesticide. The nasturtium is sprayed or sacrificed for the benefit of the growing beds or the whole greenhouse. Besides being a trap for insects, they are also edible. Their best part is the flower. The tail of the flower is full of nectar and has a great flavor, like a sugar-sweet mild radish. The sweet taste of nasturtium flowers is stimulating, and they add nice color to a salad.

When growing any flowers in the greenhouse, be sure there's not an overabundance of nitrogen in their soil. Heavy amounts of nitrogen promote leaf growth at the expense of flower production. On the other hand, bone meal and high phosphorous fertilizers help stimulate flower production. So do what's appropriate for your plants.

By using outside techniques, most common garden flowers will grow well in the solar greenhouse during the summer. But in the winter greenhouse it is important to grow only those that can survive the cool nights and still bloom.

The following is a list of hardy, flowerng plants for your winter solar greenhouse. It is best, however, to avoid planting any of these in the dead of winter. Plant in late summer or early fall for winter flowers, and early in the spring for late spring flowers. Late summer planting is preferable. If winter planting must be done, place the planted seed in a warm place (70°F, 21°C) for best germination.

Allyssum

Good border plant; start from seed. It grows low and smells good.

Begonia

Provide partial shade.

Calendula

Blooms all winter and gets about 1' high. Always remove old blossoms. Flowers are used in soups.

Prune
Here

Carnation

Start from seed or rooted cuttings. Provide a cross hatch horizontal, multilevel trellis for support. To get the largest flowers, pinch out all but one flower bud per stem. High heat (above 80°F, 27°C) will cause reduced growth and poor quality flowers. Sudden cold will also cause poorly shaped flowers. Cut flowers for sale to florists, restaurants, etc., may provide some extra income. Plants can be productive up to two years.

Chrysanthemum

Try starting cuttings from store-bought plants (see *Plant Propagation*). For best growth pinch out the growing tips. Provide full sun. Flowering is related to the length of night, and occurs only in fall and spring.

Geranium

Well suited to the solar greenhouse environment, they are able to withstand very high and low temperatures, even on the same day. They will flower all year long and do best in full to partial sun. They are propagated by cuttings or seed. Cut them back if they get tall and lanky. There are thousands of varieties from which to choose. Different types include: colored leaves, dwarfs, rose-flowered, ivy leaf and scented. Scented geraniums are always interesting; the range includes rose, lemon, strawberry, coconut, orange, apple, pine, chocolate, mint, nutmeg, almond and anchovy. Well, maybe not anchovy. According to one supplier, scented geraniums have been used as teas or for flavoring in cooking. None of the varieties have been reported to be toxic, but to be safe, go easy on eating geraniums.

Geraniums have great potential in a commercial solar greenhouse. Two good catalogs for geraniums are:

Cooks Geranium Nursery
712 North Grant
Lyons, Kansas 67554

Carobil Farm and Greenhouse
Church Road, Rt. 1
Brunswick, Maine 04011

Marigold

Well known for their insect repellent properties, they can be grown year-round in the solar greenhouse. For interplanting and borders, use the dwarf-French types. In the winter, marigolds tend to have short lives and look old much faster. Always have a few seedlings to plant in empty areas. For large cut flowers, grow the tall African varieties. However, the African varieties don't do as well in the cold as do the French types.

Nasturtium

As previously mentioned, not only can this plant be used as a trap crop for insects, but the flowers are edible. Plant nasturtiums on the edges of your raised beds and let them trail over the edges. Dwarf varieties are more manageable and don't take too much space. Nasturtiums are also good in hanging pots. Seeds will rot in cold wet ground, so try germinating them in a warm place and then transplant. The Alaska variety has beautiful leaves as well as flowers.

Pansy

Pansies are faithful winter bloomers—and I'm not referring to a brand of insulated underwear. I've had good luck bringing in plants from outside in the fall. The Swiss giant varieties have long stemmed blooms that are ideal for cut flower arrangements. Majestic giants are noted for their heat tolerance.

Snapdragons

Having great potential as a commercial solar greenhouse crop, they do fine in the winter with a great yield of beautiful, delicately scented flowers. The main trick for winter is to grow *only* those varieties that are listed for "forcing" or "greenhouse culture." Check the catalogs closely. Varieties developed for outside will grow bushy and produce few flowers in winter. Start seed in early August for winter flowering. Provide a horizontal trellis (also see Carnations) support for straight flowering spikes.

Cut Flowers

A wintertime benefit of having a solar greenhouse containing flowering plants is bringing some of the flowers inside to brighten up those dreary winter days. The color and scent of a bunch of flowers can turn the entire day around.

Cut flowers remain better looking for longer periods if you practice the following procedures:

1. Cut with a sharp knife in the late afternoon. This is when the flowers, stems and leaves have the highest sugar content. That's their food, and it keeps them alive longer.

2. Immediately place in warm water (not hot) that contains 1 tablespoon of sugar and either 2 tablespoons of vinegar or 1 tablespoon of lemon or lime juice per quart. The warm water is taken up better by the plant and the vinegar (lemon or lime juice) makes the water more acidic and therefore less susceptible to rotting organisms. And the sugar is food for the blooms. A mixture of 1 part soda pop to 1 part warm water also works well.

A Word of Caution

Many flowers and houseplants are poisonous when eaten. Please be sure your children understand what is food and what isn't. All kids go through a period when everything goes in the mouth. Keep any questionable plants out of reach, O.K.?

Herbs

Herbs are enjoying a well-deserved increase in popularity. Though often considered "exotic," don't be fooled; for the most part, herbs really are very easy to grow. Growing herbs in the solar greenhouse (hopefully) will provide you with a new opportunity to learn more about their many amazing properties. Herbs can provide teas, medicines, tonics for natural health, home remedies and fresh flavorings for cooking and salads. They may even be used as cosmetics. Herbs also can be made into pest repellents and insecticides and they have beneficial effects when interplanted with food crops (see both *Crop Layout* and *Pests and Diseases*). Most of us know that food tastes better when cooked with herbs and many people now believe that food takes on a better flavor when it's grown adjacent to them.

Because there already exist so many fine books on herbs, I won't go very deeply into the subject. There are, however, some special considerations when growing herbs in a solar greenhouse. In the winter solar greenhouse, most herbs can survive and be productive. But in general, the most hardy herbs for the winter are perennials and biennials. Tender annuals such as basil are the hardest to overwinter and may die in the cooler temperatures. At the other extreme, the winter solar greenhouses may not get cold enough to trigger flowering in certain herbs; lavender is a good example. So in that case, I suggest growing the herb in a container and leaving it outside from about October through December or January to trigger flowering.

People, especially children, are always pleasantly impressed when you take them on a small tour of your herbs. I recently gave a tour to a class of first graders. When they smelled the mint, they said it was toothpaste; when they smelled the dill, they swore it was pickles; and the fennel, they *knew* was disguised black licorice!

Herbs have great possibilities as a cottage industry. A medium-sized greenhouse can produce many herb plants for sale. Dried herbs and herbs processed into oils also may be sold or traded. An herb business could even be expanded into growing rare medicinal herbs for medical research. But the best use of your greenhouse-grown herbs is for your own needs. What could be better than to pick fresh herbs for a Christmas dinner, to be followed with some home-grown fresh herbal tea?

Most herbs you plant to grow through the winter are best started the previous spring. That will give the plant time to produce a well-developed root system that will promote more productivity during the winter months. Herbs that are started in the fall and winter grow very, very slowly, taking a long time to produce. And as with most seedlings, they are harder to germinate and get established in winter.

Place perennial herbs in areas that will not be disturbed during seasonal plantings.

Herb Processing

Herbs may be processed in a number of ways, including drying and freezing. Many of the books on herbs explain this in depth. You may wish to construct a solar dryer to dry the herbs. Usually it is hard to get herbs to dry in the solar greenhouse because the humidity is frequently too high. And they may even grow dangerous molds. So after cutting, always dry herbs in a place with low humidity—not in the greenhouse.

Using your herbs fresh is a real treat. Many people have never had this opportunity and are familiar only with dried herbs. When using fresh herbs—prior to cooking, making teas, etc.—be sure to bruise or crush them to bring out the full flavor. It takes 4 parts fresh herbs to equal 1 part dried herbs when cooking or making teas.

Following is a list of herbs that do well in a solar greenhouse, along with tips and comments on their cultivation. There are thousands of herbs, and I list only some common ones. You're encouraged to experiment and try those that aren't listed; you'll find that most will do very well. Why not start a few seeds today?

Aloe Vera

Aloe vera is known as "the healing plant." The clear juice contained in the leaves is used to help heal burns and cuts, and to prevent skin wrinkles. New evidence is showing that when

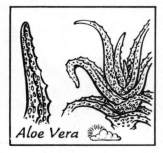

Aloe Vera

taken internally, it also heals many stomach ailments. The best thing about aloe vera is that it seems to work.

Growing it is easy. It is usually propagated from side shoot plants that arise advantageously next to a larger plant. Water thoroughly after planting. Most problems in growing aloe vera arise because it's often treated like a cactus and kept dry in a sunny place instead of being given moderate moisture levels and only partial sun. Too much sun is indicated by leaves purpling or turning a little brown. It prefers a bright place, but not full sun all day long. That should be easy to find in the greenhouse.

This plant does well in solar greenhouses and stands up to cold temperatures. However, it can show signs of rot if it is overwatered while being grown at cool temperatures. No greenhouse or windowsill should be without this amazing healing plant.

Anise

Anise is an annual herb that may be mistaken for a licorice stick. It's not that it looks like one, just that it smells like one. Anise will overwinter well in the solar greenhouse if started in the late summer for winter growth. Avoid excess nitrogen fertilization, as it may inhibit or delay seed production. Each plant requires about 1 square foot of growing space. Outside, this plant needs a long season to mature; inside your greenhouse it will thrive and mature year-round.

Basil

This is one plant that's hard to overwinter in the solar green-house, especially if your winter temperatures often fall below 45°F (7°C). But it's still well worth planting for production during spring, summer and fall. There are many varieties to choose from, including a purple leaf variety that's as beautiful as it is fragrant. Basil does fine planted in either pots or beds. Give it full sun and even watering, and harvest leaves during flowering. Pinch back flowers to stimulate more leaf production. Each plant grows to about 1½'-2' high. According to an old tradition, you should curse the seeds as you plant them. I've found it's best to do my planting and cursing after paying my phone bill. It's great therapy.

Basil

Borage

Borage grows larger than most herbs, so be sure to provide it with 2-3 square feet of growing space per plant. It will also get up to 3' high, even in winter. If you grow it in a pot, make sure the pot is at least 12'' wide. Borage produces well year-round in the solar greenhouse. Its flowers have a sweet cucumber flavor and when eaten, are said to make you happier with life. The leaves are often made into teas to give a cooling effect and provide some relief from congestion and coughing.

Catnip

Catnip is a mint relative. It is a perennial and usually is grown from seed, but it can be started from cuttings. It likes full sun. Watch out for cats because they will often destroy young seedlings and anything else nearby in their passion for this plant. It grows year-round in the solar greenhouse and produces abundant leaves. It is said that catnip can help repel that infamous greenhouse pest, the white fly. Make some catnip tea to relax; it has a great calming effect for nervous days, unless you've got a feline nature. One plant usually takes up about 2-3 square feet.

Chamomile

In the dead of winter, have some fresh picked chamomile tea from your solar greenhouse. To do so start the seeds in early summer. The seeds are tiny, so lightly cover them with peat moss to insure germination. Transplant the seedlings when they are 1'' tall. A mature plant takes up about 1 square foot of space, so each plant should be about 7'' away from other plants. Chamomile can take partial sun. It is a perennial and will grow year-round in the solar greenhouse. To harvest, cut the flower heads and crush them for fresh tea, or dry them for later use. Watch out for aphids; they love chamomile and are experts at camouflage.

Chives

Nichols Garden Nursery offers a variety developed for winter greenhouse production (see seed catalog appendix).

Coriander/Cilantro

Coriander is also know as cilantro by many Hispanics. It is an annual, but will thrive through the winter in a solar greenhouse. Plants are started from seed and do best in full sun. Both leaves and seed may be used for flavoring. Growing it for seed? If so, avoid using fertilizers high in nitrogen because high nitrogen levels will delay flowering and seed ripening, as well as reduce the total seed harvest. Each plant needs almost 1 square foot in which to grow.

Next time you cook up a pot of beans or hot sauce, throw in some cilantro leaves; it adds a great complementary flavor that's quite refreshing. The leaves smell strong but the flavor of the cilantro mellows when cooked.

Dill

Dill is an annual that is ideal for the winter solar greenhouse. It can be productive through both high and low temperatures, and does fine in partial shade. Dill plants may reach heights of up to 8' but there's a shorter dwarf variety called Bouquet. Each plant should be about 8'' away from any other plant. Anticipate its long shadow when you plant it. This plant can be prolific and will easily reseed itself if allowed to go to seed. If this happens, you may soon have thousands of seedlings sprouting, so consider harvesting before the seeds drop to save yourself hours of weeding. Both foliage and seed may be utilized, and dill leaf is excellent in salads.

Fennel

Except for its celery-like stalk, fennel greatly resembles dill. Just about the whole fennel plant is eaten—seeds, leaves and stalk. Like anise, this plant tastes like licorice. It's a perennial, and is usually started from seed. It grows abundantly in the winter solar greenhouse and can tolerate partial shade. It grows 4'-5' tall and takes up about 1 square foot of bed space. It's excellent as flavoring in soups and salads.

Garlic

Garlic grows year-round and tolerates a wide temperature range. It can be started from store-bought divided bulbs. Plant about 2'' deep. It doesn't take up much space so if you like garlic now you can have it fresh anytime. I cut the green tops off and use them much like chives or green onions, leaving the bulbs to produce more greens.

Lemon Balm

This hardy perennial is relative to the mint family, but has wonderful lemon-flavored leaves. It can be started with either seeds or cuttings and survives solar greenhouse winters very well. Lemon balm needs full to partial sun and at least 1 square foot of growing space. It grows about 1' tall, and rapidly becomes rootbound in small pots. This herb makes a refreshing tea—try mixing it with camomile. It's also great in salads.

Marijuana

Marijuana is among the more commonplace "herbs" in America. Conservative estimates are that 20 million Americans use it regularly. More use it occasionaly. It's almost as red white and blue as a six-pack of beer.

Home grown pot can eliminate the worry of smoking herbicide (Paraquat) treated leaves which are very damaging to the lungs. It also ends an association with dealers, the black market, the mafia and exploiters. Above all, it's free. Just one problem to consider before you plant your seeds . . . it's illegal. The penalty differs depending on your local laws. And getting caught would kind of ruin your day, wouldn't it? While I don't recommend its cultivation or use, people often ask if they can grow a few plants in their solar greenhouse. And because many people will try to grow it anyway, here's some information.

Marijuana is a warm season crop, preferring temperatures around 90°F (32°C) and doing poorly below 50°F (10°C). Seeds need a soil temperature around 70°F (21°C) to germinate well. Grow plants in full sun, and space them about 2′ apart. They will eventually shade other plants, so placing them against the southeast or southwest corner will help minimize this problem. Seedling diseases are often a problem so read *Pests and Diseases*.

To help promote large bud development, keep the soil high in phosphorus; work in bone meal or ground phosphate rock or super phosphate. Fertilizers such as tomato or African violet plant foods will also do. High nitrogen soils or fertilizers produce many leaves at the expense of buds. THC, the substance that gets people high, is increased in the plant during dry periods and is concentrated in the buds. For this reason, it is common to let the plants stay on the dry side for 2-3 weeks before harvesting. Many people even let them die from wilting after a long artificial drought. Cruel, but effective. Harvesting may be done at anytime, but the crop is most potent during its flowering stage.

Winter crops are possible only if temperatures are kept relatively high (well above 50°F, 10°C), but there is a common problem of plants flowering when they are too small. Early flowering will often reduce the total leaf and bud yield and the overall potency of the plant. Flowering is triggered by long nights—nights longer than 10 hours. But this can vary with different plants from different stock. You can fool plants and prevent early flowering by leaving a light on within 10′ of the plant. One 60 watt incandescent bulb will do. Plug it into a timer so that the plant sees a total of 15 hours or more of light including the daylight hours. This light will not grow your plants faster; it will only help control the flowering response.

All sources agree that good plants come from seeds of good plants. So plant only seed from proven herb. One sub-species related to the common marijuana plant (Cannabis sativa) is a native of Afghanistan. It flowers earlier, has fatter leaves and grows a bit shorter than common sativa. It is called Cannabis indica. It is the common variety grown in northern California, and seeds are hard to come by. Cannabis indica is definitely better suited for the solar greenhouse. When you're ready to harvest the plant, dig it out of the soil, roots and all. Wash off all the soil. Hang the plant upside down in a dry place.

If you're going to grow it, it may be wise to avoid clear glazings such as glass, and to minimize showing off your greenhouse.

Mint

There are many varieties of mint. These perennial plants do so well in the solar greenhouse all year-round that they can spread rapidly and become almost a weed. Be sure you don't let this happen. To contain it, you may have to put in edging (a barrier) 1′ down into the soil around the plant. If not, it'll take as much space as it can get away with. Mint does well in shade and likes a lot of water. It can be started from seeds, cuttings and transplants. It gets root bound very quickly if grown in containers.

Oregano

Oregano, a perennial, produces year-round. Propagate from cuttings or start it from seed. The seed is small, so just barely cover it with soil and keep it moist. It is a low-growing plant and will hang over the edge of a bed or a large pot. Oregano does very well in containers. Best quality leaves should be harvested during and after flowering, though leaves may be harvested at any time. Oregano usually takes up about 1 square foot of space, grows low to the ground and likes full to partial sunlight.

Rosemary

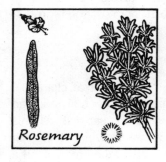

Rosemary

This plant is an evergreen perennial. It grows slowly, about 1′ per year, but is a beautiful plant that provides great flavoring. It grows upright and resembles a pine tree. It can be started from seed or cuttings, and cuttings are most successful if taken in late summer. Give it 1 square foot for each plant. It does best in full sun. It's nice to have at least one rosemary plant in the solar greenhouse for its beauty and year-round source of fresh leaf. It's reported to have medicinal and cosmetic qualities besides being a flavoring. Also, it is traditionally believed that where rosemary thrives, the woman is dominant. Watch for results.

Sage

Sage is a hardy perennial that easily survives solar greenhouse life. It is propagated from seed or cuttings. Locate it in a place that receives full sun. It also likes a well-drained soil. After two or three years, it becomes woody and sprawling. Sage grows about 1½′ high and needs about 1 square foot of space. Leaves may be used year-round as flavoring or in a healthful tea. The flowers are a beautiful shade of blue and will often bloom throughout the winter. Chewing sage flowers is a good substitute for chewing tobacco.

Summer Savory

Savory is one hardy annual that grows through the winter, but it lives only one full year. Start seeds in late summer. Savory needs sun and a lot of moisture. Keep plants 10″ apart. They will grow about 2′ tall. Try savory tea; it tastes like what its name implies.

Summer Savory

Tarragon

Ah, fresh tarragon all winter long. No problem in the winter solar greenhouse. It is usually started from either cuttings or from plants purchased from commercial growers. I found a neighbor who let me divide her plant and take a portion with good intact roots. Seed is not only hard to find but also hard to germinate. It grows 2′ high and needs about 1 square foot of bed space. It tolerates full to partial sun. Tarragon is a perennial, so locate it in a place that will not be disturbed. Besides using it for food and vinegar, I like to throw the fresh leaf into salads.

Thyme

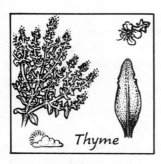

Thyme is a hardy perennial that overwinters well in the solar greenhouse. There are more than 40 varieties, differing in shape, size and flavor. The most common has small leaves and creeps low, so try it as a border plant. It also does well in 1-5-gallon pots. Thyme likes full to partial sun. Use the leaves when the flowers begin to open. In years gone by, thyme plants were found in almost every garden and were said to be the home of good spirits.

Permaculture

Gregory Bateson once described life on this planet as being ''on a river of change.'' Nothing in our lives seems to be permanent or forever. Realizing this makes me feel good and bad, depending on my present attitude about my life (which also constantly changes). All this holds true for plants, though some plants naturally live for only a few weeks while others can survive for hundreds of years, almost seeming permanent. I have classified the life cycle of a plant into three catagories:

     Annuals=Plants that live one year or less. During this time the plant grows, flowers, produces seeds and dies.

     Biennial=Plants that grow only leaves and roots the first year. In the second year they flower, produce seeds and die.

     Perennial=Plants that live for *more* than two years, often flowering and producing seeds each year.

Most of our food producing crops are annual or biennial. Agriculture systems based on annual and biennial plants require soil to be totally worked over almost every year, regularly disturbing the agricultural ecology. Quite unlike nature.

When we think of perennial plants most of us think of trees. But there are also many perennial shrubs, vegetables and grasses.

Imagine most of America's farmland filled with trees, and other perennial crops. They could eventually supply us with many of our agricultural needs: fruits, vegetables, fibers, fodder and, of course, wood for fuel and shelter, not to mention paper for solar greenhouse food books.

This lush, productive Nirvana may sound like a dream, but many agricultural futurists believe we can make outside crop production more efficient if we depend more on perennial food crops than annual crops. Why? Because perennial crops utilize a permanent root system rather than having to establish new plants each year. The word commonly used for this type of agriculture is permaculture.

Permaculture is a relatively new term, combining permanent plus agriculture. The value of permaculture lies in its permanence and potential for working with nature rather than fighting it. It is a low maintenance, whole systems approach to agriculture. Envision a shrub, planted once, that grows for 10 years while continually producing spinach-like leaves in great abundance. Compare this to planting spinach 20 - 30 times in 10 years, each time waiting for the seed to germinate and the root system to develop before the harvesting period even begins. Then you find that just when it really starts to yield, it goes to seed and dies. You have to start all over again. Not very efficient, is it?

In the solar greenhouse, those permaculture crops with the highest potential for top yields are, for the most part, totally unfamiliar to most people. Unfortunately, it's very hard to get people to eat new types of foods. Ever tried breadfruit, tamarind, or naranjilla? Maybe in the year 2042 they'll be as common as apples and oranges.

Much research needs to be done on the horticulture of such potential crops. It seems that many of the perennial crops familiar to us are not very good food producers compared to traditional annual crops. Although tomatoes, peppers and eggplants are usually grown as annuals, they're really perennials that have the potential to grow for many years . . . as long as they don't freeze. Research has shown, for example, that tomato production drops off after the first five months. That's why most growers replant the crop or grow it as an annual. Tomatoes, peppers and eggplants are all native to tropical climates. Both the familiar and unfamiliar permaculture crops best suited for the greenhouse also tend to be tropical or sub-tropical in origin. This works out well because the environment created within a solar greenhouse is usually sub-tropical, that is, an environment in which temperatures approach but never fall below freezing.

If you are interested in locating experimental permaculture crops for the solar greenhouse and need seed or information, turn to the end of this chapter for a list of places to check out.

It's unfortunate that there is little, if any, greenhouse research or funding going into the increased food potential of unfamiliar crops. I encourage all of you with curious hearts and minds to do your own research on new perennial food producers. If you come across any interesting plants with potential, please contact me and we'll get the word out in future editions.

Uncommon Perennials

Let's look at some of the possibilities of various unheard-of crops. This is just to whet your appetite, so you begin to think about unorthodox crops.

Chaya (cnidoscolus aconitifolius)

This drought-tolerant and fast growing perennial shrub produces spinach-like greens that *must* be cooked before eating. The leaves are reportedly high in Vitamin C, protein and minerals. According to the National Academy of Sciences, the horticulture of chaya has never been studied. Any takers?

Naranjilla (solanum quitoense)

This dessert fruit is native to Columbia and Ecuador. It is said to have a flavor of both pineapple and strawberry. Are you listening, Sunkist? Like humans, it takes about nine months to bear fruit and then produces tennis-ball size fruits year round. Unlike humans, however, it only produces for a little more than 2 years. It can reach a height of 5′ and is quite productive.

Spirulina (spirulina platensis and spirulina maxima)

Spirulina is a high protein blue-green algae. It was originally cultured by the Aztecs in shallow ponds and used as a main source of protein. It grows best in alkaline water with a pH between 7 and 8. It prefers to grow at temperatures of 87°F (31°C) and higher. *Extreme caution* must be taken to prevent contamination by toxic micro-organisms. For this reason I would be wary of eating any home grown algae before it's been positively identified. There's no apparent obstacle to devising thermal mass containers to provide an ideal growing environment for algae. It could be harvested with nets, dried, and then eaten as high protein food. There may be other types of algae better adapted to the solar greenhouse which could grow with even lower temperatures; it's just a matter of finding out.

More Exotica

The possibilities are limitless; breadfruit, papaya, mango and tamarind (all interesting candidates because all have edible leaves and fruits), as well as undiscovered foods, herbs and medicinal crops. Many of these can be beautifully adapted to the solar greenhouse. There is much work to be done here; we all need to experiment and learn.

Familiar Tropical Crops

Imagine a totally balanced ecology of insects, spiders, animals, annual food crops, and a large selection of edible permaculture crops with the end result being food, herbs, medicine and joy. Maybe someday there will be solar greenhouse research institutions that will have plant breeders who will incorporate great adaptability along with a wide genetic diversity into greenhouse food crops. Yields will have no ceiling. The future will be exciting.

Let's look at some familiar tropical crops, perennial in nature, which we can grow now. As mentioned before, the yield of these crops generally doesn't compare with the yields of most common annual vegetables. Is it worth the sacrifice of some space to have one prized artichoke plant or fig tree for your more exotic moments? If *your* answer is yes, here's some basic advice. Always place perennial crops near the thermal mass for moderating temperatures. And keep them in areas where the soil will not be disturbed, hopefully not in constant shade.

Artichoke, Globe

This plant, resembling a large thistle, is grown for its bud or immature flower head. Artichoke plants grow about 4′ high and up to 5′ wide. They do fine in a ground bed, but may also be planted in 5-gallon containers, such as old plastic paint buckets.

Artichokes can be started from seeds or roots that are available through many seed and nursery catalogs. I've had excellent results with seeds. They will produce the globular buds primarily in the spring and fall. Feed the plants manure tea or some other source of nitrogen if the older leaves begin to yellow. They also benefit from bone meal. Sometimes plants will completely die back. Don't worry, usually they'll soon send up a new shoot and start over again. Be sure to harvest the globe while the bud is tight (before it begins to open up). Greenhouse-grown artichokes are the sweetest you'll ever eat.

Avocados

Here is your chance to go for the big time with your little avocado seedling. Avocados prefer a relatively cool, dry, climate. Plant them in soil that is very well drained because they are susceptible to root rot.

There are many different varieties of avocados. The small round smooth-skinned fruits are known as the Mexican varieties. The larger pear-shaped types with the dark smooth skin are known as the West Indian varieties. The medium sized dark rough-skinned variety is known as the Guatemalan. I like the Guatemalan best. Most commercial avocados are hybrids of all of the above. For best pollinating results, grow two very different looking types. Cross pollinate betwen the different types by using a small paint brush to transfer pollen from one tree's flowers to the other's.

Avoid touching the leaves. Avocados seemed to be plagued by a variety of leaf and root diseases and give few fruits in the greenhouse. For these reasons, I recommend growing them only as a novelty. With that attitude, it will be a nice surprise if you have good luck and find yourself in guacamole heaven.

Banana

Bananas won't survive very well when the temperature falls below $50^{\circ}F$ ($10^{\circ}C$), making them poorly suited to the winter solar greenhouse. But if you want to try, they can be ordered from mail order nurseries in the southern United States. They like a warm sunny place. Be sure to grow only the edible varieties, as there are many ornamental ones that aren't worth your time and energy.

Citrus

Almost any citrus crop will grow in the solar greenhouse. You can start them from supermarket seeds, but generally such plants will produce sour fruit. Instead, I recommend purchasing the plants from nurseries or by mail order. As with most of the crops mentioned in this section, citrus in the greenhouse seems to do best near the thermal mass. And be sure to avoid heavily shaded spots.

A common problem that arises is chlorosis (when new growth turns yellow between the veins). Raw manures, too much nitrogen, high soil pH and salty soils all contribute to this problem. Chlorosis can be solved by applying some iron chelate or by trenching-in peat moss or leaf mold compost. The chelate, which is faster acting, is available at most garden stores.

Brush the blossoms with a small paint brush to bring about pollination. I like growing a few citrus plants just to smell the orange blossoms in winter.

Coffee

Yes, you can grow it, but don't plan to be drinking your own java for some time. Yields will be slim. Like banana plants, coffee has trouble with temperatures below 50°F (10°C). Grow it near the mass, but unlike banana plants, it will appreciate some shading. After the plant is around 5′ tall, pinch off the tall vertical tips because flowers and beans occur only on horizontal branches. Coffee plants like growing in sandy soils, and don't like manure fertilizers at all. Coffee has low tolerance for salty soils (indicated by leaf tips turning brown) and for soils with a pH higher than 6.5.

If you are lucky and get some of those coffee beans produced, soak the beans in water for 5 - 10 days, then roast and grind. Mmmm, good.

Figs

Figs are more productive than most of the crops already mentioned. However, commercial fig varieties will not set fruit unless there is a special pollinating wasp present. But don't despair; there are varieties available that will set fruit without any need for pollination. These include: Mission, Adriatic, Kadota, Brown Turkey, Everbearing, Conradia and Celeste.

Figs seem to prefer soils that have some clay in them. A fig plant grows into a tall tree, so be conscious of where its shadow will be cast when it grows up. I planted mine against the north wall water drums, and to keep it from shading the mass, I didn't let it get bushy until it grew taller than the drums. You may also grow it as a bush by keeping the tips pruned. In the winter it may or may not lose its leaves. During the winter months it won't grow and may become more susceptible to insects, mites or diseases. So don't let pests get the best of your plant during this time. It will usually regain its health come spring.

Fig plants are available from nurseries or you can propagate your own from cuttings (see *Plant Propagation*). Harvest the figs when they are dark and soft, but before they start to split. They will be the sweetest you ever ate! Whenever you break the skin of a fig tree—either for harvesting or pruning—it will exude a latex-type juice that irritates some people's skin, so you may want to wear gloves.

Depending on how large and how old your purchased plant is, it will take 2 - 4 years before you're ready to harvest fruit. If you like figs, it's worth the wait as long as the plants don't take up too much space. Two-story greenhouses have an advantage here because they can grow tall.

Grapes

Greenhouse grape production has long been a hobby of Europeans. In the greenhouse, grapes benefit from a protected environment and you can grow the southern varieties that are not cold hardy. Grapes may be susceptible to mildews in the greenhouse, so try to get varieties that are resistant to these diseases. Pollinate flowers with a brush, and make sure there's a steady flow of air during flowering.

The yields are impressive, but whether it is worth tying up the space (about 4½ square feet of bed space and up to 8′ high per plant) all year long is up to you. To use space most effectively, it seems best to grow grapes against an east wall or west wall, pruning for both vertical and horizontal growth. (See a good fruit production book for pruning specifics.) Chicken wire or any wire fencing makes a good trellis.

Pineapple

Pineapples will grow and survive in most solar greenhouses, but the amount of food you'll get for the space and time won't be much.

Start pineapples by twisting off the tops of store-purchased pineapples and letting them dry in a shady place for about 1 week. Then place the pineapple top in a mix of half sand, half potting soil. It will help to brush a small amount of rooting hormone on the bottom of the pineapple top before planting (see *Plant Propagation*). After a plant is well rooted and has produced many new leaves, you can help trigger fruit set by treating the plant with ethylene gas. This gas is given off naturally by ripe fruit. To treat a pineapple, place a freshly peeled banana skin next to the pineapple and cover both the banana skin and the growing pineapple with a plastic bag. A ripe apple will also work. Leave the plastic bag over the plant for about 5 days. The gas naturally given off by the banana peel or apple will often trigger fruiting of the pineapple. You may need to stake the plant as it begins to set fruit. Generally, however, it is a hard plant to grow and get food from.

Tea

A tea plant is grown as a small shrub, often grown in India, Sri Lanka, China and Japan. Though commercial growers keep the plants small, they can grow as high as 30′ - 40′.

You can grow tea in the solar greenhouse, although it's sensitive to frost. But sensitivity varies among varieties. Tea plants are usually planted from seed because it's almost impossible to obtain cuttings. The seeds are large, however, and may take up to 1 year to germinate. If you can get hold of cuttings, they're best. It will take a few years to realize your harvest from the plants, but if you have an extra corner, it may be worth the wait. Keep the soil damp around the seed. When you're ready for the harvest, here's how to process the leaves:

Black Tea—Crush the leaves, place them in a sealed, clean plastic bag for about 10 days, then bake the tea at 190°F (88°C) until the leaves are dry.

Oolong—Crush the leaves, place the leaves in a sealed, clean plastic bag for only 3 days, and then bake at 190°F (88°C) until dry.

Green Tea—Crush the leaves and immediately bake at 190°F (88°C) until the leaves are dry.

Information Sources for Permaculture Crops

The Future is Abundant, A guide to Sustainable Agriculture, 1982 Ed. by Larry Korn, available from Tilth, 13217 Mattson Rd., Arlington, WA 98223.

Permaculture One, 1978 by Bill Mollison and David Tblingsen, available from International Tree Crops Institute, Inc., Box 888, Winter, CA 95694.

Permaculture Two, by Bill Mollison, 1979, available from International Tree Crops Institute, Inc. Box 888, Winters CA 95694. Both *Permaculture One* and *Two* are the "bibles" of permaculture, but they are mostly concerned with the outside environment. However, both books are a good place to begin.

Permaculture Journal, (Journal of the National Permaculture Association), available from Permaculture, 37 Goldsmith Street, Maryborough, Victoria 3465, Australia.

Underexploited Tropical Plants with Promising Economic Values, National Academy of Sciences, 2101 Constitution Avenue, Washington, D.C. 20418. A good book for those interested in a wide variety of promising plants for the greenhouse or tropics.

Dump Heap (The Journal of Diverse Unsung Miracle Plants for Healthy Evolution Among People). This publication was the first to propose solar greenhouse permaculture crops. 2950 Walnut Boulevard, Walnut Creek, CA 94598. Subscription: $7.00 per year.

Mayaguez Institute for Tropical Agriculture, P.O. Box 70, Mayaguez, Puerto Rico 00708. Send for publications list.

Tropical Seeds

Casa Yerba, (Rare herbs, tropicals), Star Rt. 2, Box 21, Days Creek, OR 97429, Catalog: $1.00.

Banana Tree, 715 Northhampton St., Easton PA 18042. This is where you find banana plants.

Spangler's Exotica Seed, 820 S. Lorraine Blvd., Los Angeles, CA 90005. All around source for tropical and sub-tropical food plants. Informative catalog.

Hurov's Tropical Seeds, Box 10387, Honolulu Hawaii 96816. Extensive listing of tropical species by scientific name. Seeds available as seasons permit. Send query first.

Thompson and Morgan, 401 Kennedy Blvd., Somerdale, NJ 08083. Only major seed house with innovative greenhouse and tropical selections. Passion fruits, banana, coffee, other oddities. Costly and few seeds, but good selection.

Hudson's World Seed Service, Box 1058, Redwood City, CA 94064. Big selection of all kinds of plants, including a few tropical and warm season oddities.

County Hill Greenhouse, Rt. 2, Corning, Ohio 43730. Extensive catalog of tropical plants; many rare and newly discovered. Catalog: $2.00.

Spring Tranplants for Outside

There can be a wonderful connection between your solar greenhouse and your outside garden. Giving plants a head start in your greenhouse will greatly increase the food and flowers that are produced outside. And the further north you live, the more important this becomes. Even a small greenhouse can produce hundreds of seedling transplants for outside—enough for you and your neighbors to enjoy.

Besides creating higher outside food yields, growing your own spring seedlings means you won't be buying them. And your plants generally will be of better quality than store bought transplants. I've come across many people with small greenhouses who sell their plants to neighbors, local stores and food co-ops. They don't get rich but it brings in some extra spending money. You may want to try it too.

Getting Started

First take three steps back to *Plant Propagation* for the basics in starting seeds.

For larger seeds, planting directly into the container you plan to grow them in works fine. Because seeds are relatively cheap, I usually put two seeds in each small pot. If both germinate, I pinch one out, leaving the best looking one. This two-seed method helps insure that something will come up in each pot.

I plant smaller seeds—which are often harder to germinate because they easily get buried too deep or too shallow—in rows in a wide flat. After they germinate I transplant them into the pot they'll grow in until they are ready for the outside. Be sure to read *Pests and Diseases*.

Another way to start garden plants is to use cuttings, as discussed in *Plant Propagation*. Cuttings can be rooted in less time than it takes to grow a good sized plant from seed. This works well for herbs, hybrid tomatoes and many flowers.

Containers and Soil

For most spring seedlings I recommend planting in a pot at least 2" x 1½". You can use either pots manufactured for seedlings or recycled containers ranging from individual pots made from juice cans and paper cups to multi-plant containers such as egg cartons or milk cartons cut in half lengthwise. Be sure to poke a hole in the bottom of homemade containers for water drainage.

Manufactured containers are usually made of plastic or compressed peat moss. It's easy to transplant the peat pots by just popping the whole pot into the soil without disturbing the roots. But I've come across quite a few peat pots that never decomposed in the garden, leaving roots unable to grow. Cutting a few slashes into the sides of the pots prevents this. Be sure the *whole* peat pot is buried; if *any* of it is above ground, the roots under the surface may dry out because of a wicking action that draws moisture from the pot to evaporate in the air. If you are prone to accidentally skip greenhouse waterings, stick to plastic or homemade seedling pots because peat pots always dry out faster.

Plastic pots come singly or multi-celled. Both plastic and homemade pots work fine for transplanting, but with the plastic ones, you must take a little more care not to disturb the roots. Plastic pots can be recycled for a few years if they don't get ripped. They cost about the same as peat pots and require about the same energy in the manufacturing process.

If you plan to sell seedlings in spring, use manufactured pots because people are more attached to them than recycled containers. The manufactured seedling pots aren't that expensive—often a few cents each. However, lower prices for these pots are obtained at commercial greenhouse suppliers in larger cities.

Soil for seedlings should be either commercial potting soil (best and easiest), sterilized soil or virgin soil that's never been planted before. See *Plant Propagation* for homemade soil mixes for seedlings.

Plant Size and Transplanting

When you grow plants from seed try to time it so they are not much larger than three or four times the size of the pot when you're ready to transplant. If you want to grow a larger plant for transplanting into your garden, better get a larger corresponding pot. But remember, a larger plant doesn't always mean a better plant when it comes to spring transplants. With larger plants there is generally more transplant shock and this may permanently damage a plant's productivity. Also, research has shown that a large 1-gallon pot with a big blooming tomato plant will actually produce less total yield than a non-blooming 8'' plant with a stem width the size of a pencil.

Warning: When growing transplants, keep your eyes open for aphids and other insect pests on the tips of plants and on the undersides of leaves. If you see them, follow the advice in *Pests and Diseases*.

Hardening Off

Young plants grown in a protective environment grow very rapidly. But at the same time, they become very tender, making them subject to substantial transplant shock no matter how talented you are at transplanting. You can reduce this shock by putting your seedlings through an intermediate period to help them better withstand transplanting. This period is known as ''hardening off.'' For a week before actual transplanting into your outside garden, totally discontinue any supplementary nutrient feeding. Also cut back *slightly* on watering, and a few days before transplanting, set your plants outside in direct sunlight during the day. You can also leave them out a few nights as long as the evening low temperature isn't below 45°F (7°C). Take care; plants will dry out faster outside. These treatments will greatly reduce transplant shock but are rarely done to storebought spring seedlings. Once outside, transplant shock is also reduced if seedlings are protected from wind or direct sun with a shingle or cardboard wind break placed so that it casts a shadow over the plant. The plant should be able to stand up to the elements solo after a few days.

The following is a *general schedule* for timing the propagation of your garden transplants. You'll have to fine tune it for you own area by asking advice from experienced area gardeners or learning from your own mistakes. But the best way to fine tune this schedule is to record the day you planted each crop and later analyze the results. Is the plant too big?—then plant it later next year. Too small?—plant it earlier. Record keeping will help make you a pro at seedling production. Remember, 65°F (18°C) is a good temperature for seed germination.

	Spring Transplants for Outside		
Crop	**Time From Planting Until Set Out**	**Propagation Method**	**Comments**
Geranium	5 months; 3 if propagated by cuttings.	T or D or C	Transplant while small.
Pansy	4 - 5 months	T	Very susceptible to damping off diseases. Avoid warm temperatures.
Snapdragon	4 - 5 months	T	Try to grow at around 60°F (15°C).
Petunia	4 months	T	Very small seed; be careful.
Carnation	4 months	T or D or C	Won't do well in areas with high summer temperatures.
Peppers			
Hot or Sweet (see tomatoes)	4 months	D	Try to keep temperature above 50°F (10°C)
Eggplant	4 months	D or T	Try to keep temperature above 50°F (10°C) (see tomatoes).
Shasta Daisy	3½ months	D or T	Keep cool, below 68°F(20°C).
Tomato	3 months	D or C	If you use cuttings, don't use ones you suspect of being diseased. Smokers should wash hands thoroughly before working with tomatoes.
Herbs			
Oregano			You will need stock plants on hand for the cutting method.
Mints			
Sage			
Thyme	3 months	T or C	
Lemon Balm			
Catnip			
Tansy			
Tarragon			

Continued . . .

Chart Codes:

   T—Start seed in flat and transplant after first true leaves appear.

   D—Plant seed into the container that the mature plant will grow in. Plant at least two seeds per pot and pinch out the one with the weaker stem, leaving the best one.

   C—Start from cuttings. But you must have a stock plant to begin with (see *Plant Propagation*).

Crop	Time From Planting Until Set Out	Propagation Method	Comments
Spring Transplants for Outside			
Herbs			
Dill			
Anise			
Fennel	3 months	D or T	
Summer Savory			
Coriander			
Chamomile			
Calendula	3 months	D or T	Not good in areas with extreme summer temperatures.
Marigolds	3 months	D or T	Likes bright light.
Zinnia	3 months	D or T	If grown cool they are more susceptible to disease.
Impatiens	3 months	T	
Alyssum	2 months	D	Five to six seeds per pot—*don't thin!*
Cole Crops			
Cabbage			These crops can be set out four weeks before the last average frost date. Grow in cool temperatures.
Cauliflower	1 month	D or T	
Broccoli			
Zucchini			These crops are hard to transplant so grow them in peat pots to lessen transplant shock. Use a pot at least 2½'' wide.
Cucumber			
Watermelon	1 month	T	
Cantaloupe			
Squash			
Pumpkin			

Chart Codes:

T—Start seed in flat and transplant after first true leaves appear.

D—Plant seed into the container that the mature plant will grow in. Plant at least two seeds per pot and pinch out the one with the weaker stem, leaving the best one.

C—Start from cuttings. But you must have a stock plant to begin with (see *Plant Propagation*).

Note: If seed is not up within 2-3 weeks, check for damping off diseases, improper moisture or damaging temperatures. Utilize the different micro-environments in your greenhouse to give each crop its specific temperature and light needs. (See *Crop Layout*).

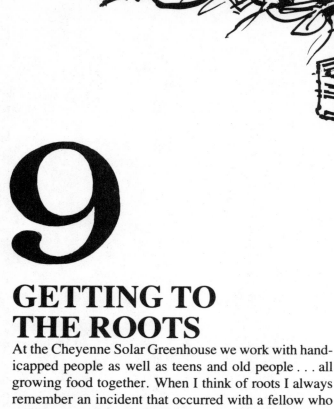

9
GETTING TO
THE ROOTS

At the Cheyenne Solar Greenhouse we work with handicapped people as well as teens and old people . . . all growing food together. When I think of roots I always remember an incident that occurred with a fellow who was mentally handicapped and very childlike, though he was about 38 years old. He was at the greenhouse to benefit from horticultural therapy (plant therapy). Unfortunately, he had a great fear of roots. He often said ''I think roots are scary, don't you?'' He was always afraid to touch them. It was odd for me because I was hard pressed to come up with a reason that he could grasp why roots shouldn't be scary. I searched my memories of childhood and remembered when there were parts of plants that scared me, too. But, I don't think anything I explained to him changed his mind about roots.

One day, however, I had him adding some compost to the soil for an early spring planting. I left him to work by himself on the bed for the morning. Later, when I looked at the bed I saw he had done a great job

except for a curious looking something in the corner of the bed. I pointed to this big, many-branched root sticking out of the soil. "What's that?" I asked. He said it was an upside down tomato plant. "I just wanted to see how it grows this way," he said very proudly. I dug around the root and sure enough there was a whole tomato plant buried under the ground. (He had found it in the compost pile). I told him it would be interesting to see what it did and we left the upside down plant in the bed. His fear was totally gone from that day on; he had found his own solution to his problem with roots.

The primary difference between a greenhouse and an outside garden is that most greenhouses produce year-round. This means year-round depletion of soil nutrients, leaving no time for soil to rest and regenerate. When greenhouse plant growth slows as temperatures get colder in fall and winter, the plant's use of soil nutrients also slows. Still, a substantial amount of nutrients may be taken up by roots. Greenhouse soil requires special attention between crop plantings; that's when you return to the soil certain elements you've removed in your last harvest. Plant nutrition and soil science is vastly complex. There are numerous books which can help you get a thorough understanding of plant and soil nutrition. It's my intention here to give you the information you need to know when something is going wrong, how to deal with it, and how to maintain soil fertility.

The approach I recommend is the minimal use of synthetic fertilizers, relying mainly on biological sources of nutrients. Once in a while, however, chemical fertilizers will come in handy, especially when growing plants in small containers, or for hydroponics.

Maintaining proper nutrition for your plants requires testing for pH, salt content and organic matter, as well as specific elements such as nitrogen, phosphorus and potassium. You'll need to be aware of symptoms indicating nutrient difficiencies or excesses. Nutrient excesses are very common because people often overdo things.

Basic Requirements For Healthy Soil

Aeration: Roots need air as well as water; they'll suffocate from overwatering. Sandy soils and soils containing decomposed organic matter help aeration. Earth worms also greatly help aerate soil. Bring some worms in from your outside garden; they'll love it in the greenhouse and will increase rapidly. And if you fish, here's a great supply of worms.

Organic Matter: Organic matter is the result of the decomposition of things that were once alive, including plants, food scraps, manures, leaves, etc. It has multiple beneficial effects on soils, for example:

1. Adds nutrients.
2. Increases water holding ability.
3. Holds mineral nutrients available for root uptake (much like a sponge).
4. Promotes beneficial microbial life.
5. Helps aerate soil.
6. Keeps soil diseases and nematode infestations to a minimum.
7. Decomposition adds CO_2 to the air, which increases plant growth (see *The Solar Greenhouse Environment*).
8. Buffers the soil pH, that is, helps raise low pH and lowers high pH.

Moisture Holding Ability: Soil needs to retain water for the roots. Two substances primarily hold water in the soil: clay and decomposed organic matter. Organic matter is my preferred choice. See recommendations for organic ingredients for your soil later in this chapter.

Drainage: Greenhouse soils should drain well. This is your only defense against overfertilization and salt problems (both of which are common). Draining is basically a matter of adding sand. See bed construction details in *Interior Layout Design*.

Proper pH: This is not the name of an acne medication! pH is a term describing the acidity level of your soil, shampoo or creme rinse. It ranges from 1-14. Seven, the halfway mark, is the neutral point.

Try to keep your soil very close to neutral. A professional soil test will usually include a pH analysis. You can check it yourself by using litmus paper, which can be bought at drug stores. Buy the type that measures around 6.0 - 8.0 pH. Mix one part soil to two parts water, stir around, and dip the paper into the solution. It will turn a color which will indicate a specific pH. Compare your color to the color key on the box the paper came in. When pH is below 6.5 or above 7.3, it is often much harder for roots to use minerals and nutrients in the soil even though they are present in adequate amounts. This is why a high and a low pH may look like a nutrient deficiency. High pH can be corrected by adding well-composed organic matter and/or gypsum. Low pH generally is corrected by adding wood ash or lime. See general gardening books for more information on this.

the pH Scale

14
13
12   Alkalinity
11 } Very strong
10 } Strong
9 } Moderate
8 } Slight
7
6   Slight
5 } Moderate
4 } Strong
3 } Very strong
2
1   Acidity

Range of good growth

Healthy Soil Microbial Life: Microbes (microscopic organisms) such as bacteria and fungus are generally beneficial to plant growth. They are what decomposes organic matter into more basic compounds. Microbes are important in controlling diseases as they often feed on harmful disease-causing organisms much like lady bugs feeding on aphids. They are also essential in many soil reactions that make nutrients available to roots. When microbes are in short supply, such as in some hydroponic media or soils low in organic matter, there seems to be increased disease, nematode (root destroying critters) or nutrient problems. The regular addition of decomposed organic matter will provide a healthy environment for microbial life.

Low Salt Content

Salt is a broad term which doesn't refer to just table salt (sodium chloride), but describes the result of a chemical reaction which occurs when acid compounds react with alkaline compounds.

Synthetic nitrogen fertilizers and organic manures are noted for their potentially high salt content. Salt problems occur when high levels of fertilizers are used in soils that have poor drainage. So be vigilant. It's almost impossible to escape some salt accumulation, but luckily, salts move with water. With heavy water applications you can leach them out to a level below the roots. This is why well drained soil is important. Salts will accumulate in the root zone of poorly drained soils; therefore there should always be holes in the bottom of growing containers. Salt concentration rises as your soil becomes drier. If a lot of water has been evaporating from your soil, you may actually see white salt crystals on the soil surface.

Symptoms of Salt Damage

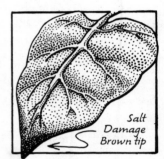

Salt Damage Brown tip

1. Leaf tips or margins browning.
2. Leaf drop.
3. Soil surface has buildup of white crystals (almost looks like table salt).
4. Slow growth.
5. Root damage.

Preventing Salt Damage

1. Go easy on fertilizing. Follow recommended rates; more is not better.
2. Avoid raw manures.
3. Soak old clay pots in water for a day before replanting in them.
4. Be sure soil drains well. A relatively high sand content helps. Make sure containers drain water out bottom holes.
5. Leach soils that show symptoms of salt damage; two or three heavy waterings usually do the trick.

Nutrients

I usually recommend that greenhouse owners stick to organic type fertilizers for the following reasons:

1. As far as amounts go, they are harder to make mistakes with.
2. They usually contain a well-balanced amount of nutrients including many micro-nutrients which are often lacking in chemical mixes.
3. As organic fertilizers decompose, carbon dioxide (CO_2) is produced. Increased CO_2 levels increase plant production. CO_2 is often low in winter greenhouses.
4. The healthy microbial life which thrives on organic fertilizer will help keep many diseases in check.

5. Nutrients are released more slowly and over a longer period of time.

6. These fertilizers may be produced at home by recycling organic wastes (food scraps, leaves, etc.).

7. It meshes well with a raised bed layout.

Synthetic commercial fertilizers will work if you don't have organic ones on hand. (Hopefully you're not just being lazy.) I prefer using synthetic fertilizers with plantings in containers where the root area is already artificially limited. It's less trouble. If you use synthetic fertilizers for any purpose, try to stick to the more efficient slow release types such as Plant Tabs, Osmocote, or Jobs plant food sticks. Water soluble house plant fertilizers also will work fine in your greenhouse beds, but don't overdo it.

Chemical plant foods always have 3 analysis numbers listed somewhere on the package. It'll say something like 5-10-5, 15-10-20, etc. This is the percentage of nitrogen, phosphorus and potassium, *in that order*. Try to get the highest percentage for your money. The lower the numbers, the less you get. Except for leafy crops, try to stay away from fertilizers high in nitrogen (the first number). Equal numbers are generally a good balance. For fruiting, flowering and seedlings, use plant foods with more phosphorus (a higher middle number) than nitrogen (the first number), such as 5-**10**-10 or 10-**20**-25. Phosphorus helps root and flower/fruit development. African violet food is very high in phosphorus. This fertilizer, when diluted in half, makes a good food for seedlings.

The best way to tell if there is a soil problem is by having a soil test done either professionally or with a home testing kit. Plants vary in how they express nutrient problems, but usually by the time you visually see the deficiency, a lot of yield will have been lost because plants are slow to show you what's been bothering them. Often a plant won't conform to textbook symptoms. Sometimes I think plants are rebellious just for the fun of it. Keep this in mind when using the charts on the following pages. This description of *general* symptoms, may be of some help.

Note: Before adding fertilizer to correct specific deficiency symptoms, especially ones you've never dealt with before, please be sure you have confirmed the symptom with a soil test or you may end up with an excess worse than the deficiency. This is especially true with micro-nutrients. Soil testing is often done at reasonable rates through state agricultural colleges. Check with your county agricultural extension service for more information and soil sampling procedures.

By regularly adding common ingredients to soil you can usually provide every element needed for plant growth. The following is a list of ingredients grouped into two classifications, organic (derived from living things) and inorganic (derived from non-living things). After this list are some possible schedules for maintaining plant fertility and healthy soil.

Major Soil Nutrients
(those needed in large quantities)

	Function	Contained in	Excess	Deficiency
Nitrogen (N)	Required for leaf growth. Important for protein and amino acid production.	Manure, fish and ocean wastes, food scraps, blood meal, urine, compost.	Luxuriant leafy growth, dark green leaves, few flowers or fruit. Look for salt damage. Leaf tip burning.	Light green to yellow leaves occurring on older, lower leaves. Yellow leaves may fall off. Stunted growth.
Phosphorus (P)	Seedling hardiness, fruit and root production, helps disease resistance.	Steamed bone meal, ground rock phosphates, manure, compost.	Very rare.	Red to purple colored leaves. Dwarfed plants, small leaves, few fruits, leaves drop early.
Potassium (K)	Regulates water movement within plants. Helps with cold hardiness, starch and sugar production.	Wood ash (see recommendations later in this chapter), granite dust, compost, manure, kelp.	Will create a magnesium deficiency. Not common.	Lower leaves mottled, with dead areas. Yellowing begins at leaf edge and continues toward the center. Weak stems. Rare in many arid soils.
Calcium (Ca)	Cell wall and enzyme production.	Bone meal, egg shells, dolomite, gypsum, lime and milk.	Not very common. Will cause deficiencies of potassium, magnesium, iron.	Yellow, hooked, plant tip. Tips may die back, short roots. Blossom end fruit rot on tomatoes. Centers of lettuce and celery may rot.
Magnesium (Mg)	Chlorophyll production and respiration.	Organic matter, some commercial plant foods.	Causes other micronutrient imbalances.	Yellowing between veins on *older lower* leaves, which may eventually turn brown. Common in acid soils. Common on shade-loving houseplants set in sunny place.
Sulfur (S)	Protein production.	Ground sulfur, rain near coal-fired power plants, gypsum.	Causes acid soil.	Light yellowing on new leaves *including yellow veins*.

Micro-nutrients

These are essential but needed only in very small amounts, hence over-applying is easy to do. There are usually adequate amounts in organic matter. Deficiencies may be just a result of high or low pH, or high salt accumulation.

	Function	Contained in	Excess	Deficiency
Boron (B)	Cell wall formation, carbohydrate transport.	Organic matter.	Slight excess will kill plants. May occur in acid soils, so keep soils neutral	Tips of the plant die. Cabbage family plants develop hollow stems.
Copper (Cu)	Enzyme and photosynthesis regulation.	Seaweed, kelp, manure, compost.	Rare. Causes iron deficiency.	Leaves look bleached. Light-colored veins.
Iron (Fe)	Chlorophyll formation.	Organic matter, iron chelate, iron sulfate (both chelate and sulfate are purchased at garden supply centers. Chelate is longer lasting; follow recommended rates).	Darker green foliage; then turns into magnesium or zinc deficiency.	Yellowing between veins on newly developing leaves. Old leaves remain green. *Often due to high pH* or poor drainage.
Manganese (Mn)	Helps in photosynthesis and respiration.	Manganese sulphate, organic matter.	Similar to deficiency; dark spots present, crinkling and cupping of leaves.	Much like iron, but even the smallest veins remain green while all new growth turns yellow to white. Old growth remains green.
Molybdenum (Mo)	Nitrogen fixation, nitrogen metabolism.	Usually corrected by raising a low soil pH to neutral.	Slight excess causes death.	Stunting, similar to nitrogen deficiency, common in acid soils below pH 6.0.
Zinc (Zn)	Chlorophyll formation, bud development.	Zinc sulphate, organic matter.	May result in other micronutrient problems. Sometimes resembles iron deficiency.	Top leaves remain very small; stunting, dwarfing. Mottled yellow leaves.

Organic Ingredients

Peat Moss.   Peat moss is the remains of dead plants that have partially decayed and may be hundreds of years old. Because it's often quite low in any nutrients, it is not a fertilizer, but is mainly a soil conditioner. It increases soil aeration, water absorption and it helps soil hold other nutrients that would normally leach out or remain unavailable to roots. Some peat moss may have fertilizer added to it. The label will tell you if that's the case.

Sphagnum peat, the most commonly available, is usually mined in Canada. It's a limited resource being depleted more quickly than it is being replenished naturally. In some countries, peat is also burned as a fuel source for cooking and heat.

Peat moss is sold in different grades depending on its degree of decomposition. The grades H3, H4 and H5 are preferable for greenhouse soils. It's a particularly good addition for soils low in organic matter. As much as 1/3 of the total volume of your soil can be peat, as long as there aren't large amounts of other decomposed organic matter already present. Excess peat may cause an acidic reaction in your soil and may result in your soil becoming easily waterlogged. Peat varies in pH from 4.0 to neutral (7.0 pH). It is somewhat expensive compared to other organic soil conditioners, and because it is a limited resource, the price will probably keep going up.

Manure.   Manure is both a soil conditioner and a fertilizer. Due to its high content of soluble salts it can burn crops. Manure should *never* be applied fresh. Always compost it for at least one year, or find some old stuff.

Manures vary greatly in nutrient content. The age and type of manure create very different fertilizer amounts. Generally the older the manure, the less nutrient value, but even old manure makes a great soil conditioner, much like peat moss. Rabbit and poultry manure are about twice as rich as that of horses, cows and pigs. Sheep and goats sit somewhere between the two.

It's hard to give accurate recommendations for applications because even the same type of manure may vary a great deal. But I'll do it anyway.

Before each planting in soil beds 2' deep, I usually add about a 1'' thick layer of poultry or rabbit manure, or 1½'' of sheep and goat manure, or 2'' of horse, cow and pig manure. Blend it in throughout the soil. To eliminate hot spots in your soil be sure to break up the manure into fine pieces. If it stays in large clods, you'll probably have some salt problems and possibly an isolated type of iron deficiency.

Manure is usually higher in nitrogen than in phosphorus and potassium. I like to mix it with a bit of bone meal and some wood ash to make a complete fertilizer. In highly alkaline soils (pH above 7.3,) always forget the wood ash.

Sewage Sludge.   Many cities sell their sludge in a dried and bagged form. Some brand names are Milwaukee's Milorganite, Vancouver's Grow-Rich, Chicago's Chicagrow and Boston's Metroloam. Other cities may offer it free or at a low cost. Cities vary in their treatment and content of human waste. Some non-commercial sludge may need to be composted before using. Talk to your sewer plant operator about the safety of their sludge on edible crops.

Sludges in some cities may contain toxic heavy metals. A common one is cadmium, which doesn't leach out of soils and is absorbed by plants, most readily by plants in acid soils (pH below 6.8). The commercially available sludges usually don't have a heavy metal problem.

If you're concerned, have a local soil laboratory analyze sludge for heavy metals, and if it tests safe, apply it to a 1'' depth and mix well into the soil. To prevent heavy metal plant uptake, maintain soil at 7.0 pH or higher. As should be common practice, *always wash all produce before eating it*. Sewage sludge is quite low in potassium so an additional source may have to supplement it.

Leaf Mold.   Leaf mold is simply composted leaves; it's very high in micronutrients. It is an excellent source of organic matter but is low in major fertilizer contents. Use well-rotted leaves as you would peat moss.

Fish Emulsion.   This material is very high in nitrogen so use it sparingly on greenhouse fruiting crops. It's excellent on leafy crops, though the major drawback of fish emulsion is the smell, and the cost may be high depending on how landlocked you are.

Bone Meal.   Available raw and steamed, it contains mostly phosphorus, with some calcium and a trace of nitrogen. It should be worked in throughout the depth of the soil. Bone meal's great for fruiting crops, especially tomatos. It also helps flowers bloom beautifully over long periods. It is usually added at 1 lb. per 10 sq. ft. Compared to garden stores, agricultural feed stores sell it cheaper in 50 lb. bags. Steamed bone meal is slightly faster acting.

Sawdust.   Sawdust can make a fine soil conditioner if the following precautions are taken.

1. Never use sawdust from cedar, redwood or walnut. They contain plant toxins.
2. Soil organisms steal soil nitrogen to breakdown raw sawdust. The organisms grab the nitrogen right out from under the poor plant roots, often leaving plants with a nitrogen deficiency. To prevent this, either add compost, manure or some other additional source of nitrogen. Sawdust and manure make excellent composting companions, creating a superb fertilizer and plant conditioner for the greenhouse.

Wood Ash.   Wood ash is added to soils to raise a low pH and to add calcium, potassium, phophorus, magnesium and a little sulfur. The exact amounts of nutrients added to a plant vary from species to species. Wood ash is about two-thirds as effective as ground limestone in raising a low (acid) pH to neutral. If you live in arid areas where high pH soil (alkaline soil) is a common problem or have an alkaline soil above 7.0 pH, you should probably avoid using ash. If, however, your soil is acidic (below 7.0 pH), ash will help. It's commonly added at a rate of 1 lb. per 10 square feet. If you mix it with ½ lb. blood meal, 1 lb. of bone meal and 4 lbs. of peat moss or leaf mold, you will have a well balanced fertilizer. Wood ash spread around the base of plants also can keep slugs away.

Coal ash is not good for soil or plants and should be avoided.

Blood Meal.   Blood meal does contain some phosphorus, but it is basically a nitrogen fertilizer. It is added at ½ lb. per 10 square feet. It can be expensive.

Compost.   Composting is a great way to deal with plant wastes. It can be used as an excellent soil conditioner because it's pure decomposed organic matter.

There is enough written in most gardening books on composting procedures. For the greenhouse specifically, just be sure all greenhouse compost is headed for use in your *outside* garden soil, and both outside garden compost and food scrap compost are used as the sole compost in your greenhouse. This parallel cycle will help break up possible disease infestations.

For small greenhouses I recommend not taking up precious space for a traditional compost pile. Instead do it outside or create a compost mulch for CO_2 fertilizing as outlined in *The Solar Greenhouse Environment*.

In all the compost piles I've seen and worked with, the most common problems include not enough carbon-type materials (see compost mulch discussion in *The Solar Greenhouse Environment*), and poor aeration or overwatering.

Inorganic Materials

Sand.   Sand is basically ground up rock; it contains no fertilizing ingredients. It is added to soil to help drainage and aeration, and will greatly aid soils high in clay. Sands vary in pH depending on the parent material. Greenhouse soils should always be on the sandy side, but ocean sand should be avoided because it's too high in salts.

Perlite.   Perlite is used for the same reasons as sand: drainage and aeration. It is many times lighter than sand. It's mined as an ore, then heated till it expands like popcorn. Perlite has no nutrient value and a neutral pH. It has two minor disadvantages:

1. It's dusty, so wear a dust mask or moisten it first to keep dust down when mixing it in.
2. It floats to the top in some potting mixtures.

Rock Phosphate.   This calcium phosphate mineral is ground to a fine powder and added to supply phosphorus to the soil. It is a *very* slow release material, even slower than bone meal.

Super Phosphate.   This is basically rock phosphate that has been treated with an acid to speed its action in the soil, making phosphorus more available than either bone meal or rock phosphate. There is some worry that initially it can have a very acidic reaction in the soil. It is recommended that super phosphate be mixed in very evenly and thoroughly. Twenty percent super phosphate is added at a rate of 5 lbs. per 100 square feet.

Vermiculite.   This mica-type mineral is mined, heated and expanded much like perlite. Each piece is silver-colored and looks like a miniature accordion. Unlike perlite, vermiculite can hold water (up to 300% by weight). And much like organic matter, it has the ability to hold some nutrients in the soil for plant roots. It also helps soils resist changes in pH and like sand, it improves drainage.

Vermiculite contains some potassium, magnesium and calcium. You should use only horticultural grade vermiculite; it's available at greenhouse and garden supply stores. Construction grade vermiculite, used for roof insulation, shouldn't be used in the greenhouse because often it is coated with small amounts of oil that may be harmful to young roots.

Gypsum.   Gypsum is used to lower high pH and to improve drainage. People often mistakenly think it raises pH. It will help improve clay soils by loosening them. It also contains calcium and sulfur. It is an ancient fertilizer used by the Romans.

Limestone.   Ground limestone is commonly used to raise low soil pH. The amount needed to raise the pH one unit is approximately 1 lb. per 10 square feet. The amount will vary depending on how finely ground the limestone is and how much clay is contained in the soil. Add more limestone with soils higher in clay or when using more coarsely ground limestone. Follow your soil test recommendations. See Wood Ash for raising pH.

Maintaining Soil Fertility

At least twice a year, or whenever a crop is harvested and removed, rework your soil and replenish what nutrients you have removed. There are a number of fertilizers and soil conditioners to choose from and add. Here are several options, though you may want to devise your own based on experience, local soil conditions, and soil test results. For initial bed preparation refer to *Interior Layout Design*. For specific amounts of a nutrient or conditioner to add to soil see the preceeding discussion of each. Also, the package the material comes in will tell you how much to add for a given space.

Option #1

Remove 3'' of soil from the top of the bed. Add 2'' of well decomposed compost, bone meal, and wood ash (only if needed) to correct a low soil pH. Blend it in to the full depth of the bed (Remember, 2' deep beds are recommended).

Option #2

Replace 3'' of soil with 2'' of decomposed manure (less if poultry) and 1'' of leaf mold or peat moss. Also add bone meal or ground phosphate rock. If soil is acidic, add wood ash. Blend all throughout soil depth.

Option #3

Remove 2''-3'' of soil depth. Add blood meal or fish emulsion, 1'' peat moss, 1'' vermiculite, bone meal, and blend in throughout soil.

Option #4

Remove 2'' of soil. Add 5-10-5 commercial vegetable fertilizer, 3'' of peat moss or leaf mold, and blend in thoroughly.

Note: Each time you work the soil be sure that it is loose to a depth of about 18''. Compacted soil grows poor plants no matter how much nutrients are in it.

Crop Needs

Different crops have differing needs. Here are some general guidelines:

- Summer crops will need slightly more total nutrients, especially more phosphorus.

- Winter crops can get by with less phosphorus, but need slightly more nitrogen.

- Squash, cucumber and melon crops are heavy feeders and need about 30% more nitrogen.

- Tomato crops respond well to slightly lower nitrogen and higher phosphorus applications, especially bone meal.

- Peas, beans and flowers respond to lower amounts of nitrogen and steady levels of phosphorus.

- Most crops will benefit from a shallow compost mulch—see *Interior Layout Design*.

- Plants in small containers will benefit from regular feedings of a commercial houseplant type fertilizer at manufacturer's recommended rates. Blood meal, fish emulsion and bone meal will also work well for containers, but try to avoid feeding very small seedlings unless you suspect a specific deficiency.

- Don't fertilize germinating seedlings.

Hydroponics

With hydroponics, plants are grown without soil, using a water-based nutrient solution. Usually the plant roots are grown in an inert aggregate material such as sand or gravel with nutrients added in solution. For healthy growth *all* of the essential elements must be supplied by the nutrient solution in proper quantities.

It always makes me smile to hear hydroponics mistakenly called "hydrophonics." Hydrophonics is water music (or music under water) and has nothing to do with plants. But after hearing it so often I too find myself slipping into "Hydrophonics." It sounds like more fun to me anyway.

Despite widespread publicity these days which often leads people to believe hydroponics is a revolutionary new discovery, the basic technique was formulated well over a century ago. I've read many articles, publications and advertisements which convey the impression that plant growth and yields will be greater with hydroponics than with soil systems. Most research, however, indicates that with similar favorable conditions, yields actually will be much the same. Plants cannot be spaced any closer together because light, not nutrition, is the primary limiting factor. Also the nutritional value or overall quality of hydroponic produce is not superior to soil-grown food.

So why hydroponics? The main advantage is that it can be automated, which saves labor. This is great if you're in the greenhouse business because labor is a major expense. For home greenhouses, the expense of setting up hydroponics usually makes it impractical. Nutrients must be constantly replaced so there's the recurring cost of synthetic fertilizers. But for large operations, hydroponics may pay off.

Regarding nutrients in hydroponics, there has been a good bit of work done on the use of organic materials rather than synthetic fertilizers. This usually involves an extensive process of making manure teas, diluting emulsion or blood meal, etc. To me, the organic systems seem to create more work than required by a simple soil system (employing organic fertilizers). The results of organic hydroponics are also quite variable because organic materials vary greatly in their nutrient content.

Commercial hydroponic nutrient solutions may be purchased pre-mixed or you can mix them yourself. There are a number of excellent books (listed at the end of this chapter) that contain recipes for mixing your own.

Although hydroponic culture can be successfully used in the solar greenhouse, first consider the pros and cons.

Hydroponic Pros:

Labor saving.

Easily automated.

Plants receive proper nutrition.

Eliminates need to weed, water, cultivate.

Can use space more creatively.

Hydroponic Cons:

You'll need to regularly purchase nutrient elements.

Not forgiving of any mistakes in mixing and adding fertilizers.

Crops are often more susceptible to disease and insect pests.

No wonderful sweet smell of soil, which is invigorating in the winter.

Does not produce any CO_2 to help plant growth.

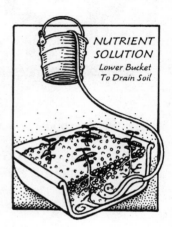

NUTRIENT SOLUTION

Lower Bucket To Drain Soil

Hydroponic plant systems require fancy plumbing, pumps and timers; but there are a couple of simple methods for those on limited budgets. A gravity feed gravel system is quite simple. A 1' foot deep box is filled with pea sized gravel. The box has only one drainage hole. The nutrient solution is fed by a bucket with a hose attached to the drainage hole. When the bucket is set higher than the box the solution drains into the box. Then the bucket is set lower than the box so that the solution is drained back into the bucket. This is done about 2 or 3 times per day. The nutrient solution should be changed once a week.

Straw Bale Culture

This system is nice because it uses an organic source (a straw bale) for the rooting medium. It's kind of a cross between hydroponics and organic soil culture. I like it because the bale decomposes in time; and as it decomposes, it gives off heat and CO_2 much like a compost pile. It has great potential for the solar greenhouse and is a common procedure in Europe. It's not advisable for perennial crops, however. On the average one bale lasts about 10 months.

Here are the steps involved in bale culture:

—Spread a 3'' layer of chicken manure (it can be fresh) on top of the bale.

—Keep the bale thoroughly moist for two weeks.

—Dig out a pouch (about 4'' deep and 4'' in diameter) into which you plan to set plants. Fill it with potting soil.

—Wrap the entire bale, except the bottom and the plant pouches, in polyethylene (cheap kind is fine; and black is preferred).

—Bale will heat up to over 100° F (38° C).

—Plant your plants or seedlings in the soil pouches when bale cools to 75° - 80° F (25° - 27° C).

—Water daily with hydroponic solution.

—Space plants as you would in a soil bed (usually only two tomato or cucumber plants per bale).

An alternative to the initial chicken manure treatment is to use a high nitrogen fertilizer. Four cups of regular lawn food (22-6-6 or some similar analysis) works well. *Don't use any lawn food that has herbicides in it* like "Weed and Feed." Keep the bale moist for 2 weeks and then proceed with wrapping and planting as outlined above. If the bale initially fails to heat up, add more fertilizer.

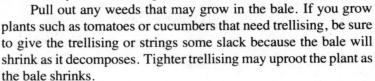

Pull out any weeds that may grow in the bale. If you grow plants such as tomatoes or cucumbers that need trellising, be sure to give the trellising or strings some slack because the bale will shrink as it decomposes. Tighter trellising may uproot the plant as the bale shrinks.

With the heat and CO_2 produced by the straw bales, you will be able to have higher than normal fall and winter yields. One potential problem with straw bale culture is herbicides. I've heard reports of people utilizing straw bales made from hay that was treated with a broad leaf herbicide. This could kill most vegetables growing in the bale because most are broad leaf plants. Check with the person who grew the hay to be sure this isn't the case.

Here are some books about hydroponic culture:

The Passive Solar Greenhouse and Organic Hydroponics: A Primer by Rick Kasprzak, 1977 from RLD Publications, Box 1443, Flagstaff, AZ 86002.

Hydroponic Gardening by Raymond Bridwell, Woodbridge Press, 1972.

The Survival Greenhouse by James Dekorne, 1975, Walden Foundation, El Rito, NM.

Home Hydroponics and How To Do It by Lem. Jones, 1977, Ward Ritchie Press, Pasadena, CA.

Beginners Guide to Hydroponics: Soilless Gardening by James Sholto Douglas, 1976, General Publishing Co.

Hydroponic Food Production by Howard Resh, Woodbridge Press, 1978.

Hydro-Story by Charles Sherman and Hap Brenizer, Nolo Press, 1976.

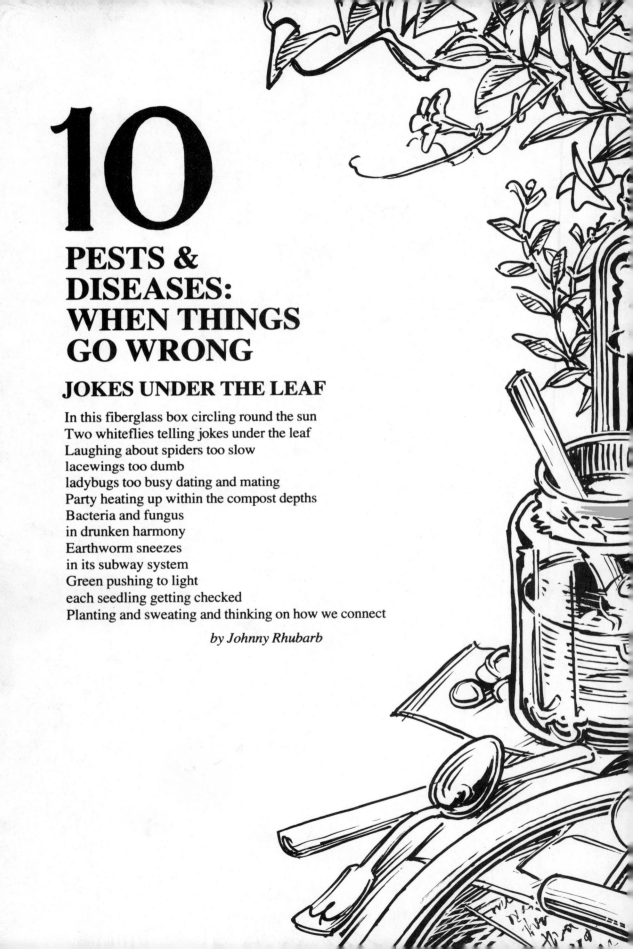

10

PESTS & DISEASES: WHEN THINGS GO WRONG

JOKES UNDER THE LEAF

In this fiberglass box circling round the sun
Two whiteflies telling jokes under the leaf
Laughing about spiders too slow
lacewings too dumb
ladybugs too busy dating and mating
Party heating up within the compost depths
Bacteria and fungus
in drunken harmony
Earthworm sneezes
in its subway system
Green pushing to light
each seedling getting checked
Planting and sweating and thinking on how we connect

by Johnny Rhubarb

It's when your first plant dies or becomes sickly that you fully realize your greenhouse is a miniature ecological environment that won't always do as you wish. You can fight it with a war-like extermination attitude. You can let it go to hell with pests and diseases running rampant, or you can manage it ecologically, trying to create new balances and microenvironments to produce the desired result . . . food.

Joan Loitz, a solar greenhouse pioneer who has written extensively on pest control, says that all new greenhouses go through a "honeymoon" period. It usually takes 2 - 8 months before the first pest or disease attacks. The first pest usually shows up just when people begin to get cocky about how pest-free things are. After that, watch out. It will be constant excitement, with a few new pests or diseases regularly finding a way to prevent boredom in your greenhouse. Some will be easy to deal with, while others will be quite challenging.

The first step when things go wrong is to learn to *look* at your greenhouse. It's so easy to look and not see. Don't even attempt to figure out the problem if you're feeling rushed or nervous. A calm, relaxing time of day is best. When something goes wrong, determining the cause requires looking closely at individual leaves as well as examining the greenhouse for general trends. Looking closely is helped greatly by a magnifying glass. The type used for reading will do. Low cost hand lenses (10x) are also a great tool; usually they can be found at college book stores because they are often used in labs. When looking closely, don't just look at the top of the leaves near the aisle, but *look under the leaves* and into the far corners of the beds. Try to do this regularly. I like to do it before my day gets going, walking around the greenhouse with my coffee cup in one hand and my hand lens in the other.

Greenhouse problems are usually caused by an organism (disease, insect or human); the environment (heat, light, soil nutrients, etc.); or combinations of both, making it seem mighty complex. Sometimes insects are not a problem in themselves but may be spreading a disease as

they feed. I have seen situations where too much nitrogen in the soil caused soft lush growth, which in turn attracted aphids, a common greenhouse pest. The aphids then spread a leaf disease around as they fed. Is this a soil, aphid or disease problem? Its all connected. Nutrient imbalances may mimic a disease by causing yellowing or leaf splotches. And some sprays used to control pests turn out to be toxic to some plants, causing more damage than the original pest—a case of the cure being worse than the disease. As the saying goes, "everything is connected to everything else." The greenhouse is no exception.

The susceptibility of a plant to a pest or a disease is directly related to its health and age. Parsley, for example, is a biennial that produces leaves the first year and a seed stalk the second. Every time I forget to pull out the parsley before the second year, bugs jump all over it. It appears that something clicks in the second year that makes the plant susceptible.

When a plant is under stress, it also becomes more susceptible. Stress is caused by a number of environmental factors: temperature, light, nutrients and water. When these factors are not at their optimum, stress results. I once kept an eggplant bed alive long into the winter even though the daily temperatures were very cold. Eggplant prefers constant *warm* temperatures. The longer it lived into the cold winter, the more pests and diseases were hampering it. It really shouldn't have been growing then. Kohlrabi, a cabbage family crop that likes *cool* winter temperatures, would have done better. But one year I planted kohlrabi in the hot summer greenhouse. It soon had bugs all over it while the more heat loving crops like tomatoes and cucumbers were pest free. The kohlrabi was under stress and the wily pests knew it.

Rather than trying to understand what's going on, many people just resort to poisons. Spraying poisons can adversely affect human health and create a pest resistance to the poisons. It also can cost ''an arm and a leg.'' Short and long term effects of chemicals on human health are constantly being questioned; rarely a year goes by that another chemical isn't pulled off the shelves because of safety questions. In 1978 alone, 40,000 pesticide poisonings were reported. California officials believe only 2% of farmworker poisonings are reported. Scientists are uncertain as to whether there is *any* level of pesticides that can be tolerated without threat to human health or the environment. The use of pesticides is especially shortsighted when comparing their often limited effectiveness against all their costs. Home food production may be our only form of independence from pesticides.

The more we spray, the more insects become resistant to the chemicals. And they can even begin to benefit from them. Compared to 1965, twice as many insects (including many greenhouse pests) now have developed resistance to sprays. Also, when massive spraying occurs it kills the many beneficial insects that often prevent harmful insect populations from developing. Not all bugs are bad! The use of beneficial insects to control harmful ones is known as biological control, and I'll go into it later.

Because solar greenhouses are usually attached to the home for heating purposes, we must be especially careful how we go about controlling pests and diseases. What works in an outside garden may not work inside. Here's a comparison of outside and inside pest control.

Outside Garden

- Repellents actually repel pests out of your garden onto a neighbor's property.
- Due to the action of pure unfiltered sun, pesticides break down faster.
- Wind can blow your pesticides into someone else's garden.
- There are more naturally occurring beneficial insects outside.
- Purchased beneficial insects often fly away with the first wind.
- You can stand upwind while spraying, breathing fresh air.

Attached Greenhouse Garden

- Repellents have only limited use because the environment is enclosed.
- Sprays easily get into household air.
- Beneficial insects released inside the greenhouse will usually stay there.
- Spraying pesticides leaves no fresh air for the person spraying.
- Effects of a spray last slightly longer.
- Greenhouse pests and diseases often differ from those in the outside environment.

Your solar greenhouse is probably the closest garden you'll ever live with. Because of the many health concerns associated with chemical pesticides, it's especially important to rethink traditional methods of pest control for the attached greenhouse. The best option available is what entomologists call Integrated Pest Management (IPM). IPM involves maintaining pest populations at tolerable levels by using biological controls (beneficial organisms), cultural controls (such as crop rotation or growing resistant varieties) and pesticides only as a *last resort in spot applications*. There's more about IPM later in this chapter.

There are a number of ways to control insect pests in your greenhouse. I'll discuss each individually.

Preventative Measures

1. *Clean it up*—Keep dead leaves cleaned up and off the soil and don't let plant parts rot on the soil surface. Eliminate places where pests can thrive, including weeds, poorly managed compost piles, debris.

2. *Beware of gift plants*—This may be the best way to get a new pest to romp in your greenhouse. Don't be a hospital for a friend's sick plants. If you must take on any new plant, including a store-bought one, inspect it closely. Take it outside and spray it before bringing it into its new home. See sprays later in this chapter.

3. *Pull up plants* that are past their productive period; also those that are sickly or infested. Remove them from the greenhouse . . . carefully. You don't want to shake off the bugs on your way out.

4. *Before reusing pots, wash them* with hot water and soap.

5. *Keep air moving*—Pests love stagnant air so, even in winter, run a small fan. It'll also help move heat into your house and prevent air stratification (hot ceilings and cold floors).

6. *Maintain plant health*—When it's infested, your plant may be telling you something. Are you growing it at the right time or in the right location? Does it have the light, nutrition, water and temperature that it needs? Maybe a different plant variety would do better. Is the infested plant getting old or going to seed? Give it some thought.

7. *Intercropping (Integrated Planting)*—As detailed in *Crop Layout,* planting beds with mixtures of crops rather than a single crop keeps infestations down. It confuses both insects and diseases.

8. *Rotate crops* from year to year—don't plant the same crop in the same place in consecutive years.

Selection for Resistance

As mentioned in *Selecting Greenhouse Crop Varieties,* some plant varieties may have some resistance to insect pests. But do your own testing. You'll find one variety often will develop less of a bug problem. It's important to keep records that compare the performance of each variety. You will find your record keeping time pays off.

Environmental Pest Controls

Besides practicing what is listed as Preventative Measures, there are other ways to change the environment to your advantage and make it harder for pests to survive. Here they are:

Baits and Traps The color yellow attracts many pests, including white flies and winged aphids. Yellow fly paper will help control some populations. Homemade fly paper may be made by spreading grease (found at auto parts stores) on yellow cardboard and hanging it, or mounting it on a post in an infested area. The pests fly right into it and die. When the grease gets dusty it must be reapplied. A beneficial parasite, such as Encarsia formesia, which controls whiteflies, will also be attracted and killed by yellow sticky traps, so don't use them when this friendly parasite is present or soon to be released.

Slugs and snails are attracted to beer, so they can be controlled with beer traps. But the beer must be renewed every 2 days; and there should be a trap every 5 square feet. Put the beer in something they can easily crawl into. (It's quite labor intensive and you may find something better to do with your beer.)

Many people use crushed eggshells around plants to keep snails and slugs away. These pests don't like crawling on rough surfaces. Diatomaceous earth, wood ash (used in moderation), hydrated lime, ferrous ammonium sulphate and sawdust also make a good slug or snail barrier around seedlings.

The most common bait for slugs is metaldehyde. It's usually mixed with sawdust, but sawdust is much easier to pronounce. Unfortunately, it has all the disadvantages of a pesticide. It's poisonous and should be kept off food. Also, it can be absorbed through the skin, so wear gloves. After some time it will break down in the soil. If used constantly, slugs and snails will become resistant, so it's best used sparingly around seedlings which are particularly susceptible to slug and snail attacks. Keep it locked up and away from pets and children (not necessarily in that order).

Slug trap

Small thin boards, such as pieces of plywood, or potatoes cut in half placed on the soil surface work as a great trap for sow bugs, pill bugs and slugs. These pests are night feeders. During the day they retreat to dark moist places, hopefully under your board where you can dispose of them very easily in the morning. See Slug section in this chapter for further controls.

Mice in the greenhouse that nibble on plant leaves are a problem which can be solved by using . . . you guessed it, mouse traps. Cats or commercial baits may also work.

Future greenhouse traps may include pheromones (scented chemical sex hormones that attract pests into a trap).

Sprays for Pest Control Don't automatically assume I mean synthetic chemical sprays. There are a number of things you can spray to help keep insects down. They include:

1. Homemade Pesticides

Many garden books have recipes for homemade pesticides. They include such ingredients as garlic, red peppers, onions and dead insects. Many home brewed pesticides are basically insect repellents. They work fine outside because they repel pests from your garden to someone else's, but in the greenhouse pests often are repelled from place to place inside the greenhouse.

However, stronger home formulations such as soap and tobacco may be used. Nicotine tea, a spray made from cigarettes, is very effective. Before spraying, let it steep overnight til it's dark, and don't inhale the vapor. Wear gloves and a respirator. Don't use it on peppers or tomatoes because it may spread tobacco mosaic virus to these tobacco relatives. Take proper precautions because it's poison to people too. A mild soap spray is very effective (especially on soft-bodied insects such as aphids), and unlike tobacco, it's safe. Always use soap before you try a stronger pesticide. Mix 2 tbs. of a *mild* detergent such as Ivory Liquid or Dr. Bronner's in 1 gal. of water, or mix 1 oz. of Fels Naptha or Ivory Flakes in 1 gal. of water. Before using, test on a leaf and wait a day to be sure it doesn't burn the leaf. If it does, further dilute the mixture.

I've used a commercially available insecticidal soap that's been formulated to be hard on bugs and easy on plants and people. It's more expensive than regular soap. For more information write: Safer Agro-Chem, 3233 Vista Diego Rd., Jamul, CA 92035.

2. Botanical Pesticides

Derived from plants, they're commonly believed to be easier on our environment. These commercially available pesticides usually have a low toxicity to humans compared to many synthetic pesticides, but they also have a shorter effective life in your garden. For this reason you may have to spray more often. Unlike many botanicals, nicotine derived from tobacco has a very high toxicity to humans and extreme caution is urged if you use it. It's sold commercially as Nicotine Sulphate or Black Leaf 40®.

When spraying any commercially available botanical spray, treat it with the same safety precautions you would a chemical pesticide. You can get sick, dizzy, headachey and nauseated *just as fast* with botanicals as with synthetics. Safety procedures are outlined at the end of this section on page 172-173. Commercially available botanicals also kill beneficial insects and should not be used at all when you're using a biological control, or else use it only in very rare spot applications. Here's a list of commonly available botanicals:

A.   Rotenone—An extract of certain tropical legume plants, Rotenone is a contact and stomach poison that's active on most common greenhouse pests, including slugs.

B.   Pyrethrum—Derived from the flower heads of the pyrethrum chrysanthemum, it is produced in Africa and South America. It is a contact insecticide that is commonly combined with Rotenone in commercial preparations. It is effective on most common greenhouse pests, especially flying ones such as the white fly. Pyrethrum plant seeds are available from most seed catalogs. Home preparations may be made from the flower heads ground into a dust or brewed into a strong tea for spraying.

C.   Sabadilla—Derived from the seeds of a tropical plant resembling corn, it's a powerful contact and stomach poison that's active on most vegetable pests except some spider mites.

D.   Ryania—As with most botanicals, it's derived from a tropical plant, actually from the ground stems of a shrub. It is often used effectively on aphids and is said to be easier on beneficial insects. Unfortunately, it's usually sold as a dust. But spray formulations, when found, usually work best in the greenhouse.

E.   Nicotine—It's an age-old pesticide with high toxicity to both humans and insects. Even if you smoke cigarettes you'll still be surprised how sick you can get if you use this pesticide improperly. Its vapors are quite toxic. Keep it off your skin. It should be used only with extreme caution! See "Spraying Procedures," later in this chapter.

Botanicals are available at your local garden store or from:

Pratt-Gabriel Div.
Miller Chemical & Fertilizer Corp.
122 Sharon Rd., P.O. Box 8
Robbinsville, NJ 08691

Organic Control, Inc.
5132 Venice Blvd.
Los Angeles, CA 90019

Burgess Seed and Plant Co.
905 Four Seasons Rd.
Bloomington, IL 17862

3. Microbial Pesticides

Like biological warfare, these formulations of microbes attack specific pests by causing a disease that kills them. Luckily, microbial pesticides won't affect humans or even most beneficial insects. They usually kill only the target population. They are the only safe commercial insecticide that can be used in conjunction with biological control. The primary microbial agent that's available currently is Bacillus Thuringiensis, commonly sold as Dipel® or Thuricide®. It affects only army worms, cabbage worms, cabbage looper, tent caterpillar, gypsy moth, leaf roller, horn worms, and many other caterpillar family pests. It will not harm most other insects and is very safe for people.

Store it in a cool place but don't let it freeze. If you don't use all that you mix, don't bother storing it because diluted formulations in the sprayer won't be effective past 12 hours.

4. Synthetic Pesticides

These are totally human-made preparations known for quick results and long lasting activity. But that's a mixed blessing because the long lasting activity is also bothersome to the ecology. Also, the many strange products these pesticides break down into may be worse to ecologies than the original formulations, so I recommend the use of botanical sprays over synthetic formulations because the breakdown products are generally safer. Few synthetics are compatible with biological control methods.

There are a few synthetic formulations that are questionably safe. However, I discourage the use of these chemicals unless absolutely necessary. It should be done only as the very, very last resort. Common ones include:

A. Malathion—Controls a wide array of pests including aphids and mites. It has a relatively short life.

B. Sevin—Effective on many common vegetable pests, and according to the EPA, it has low toxicity for humans. It has been known to have backfire effects, however, by helping to cause spider mite outbreaks.

C. Methoxychlor—It kills a broad spectrum of pests, and according to the EPA it has a relatively low toxicity for humans. Works better on the larger insect pests.

Never Use *Systemic* Pesticides
or those that are *not* rated
on the label for use on "food crops"

5. Other Pest Sprays

A.   Sulfur—Sulfur is active on certain diseases (see disease section later in this chapter) and is also helpful in controlling mites. It's available as a spray or a dust and may cause some leaf burning, so always test it on one leaf and wait 24 hours to see if it's too strong.

B.   Rubbing Alcohol—This is effective against mealy bugs as well as many other insects. Spray a mixture of 1 tbl. per pint of water. As with sulfur, do a leaf check before overall spraying because it may harm the plant. Individual mealy bugs may be dabbed with a Q-tip dipped in alcohol, but avoid getting it on the plant as pure alcohol will burn leaves.

Spraying Procedures   Before even considering spraying, be sure to confirm that what you think is a pest *really* is doing damage. More than once I've come across greenhouse owners about to wipe out a bug that turned out to be a baby ladybug (it looks nothing like the adult). The young lady bugs help contol many pests. Ask yourself what damage the "pest" is doing. Get out your hand lens and check around the back beds to see what's going on.

If you've got a pest and want to spray (having decided against other listed options) pick out a safe pesticide, and be sure it will be effective. The label should tell you what it will kill—and on what crops it is cleared for. If common botanical sprays are unavailable and you need to spray something, call your nearest county agricultural extension agent. Ask them to recommend the most effective and safest spray for your particular pest. The EPA has set up a system to measure pesticide toxicity. They use "LD50" numbers. LD50 is a measure of how much pesticide it takes to kill test animals. Pesticides with the *highest* LD50 numbers are safest (that is, it takes more chemical to kill them). Use this as a measure to compare the safety of all pesticides. These numbers for various substances should be available from county agricultural extension agents. Sprays can be made more effective by adding material that will cause the spray to spread out on the leaf rather than bead up. Here's how: mix 2 tbls. of mild soap (not

detergent) per gallon of spray. Commercially prepared "spreaders," as they are known, do the same and are available from agriculture supply houses. A spray is not as effective if it beads up on the leaf. Too much soap or spreader may be harmful to leaves, so be careful; more is not necessarily better.

You can use either the common inexpensive hand-held plastic squeeze sprayer available at most garden stores or you can buy a fancy pump-up metal compressed air sprayer. Hand sprayers take a little longer and don't work quite as well, but they're adequate. You can also buy the spreader formulation in an aerosol container or hand pump Windex®-type sprayer built into the spray can.

The best sprayer available is a 1-2 gallon stainless steel hand pump—the compressed air type. Sprayers range in price from $2.00 to $50.00. Even if you never plan to use pesticides in your greenhouse, a sprayer will come in handy for spraying soap or misting leaves with water. You should get one.

Other equipment to have on hand with your sprayer includes:

1.   A chemical respirator mask—available at agriculture supply or feed stores. Even with botanicals, a paint or dust mask is not enough. The greenhouse is an enclosed environment and *you need protection!*

2. Plastic or rubber gloves because many pesticides are harmful and can be absorbed directly through the skin.

3. Goggles to prevent any spray from getting into your eyes.

4. Toothbrush. Nozzles are constantly getting plugged and an old toothbrush is the best way to clean them out. But don't reuse it on your teeth! Never clean nozzles with metal pins or the like. It will damage nozzles permanently.

Spray Techniques (including botanical, microbial and synthetic chemical sprays)

1. Read the label at least twice. It can tell you a lot about the material: how to store it, how to apply it, what it controls, what plants it's been developed for, and often how long before the food is safe to eat. Call the local county agricultural extension agent if you have any unanswered questions about a spray.

2. Seal off the greenhouse from the home.

3. Wear protective clothing: gloves, goggles, respirator.

4. Use the recommended dosage; more is *not* better.

5. Spray mostly undersides of leaves and tips of plants; that's where most pests hang out.

6. Spraying is usually best done in the afternoon or evening, with 70°F (21°C) being the temperature at which sprays are most effective.

7. Spot spray if possible; cover only infested plants. Don't miss any infestations.

8. Follow days-to-harvest guidelines given on the label or found out from your county agricultural extension agent. Even with botanicals, it may be a few days before your food is safe to eat.

9. Use soap and water to clean the sprayer after *every* use. Don't forget to spray soapy water through the hose and nozzle too.

10. Store the stuff as recommended on the label—*away from children and pets*.

11. With most botanical or synthetic sprays, wash hands and change clothes after spraying.

Dusts   Many of the common pesticides, both botanical and synthetic, are available in dust formulations to be spread on and around plants. They have the problem of not getting coverage on the underside of the leaves. There is also the problem of people inhaling the dust when applying it, so a respirator mask is helpful. With some exceptions, sprays are generally superior to dusts in the greenhouse.

One material that is found only as a dust is Diatomaceous earth. It is fine silica remains of the skeletons of prehistoric one-celled organisms. As pests crawl over this material the silica cuts up the insects' bodies and dries them out. It's effective against soft-bodied insects and slugs. Some brands are blended with a small amount of botanical pesticide to increase its effectiveness. Your pest must have physical contact with it before it works. It's usually not harmful to beneficial insects.

Freeze Out   This is where people open up their greenhouse in the dead of winter to freeze out all the pests. It's often done in desperation. I question its effectiveness. In some corner, there'll be a few survivors ready to repopulate; or they'll come back from a nearby greenhouse, in a neighbor's clothing or on a salad leaf at a pot luck. They'll fly or hitchhike, but whatever, the pests *will* return soon. You end up where you began except without the winter crop, which was frozen out. It merely postpones the problem.

Eat Them?   Eat the pests in your greenhouse? Just the idea of it will make some of you ill. If it does, skip this part. Eating bugs is probably more nutritious than what you last ate. Roasted grasshoppers have about 75% protein and 20% fat and are high in niacin and riboflavin. Grasshoppers were sold in ancient Greek markets (mostly to the poor; the wealthy preferred the domestic oak grubs fattened on flowers . . . yum). Many cultures depend on insects as their food source, roasting them, making flour out of them or frying them. The very idea of this may seem repulsive to modern sophisticates who dine on delicacies such as snails, rocky mountain oysters, frogs' legs and chicken embryos (eggs), not to mention BHA, BHT, sodium nitrite, polysorbate 80, saccharin, and artificial colors galore.

I've eaten raw aphids (usually by mistake); they are tiny sweet morsels. It takes a real infestation and a lot of time to get full; it won't ruin your appetite for dinner unless you're a heavy aphid consumer.

Slugs are very closely related to and taste similar to garden snails, which the French call "escargots." Many Europeans eat slugs to cure arthritis. People are often offended by the idea of slug eating, but it certainly would add a touch of class and elegance to your next dinner party to serve greenhouse escargots. If you can find some snail shells, no one will ever know.

I'm really not very serious about this as a pest control or a food source, but think about this. Many people are repulsed by the thought of chomping on pests for human food; shouldn't we be equally repulsed by poisoning our food, air and water with synthetic pesticides in an often-futile and many times unnecessary crusade to rid our garden of bugs. Which is truly more civilized?

Biological Control/Integrated Pest Management (IPM)

Integrated pest management is, as the name implies, a strategy for the *management* of pests, not their total annihilation. The end result is a tolerable level of pests in balance with the environment. IPM uses biological control, crop rotation, integrated planting, cultural controls, and also (but only when absolutely necessary—and very rarely) some spot pesticide spraying of isolated plants. In the greenhouse this can be tricky.

Bilogical control is the management of pest populations by use of natural enemies known as beneficial insects. The beneficial insects are classified either as predators (organisms that control the pest by eating it), or as parasites (organisms that must live in or on the pest at the expense of the pest). Predators are usually general feeders who work on many pests. Parasites are specific, usually able to control only one target pest.

Biological control is the cornerstone to IPM. In using IPM I deal with infestations by first releasing a predator or parasite to feed on it. Supplementing this action I use the spraying of home remedies, hand picking the pests off of the plants, planting resistant varieties, baits and traps, and integrated planting (see *Crop Layout*). I spray pesticides, (mostly botanicals), only as a last resort. The only exception is spraying microbial pesticides.

When an infestation occurs, first consider pulling out and discarding the infested plant, taking the plant outside if it's in a container and spraying it with a botanical pesticide, or spot spraying a botanical pesticide in the greenhouse. Spot spraying is still chancy, so it's a good idea to hang a piece of plastic around the area you're going to spray to help prevent drift, thus minimizing injury to beneficial insect populations. These insects have much less resistance to most sprays than do the pests. And when they are all killed by spraying, you must reestablish the beneficial insects all over again.

With IPM, you must ask yourself at what level is a pest or disease personally tolerable? Rather than choosing to use a chemical on a wipe-out basis, think about how to safely bring the number of pests down to a level that is manageable and tolerable. It takes more thought and detective work, but it's a joy to understand, work with, and cultivate your greenhouse ecosystem. Besides, IPM pest control is often more effective than conventional spraying. Compared to the risks of massive spraying, it is the only sane choice, especially with a greenhouse attached to and opening into your home.

Biological control is not a new science. There was a flurry of activity in researching and applying biological control techniques in the first half of the twentieth century. But with the advent of DDT and other effective chemicals developed during World War II, use of biological control measures almost came to a halt. However, there was a rediscovery of biological controls in the 1970s—and for good reasons. The expense, ineffectiveness and health questions associated with synthetic, petroleum-based pesticides are some of the best arguments for the renewed use of poisonless pest control.

In nature, biological control is a continuing action, constantly creating and maintaining a dynamic balance. Of the approximately 1,000,000 insects listed as plant feeders in the United States, only 1 percent are listed as pests of agriculture.

To acquire beneficial insects, either you must order them through the mail (see addresses later in chapter), bring them in from the outside environment, or find a local supplier. Establishing a biological balance that keeps pest populations in check requires certain environmental conditions. First, create a pesticide-free greenhouse. Next, remember that this type of control requires patience because it can take many weeks for the beneficial bugs to get established. You just have to put up with this "out-of-control" period. Their establishment is helped by not letting temperatures get above 90°F (32°C) which can happen often in solar greenhouses. High temperatures are very detrimental to insect populations, although freezing temperatures are not good for either bugs or plants. I've found that winter is generally not a good time to introduce any beneficial insects. When you release your insects, try to do so on a cloudy day. A light mist on the plants will also help, except when establishing predator mites that prefer drier conditions. Having blooming flowers in your greenhouse not only adds beauty, but the nectar and pollen contained within the flowers provides a back-up food source for many of the beneficial insects. Have a few dill, fennel, or celery flowers around because they are loved by many beneficial insects and are a good food source for them. Having a large pest population also helps to successfully establish a beneficial insect population—they won't lack for food.

Identification of both the beneficial and harmful insects is essential. To do this you will need a 10x hand lens—a cheap one will do. When your beneficial bugs arrive, get a few of them under a good light and look closely at them. Know them well. Give them your best blessings. Release them on the plants that have the highest populations of pests. Mark these plants with a tag so you can periodically check on their performance with your hand lens. Look on the underside of leaves and always check adjacent plants for indications of beneficial insects at work. Don't release any new general predator in an area where another general predator already exists. To do so will greatly lessen the chances of establishing the new predator. Watch your plants closely and don't let a problem sneak up on you. And obtain your beneficial bugs as soon as you see a high population of pests.

A good example of the benefits of establishing and spreading a beneficial insect is the white fly parasite. The *encarsia formosa* (white fly parasite) will establish itself in an area heavily infested with white flies, and you can use this place as a base of operations. For instance, if you have established the encarsia on a tomato plant to control a bad white fly problem, the plant will soon be covered with many little dark spots. The dark spots are parasitized white flies and contain young encarsia soon to hatch out of what was once a young white fly. If you spot a white fly infestation beginning in another area, pluck a leaf with the encarsia on it (with black spots) and hang it directly near the new infestation. On a daily basis, use your hand lens to follow their progress. Use similar techniques with all releases.

If biological control is something you want to be involved with, eliminate the mental programming that all bugs are bad. If you are used to using "total wipe-out" pesticides, it may be hard to be comfortable with plants that always have some pests and some beneficial insects working on them. You will have to put up with some pest damage, but it's well worth the reward of having a self-perpetuating insect control system that is guaranteed not to have harmful long-term side effects. Not only will you have a garden of plants, but also a garden of animals—all in balance.

When it comes time to purchase beneficial insects you may find that the prices seem a bit high. Keep in mind that if you are successful, you will be purchasing these critters only rarely, as they often will repopulate themselves. An alternative to paying the high price individually is to buy cooperatively. Share the cost with friends, or members of a co-op or gardening club. For people with attached greenhouses, split the smallest order of beneficial insects available, giving priority to the greenhouses with the worst infestation. Soon they may even be able to supply many other folks with the needed predator or parasite. As people become more familiar with using the biology of natural greenhouse pests controls, they will gain skill in rearing and maintaining these beneficial insects. There is a potential for developing cottage industries around rearing predators and parasites for use in solar greenhouses. I see exciting possibilities for a good deal of small-scale economic development involving the solar greenhouse.

Besides insects, other greenhouse pest control friends are reptiles such as small, harmless snakes, toads, chameleons and other lizards. These reptiles have excellent appetites for insects and may have an important place in your pest control program.  Slugs, flying pests and even a few (oops) beneficial insects will be part of their diet. Watch closely to be sure they are feeding mainly on your pests. If the reptiles' food supply gets low, they may require supplemental food, possibly available at pet stores. Experiment.

The experience of having a self-contained ecosystem existing within your greenhouse is a source of continual amazement. The fun of working in a greenhouse that produces food is doubled when you're not only growing plants, but also animals and insects living in dynamic balance. It will become a self-contained biological island (or at least a peninsula) to help bring *your* mind, body and spirit into a better dynamic balance of its own. At the least, it may help you get through a long winter.

Greenhouse Friends

Name:	**Ladybug** or **Ladybird Beetle**
Biotype:	General predator
Description:	*Adult:* 3/16'' long, oval-shaped; red-orange outer wings with dark spots. *Young:* 1/16''-1/8'' long; flat-looking; tapering to the rear; dark grey with orange spots. *Eggs:* Elongated football-shaped, 1/16''-1/8'' long; yellow; laid in bunches on the leaf.
Pest Controlled:	Feeds on many insects including aphids, white flies (young), mites, mealybugs, scale. Usually best with aphids.
How to Acquire:	Usually through the mail—may come into greenhouse naturally. Purchase by the gallon, quart or pint. One gallon is approximately 75,000 ladybugs. A pint is plenty for a small greenhouse.
Comments:	Ladybugs will store in the refrigerator for up to 3 months, but do not freeze. Use as needed out of refrigerator; release in the evening after watering. You may pluck one inner wing under the orange ones to keep the ladybugs in a problem area—it usually works. They will survive this. (Not for the squeamish.) Temperatures above 85°F (30°C) cause ladybugs to die off,

fly off, and generally have negative attitudes. Ladybugs may not be available during certain times in winter so check with a supplier. Ladybugs will feed on flower nectar and pollen during times of few pests. They may need to be periodically re-introduced into your greenhouse. Generally ladybugs aren't all they're cracked up to be in the solar greenhouse; some of this is due to high temperatures and their feeding habits. It's hard to figure. I've seen them do wonderful jobs on aphid populations. Then there are an equal number of times when the aphids almost dance in front of the ladybugs' noses; the ladybugs yawn (perhaps they're often too preoccupied with mating) and fly away without eating . . . no pest control. So I've found that they are sometimes good, sometimes not, and it's hard to say exactly why.

Name:	**Praying Mantis**
Biotype:	General predator
Description:	*Adult:* Resembles walking stick; large, up to 5'' long; brown to green. Triangle-shaped head; large forearms to catch prey.

Young: Resembles an adult, only much smaller—⅛'' and larger. Almost looks like a large mosquito.

Eggs: Born from an egg case (up to 200 eggs per case). The case resembles a wad of brown, rigid foam about 1½'' in diameter.

Pests Controlled: While young, they feed on many soft-bodied insects. As they get older, they feed on larger insects, including each other.

How to Acquire: Usually through the mail. In warmer climates egg cases may be collected from outside in late fall and winter. Look for egg cases on branches.

Comments: Hang mantis egg cases from a branch in areas with pest problems. Egg cases do not change appearance appreciably after young have hatched, so watch closely. Cases are generally available only from January through June. While young, mantises do a fine job on many greenhouse pests. Contrary to what many suppliers say, adults often begin to feed on ladybugs and may greatly deplete their population. Mantises are fun to have around and can become friendly with people. If treated gently, they will not bite.

Name: **Green Lacewing Flies** (young known as **Aphid Lion**)

Biotype: Predator

Description: *Adult:* Up to 1'' long; slender green body; large lacy wings; beautiful golden eyes; large antennae.

Young: 1/16''-1/8'' long; large jaws; tapered body down to tail; looks like small centipede without all the legs.

Eggs: 1/16'' round; found on the end of a 3/4'' long, thin, hair-like stalk.

Pests Controlled: Only young are predaceous; adults feed on nectar. Young feed on a wide variety of greenhouse pests including aphids, mites and some white flies. Aphids are the primary food.

How to Acquire: Usually through the mail. They will fly in from the outside on their own but only if your vents aren't screened.

Comments: Green lacewings are usually very good predators but are subject to be eaten by other predators and each other. For this reason, don't try to establish green lacewings in areas where you have already established predators such as ladybugs. The young green lacewing is a nocturnal predator. They're usually purchased as eggs, which may be held in the refrigerator for up to 8 days. But it's best to release them immediately. When the eggs are grey in color, they are just a few hours from hatching. If eggs have hatched when they arrive, release them immediately, as the young will eat each other. To release, scatter on leaves, in crotches of stems and as near to pest infestation as possible. Early morning application is said to be best.

Name: **Fireflies** or **Lightening Bugs**

Biotype: Predator

Description: *Adult:* ⅜''-½'' long; flat narrow beetle. Abdomen often luminescent. Range in color from black to brown; sometimes has lines of yellow or orange.

Young: ¼"-⅜" long, dark-colored; flat, well-protected back and head, equipped with strong sickle-like jaws. One or more segments may glow in the dark.

Eggs: Found on moist ground, may be glowing. Found in damp, swampy areas.

Pests Controlled:	Snails and slugs.
How to Acquire:	Not commercially available. Must be collected outside the greenhouse and released inside.
Comments:	Slugs and snails are hard pests to deal with in any greenhouse. There is a possibility that some control may be obtaned with the firefly but much more work has yet to be done with these critters. The young form is the main predator; it usually takes 1-2 years for the young firefly to become an adult. It is a great fantasy to imagine your greenhouse lit up at night by a large number of happy fireflies eating slugs for dinner. Remember, it's still experimental for the greenhouse and control information is vague. I've released them and had trouble keeping them alive for any period of time. But my experience is limited. I feel there's good potential here.

Name:	**Syrphid Fly - Hover Fly**
Biotype:	Predator
Description:	*Adult:* 3/8"-1/2". Resembles a wasp but is really a fly. Has yellow or orange rings on a black body. Has the ability to hover like a hummingbird or bee (usually around flowers). *Young:* 1/16"-3/8" . . . Looks like small grey or brown maggot or caterpillar. *Eggs:* Laid singly; oval; white; 1/32".

Pest Controlled:	Usually only young are predaceous, and have a good appetite for aphids.
How to Acquire:	Young are much harder to spot than adults. Flowers attract adults into your yard and greenhouse. They look like a wasp with a fly body (but not so segmented). Besides the orange stripes, their superb flying ability and the way they hover in the air is the best giveaway to their identification.

Name:	**Spiders**
Biotype:	General predator
Description:	Usually 4 pairs of segmented legs. Often found in webs. Abdomen strongly constricted at base.
Pests Controlled:	Spiders feed on many small flying insects including winged aphids and white flies. They also feed on other crawling insects.
How to Acquire:	Not available commercially. Can be found outside and brought in, or will arise naturally as you resist the spraying of pesticides. Smaller spiders seem

more active and better for the greenhouse. Besides, they're not so scary to people!

Comments:	Spiders are an important general predator that you should make friends with in your greenhouse. Let them live peacefully in out of the way places (corners, under benches) and they will help your greenhouse crops stay healthy. Spiders aren't insects but are often grouped under the title "beneficial insects."

Name:	**Predator Mite—Phytoseiulus persimilis**
Biotype:	Predator
Description:	Very small—1/64'', resembles pest mite but has longer legs and is reddish in color. Hard to distinguish from other mites.
Pest Controlled:	Mites only.
How to Acquire:	Usually obtained through a commercial supplier.
Comments:	This predator mite has a healthy appetite for its pesty brothers and sisters—two-spot and red spider mites. Release the mite immediately in areas of mite infestation. Keep a close watch on its progress. This particular mite is best on greenhouse crops. There are different mites available for other crops. Don't water before or immediately after releasing. Predator spider mites aren't insects but are usually grouped under title of "beneficial insects."

Name:	**Predator Mite—Amblyseius californicus**
Biotype:	Predator
Description:	*Adult:* Similar to the phytoseiulus persimilis mite, but it moves a bit slower.
Pests Controlled:	Red spider and two-spot spider mites.
How to Acquire:	Through commercial suppliers.
Comments:	If you are having a mite infestation and your greenhouse runs hot (often above 90°F, 32°C) the californicus mite may be a better choice than the phytoseiulus persimilis because it withstands higher temperatures quite well.

Name:	**Cryptolaemus montrouzieri**
Biotype:	Predator
Description:	A cousin to the ladybug, it is a blackish hairy beetle with reddish thorax and wing tips.
Pest Controlled:	Mealybugs.
How to Acquire:	Only through commercial supply houses.
Comments:	This beetle has the distinction of having helped to save California's citrus industry in the early 1900s. It feeds only on mealybugs and works well in greenhouses. Recolonization is often necessary because this beetle depresses mealybug populations to such low levels that they themselves subsequently starve.

Name:	**Encarsia formosa**
Biotype:	Parasite
Description:	*Adult:* A very small harmless wasp about the size of a large speck of dust (not easy to see even with a hand lens.) The head is black and the abdomen light yellow.
	Eggs: Black and round, about 1/32''. Found on the underside of leaves near and among young white fly populations.
Pest Controlled:	White flies.
How to Acquire:	Usually through commercial suppliers. May occur naturally or be collected from other greenhouse growers who use the wasp for white fly control.
Comments:	An excellent way to control the white fly. There has been concern that solar greenhouses are too cool for encarsia to be able to keep up with the white fly population. Ideal temperatures are 70°-80°F (21°-27°C) days and 60°-70°F (15°-21°C) nights. My experience has shown that the encarsia keeps up with white flies in solar greenhouses with their lower and more fluctuating temperatures (40°-100°F, 4°-38°C.) They seem to over-winter fine in solar greenhouses. The encarsia is very tiny and will not harm people or plants whatsoever.

When purchased, the wasps will arrive as black eggs on a leaf. Hang this leaf on a plant that has a high infestation of white flies in an area of your greenhouse that's also infested. Tag plant(s). The young wasps will hatch out of round black dots and fly to the area where many white fly young are developing. These developing white flies look like round white scale-like (1/32'') dots under leaves. The young white fly is immobile. The encarsia will lay eggs into these developing white flies by ''stinging'' each white dot. The new encarsia young will begin to grow in the developing white fly scale, feeding on and eventually killing the white fly. The white scale will eventually turn black as the wasp grows within the white fly. The wasp will then emerge from this former white fly and eventually lay more eggs into more developing white flies. In completing their life cycle, they control the white fly. They parasitize only the white fly. Establishment of the encarsia formosa is indicated by the blackening of many young developing white flies. After establishment, you can spread the encarsia to other problem areas by plucking off a leaf full of the black dots (developing encarsia) and hanging it in a new area of infestation. While establishing the wasp, don't prune the plants in the area of initial release until the wasp has begun some control of the white flies. Also, while using the encarsia in your greenhouse, don't use any control methods for white flies involving yellow sticky traps or boards. The encarsia will also perish on these boards. One small order from a supply house is usually enough for two small attached greenhouses or one large-size greenhouse (up to 1,000 sq. ft.). Establishment of encarsia may take up to 2½ months, so be patient. To over-winter the encarsia in your solar greenhouse, maintain some hardy tomato plants or geraniums near the warmest part of the greenhouse (usually against the north wall near the thermal storage). Let the encarsia and the white flies spend the winter here. As the temperatures warm up and the white flies start doing damage, repeat the spreading of encarsia eggs around the greenhouse, using over-wintered tomato or geraniums as the starting point.

Name:	**Brachnid Wasp**
Biotype:	Parasite
Description:	Brownish or black, small wasp from 1/16"-3/8". Young larva stage is parasitic.
Pest Controlled:	Aphids.
How to Acquire:	No commercial suppliers listed; you must locate them outside and bring them in. They may move in from the outside garden naturally.
Comments:	Most good parasites are in the wasp family. The brachnid is among the better parasites.

Look for copper-colored, bloated aphids as an indication of control. Try to locate aphid populations in outside weeds during the summer. Look for parasitized aphids (copper colored and bloated) among the outside colonies. Bring these parasitized aphids containing the brachnid wasp into your greenhouse where, hopefully, they will set up shop, working on your greenhouse aphids. I've had great success with this.

Name:	**Gall Midge (Aphidoletes aphidimyza)**
Biotype:	Predator
Description:	The adults are less than 1/16" in length, and have long trailing legs and translucent wings that are larger than the body. The orange-colored larvae are slightly larger than the adults; they are worm-like and taper to the head. It is the larvae that feed on the aphids while the adults feed on flower nectar and pollen.
Pest Controlled:	Aphids.
How to Acquire:	Not currently available commercially. They may find their way into your greenhouse naturally or you can bring them in from outside. There is an indepth discussion on collecting the gall midge for greenhouse pest control in the excellent booklet, *Biological Control of Greenhouse Aphids,* listed at the end of this section.
Comments:	During the winter months, the gall midge will often hibernate in the soil.

Name:	**Zebra finch (taeniopygia guttata castanotis)**
Biotype:	Predator
Description:	*Males:* orange beak and feet, black and white striping on chest and tail, white belly, orange cheek patches, chestnut flanks dotted with white spots,

black patch on upper chest. *Females:* same coloring except they lack the orange face patches, the chestnut flanking, and the black chest patch.

Pests Controlled: Aphids, worms and other soft bodied insects

How to Acquire: Pet shops and private breeders or local bird clubs.

Comments: These are predators you turn loose in the greenhouse. It's best to acquire babies and cage them while you acclimate them to your home. See a manual on their care and culture. They will need to be taught to eat the aphids and worms. Here's how: introduce infested limbs into their cage and allow them to discover the delicacies. Once they develop a taste for the insects, introduce the birds into the greenhouse. Birds introduced in warm temperatures will do fine in winter. The birds, however, will shred plant material to build nests when breeding season arrives (usually spring), so it is best to provide other nesting material for them (such as twigs, grasses, burlap shreddings, dryer lint, etc.) Be sure all string-like pieces are no longer than 3''-4''. Put the nesting material by their feeding station. Also, the little avians need vegetable matter in their diet (just as we do) for fresh vitamins and minerals; so by providing *washed* fresh vegetables (i.e. spinach, broccoli, corn, squash, cauliflower, etc.) you accomplish excellent nutrition for a creature who's mean body temperature is 104°F, plus, spare your valuable plants from possible destruction. You will get much song and delight form these birds, while employing a natural insect control.

Name: **Toads, Chameleons, Lizards and Snakes**

Biotype: Predators

Description: Reptiles.

Pests Controlled: Slugs and assorted flying and crawling insects.

How to Acquire: Pet shops, or collect from outside.

Comments: Chameleons and toads seem to feed on flying insects. They position themselves on the tops of plants in search of food. Lizards, salamanders and snakes will feed on grasshoppers and slugs. There is a lot of room for experimentation.  Be sure to put away your mouse poison; it may also kill the reptiles. If food gets low for these predators, you may have to feed them supplementary food such as mealworms, available at pet stores. These predators are not recommended for community or commercial greenhouses because these great little creatures often scare the hell out of people. Otherwise, give them a try—you may find a good friend under the scales.

Sources of Beneficial Critters for your Greenhouse

Abbott Laboratories
14th and Sheridan Roads
North Chicago, Illinois 60064

Bacillus thuringiensis

Beneficial Insect Company
P.O. Box 323
Brownsville, CA 95919

Ladybugs

Bio-control Company
10180 Ladybird Drive
Auburn, CA 95608

Ladybugs and praying mantis egg cases

Biotactics
22412 Pico Street
Colton, CA 92324

Spider mite predators

California Green Lacewings, Inc.
2521 Webb Avenue
Alameda, CA 94501

Green lacewing flies

Natural Pest Controls
9397 Premier Way
Sacramento, CA 95826

Predator mites, scale parasites, green lace wing flies, cryptolameus (mealybug predator), ladybugs, praying mantis

Norman Evans
3423 Devin Rd.
Grove City, OH 43123

Praying mantis

Ladybug Sales
Rt. 1, Box 93A
Biggs, CA 95917

Ladybugs

Mincemoyers Nursery
Route 526
Jackson, NJ 08527

Praying mantis

Organic Control, Inc.
P.O. Box 25382
Los Angeles, CA 90025

Bacillus thuringiensis

Pyramid Nursery
4640 Attawa Ave.
Sacramento, CA 95822

Ladybugs, praying mantis, green lacewing flies

Rincon Vitova
P.O. Box 95
Oakview, CA 93022

Green lacewings, ladybugs, predator mites encarsia formosa, cryptolameus (mealybug predator)

More Reading on Biological Control

A Guide to the Biological Control of Greenhouse Aphids by Mariam Klein and Linda Gilkeson, available from Memphremagog Group, P.O. Box 456, Newport, VT 05855. $5.00 The best publication yet on greenhouse biological pest control with good details on collecting your own predators and parasites from outside.

Common Sense Pest Control by Helga Olkowski. Consumers Cooperative of Berkeley, Inc. 4805 Central Ave., Richmond, CA 94804

The Bug Book, Harmless Insect Controls by Helen and John Philbrick, Garden Way Publishing, Charlotte, Vermont (1974)

Windowsill Ecology—Controlling Indoor Plant Pests with Beneficial Insects by William H. Jordan, Jr., Rodale Press, Inc. (1977)

Handbook on Biological Control of Plant Pests, Editor, Cynthia Westcott. Brooklyn Botanic Garden, Brooklyn, NY 11225. (1960)

Common Greenhouse Pests

Note: for more indepth discussion of each control mentioned here, see previously listed techniques

Name:	**Aphids**
Description:	Pear shaped and quite small with long legs and antennae. They have a pair of small "exhaust pipe" structures on their rear end. They vary greatly in color, ranging from black, grey, red, yellow or green. Adults may be winged or wingless. Females can give birth to live young without mating. Offspring can reproduce within 7-10 days. Fast, huh? Colonies are found on new buds and under leaves near veins. Especially check young seedlings. Also, ants may carry aphids to your plants.
Damage:	Aphids are sucking insects that cause spotty marks on leaves, and deformed and curling leaves and flowers. In high populations they can greatly stunt growth or even kill plants. They also secrete a sticky substance called honeydew which drips onto lower leaves. Then a black mold often grows on the honeydew. This black mold, commonly known as "sooty mold," is also damaging to fruits and leaves. Aphids may transmit plant diseases that may result in yellowing tissue and plant death.
Control:	General predators, brachnid wasps, gall midges, ladybugs, soap sprays and botanicals. Control the ants associated with aphids. Ants often herd these pests around like cows because they feed on the honeydew that aphids secrete. Ants are amazingly repeled by spreading the herb tansy around the greenhouse.

Name: **Cabbage Looper, Green Worm**

Description: Green caterpillar up to ½'' long; may have white stripe on sides. They move with a looping gait. Adults are small white moths.

Damage: The caterpillar causes small holes in leaves. May defoliate plants. Usually found on cabbage and cabbage relatives but may be on other plants.

Control: Use microbial insecticide, Dipel® or Thuricide® (safe for biological control).

Name: **Fungus Gnat**

Description: ⅛'' long, grey-black, long legs. Found near soil surface, especially where there is decomposing organic matter. Larvae are white and wormlike; about ⅛'' or smaller. Looks like a cloud of 4 or 5 dots at the base of the plant.

Damage: It is often more annoying to people than to plants. Larvae may sometimes feed on roots, which in turn may promote root rot organisms.

Control: Cultivate soil surface, dust soil with tobacco from cigarettes or Rotenone® dust if you're *sure* the gnats are doing actual damage.

Name: **Leafhopper**

Description: Small, light colored (yellow to green) up to ¼'' long. Look for them jumping and flying when foliage is disturbed. They are fast.

Damage: Cause spotting on leaves and known for transmitting diseases. Also, sucking effects similar to aphid damage.

Control: General predators give slight control; spot spraying with botanicals. I have found that leafhoppers are attracted to calendulas, which may be used as a trap crop.

Name: **Leafminers**

Description: Very small flies (1/32''-1/16'') with black and yellow markings, Adults seen flying when foliage is disturbed. Eggs are laid in leaves, through which larvae make characteristic tunnels.

Damage: Damage is usually more visual than actual to vegetable crops. Look for serpentine tunnels in leaves. That is the main indication that you have a problem.

Control: Control measures required only in extreme cases. Spray for adults.

Name: **Mealybugs**

Description: White to tan, oval shaped, about 1/3'' or less. They produce a wax-like cottony substance. Found near buds and leaf bases.

Damage: They are sucking insects causing problems similar to aphids, including honeydew secretions. They damage crops by removing plant sap.

Control: Rubbing alcohol, botanical spray, soap solution, cryptolaemus predator.

Name: **Millipede, Centipede, Symphylids**

Description: Long, slender, white to brown bodies with many legs. Up to 1'' long. Found on soil surface, often under debris. They run for cover fast when disturbed.

Damage: May occasionally feed on roots, causing stunting of plants.

Control: Practice good sanitation, keep debris off soil surface. Even when pest is present, the need for spray is rare.

Name: **Mites** (two-spot and red spider)

Description: Small (1/32''-1/16''); pale yellow to light brown to reddish; they may have red spots. Because they are spiders they have 8 legs. Get a hand lens or magnifying glass to see them. Adults may have two spots on either side of the body. This is the "two-spot mite." They look like tiny dots associated with webs found on underside of leaves and growing tips.

Damage: They feed with sucking mouthparts. Injury causes leaves to look lighter colored as if they are drying out or parched. Upper surface may look spotty or "stippled." Also look for webbing over foliage. High populations greatly reduce yield and may kill plants.

Control: Phytoseiulus and amblyseius (predatory mites) are excellent biological controls. Also try spraying soap, water (which sometimes knocks them off the plant) or botanicals.

Name: **Slugs, Snails**

Description: Slugs are slimy, dark-grey soft-bodied creatures up to 1'' long. They glide on the plants leaving a silvery reflective trail. They are usually nocturnal feeders, and are found hiding under debris. Snails are similar in habit and appearance to slugs except they have a round shell which varies in color and markings.

Damage: They eat holes in the leaf about ½''-1'' round. Often they kill seedlings and make foliage so full of holes it is unmarketable or unpalatable.

Control: Avoid mulching and keep top of soil clean. Baits and traps (see environmental controls); metaldehyde; set out small flat boards or potatoes cut in half on soil surface, in morning handpick pest from underside and destroy; diatomaceous earth will protect young seedlings.

Name: **Sowbugs, Pillbugs**

Description: Grey, flattened, oval bodies (up to 1/3'') with large scale-like plates. May roll into ball (pillbugs) or run away (sowbugs) if disturbed.

Damage: Occasionally feed on roots, seedlings and stems.

Control: Cultivation, *keep soil surface clean*, dust with ''Dipel II''® granules (a special formulation of bacillus thuringiensis), trap under boards or potatoes cut in half and placed on soil surface. Dispose of them in morning.

Name: **White Flies**

Description: Small (1/16'') white flying insects. Eggs, which usually go unseen, are very small, black, slender specks; young are roundish, flat and white. All are found on underside of the leaf.

Damage: Similar to aphids.

Control: Encarsia formosa is excellent biological control, yellow sticky traps (not to be used with encarsia control), botanicals, general predators.

Name: **Thrips**

Description: Very small; yellow to brownish; cigar-shaped; 1/50''-1/32'' long.

Damage: They suck on the leaves, causing a stippling of the leaf.

Control: Spray underside of leaf with garlic or hot pepper solution.

Name: **Nematodes**

Description: Live in soil, not visible to the eye; root feeders.

Damage: Leaves may be abnormal color, plants become very prone to wilting, discolored roots, low productivity. Hard to positively identify this damage as being attributed to nematodes. You may need an expert.

Control: Unless common in your area, nematode damage is hard to confirm. Intercrop marigolds. Work decomposed organic matter into the soil, as there is a fungus that lives in organic matter that actually is predaceous on nematodes.

Name: **Cats** and **Dogs**

Description: You know.

Damage: Plant flattening, uprooting of plants, leaves chewed on; common around catnip.

Control: You know.

If you cannot identify a pest. . .

try to capture some and put them in a small jar of alcohol. Take it to your county agricultural extension agent for aid in identification and control. Take their spray recommendations with some caution, especially if you're already releasing beneficial insects. Extension agents tend to favor chemical control.

Diseases

There are a lot of fancy, scientific definitions for plant disease but let's keep it simple. How about: *Any deviation from the normal in your plant that you don't like*. A broad definition but you probably already have an idea of what a disease is anyway.

A disease may range from causing the death of a whole plant, death to parts of a plant, a cancerous overgrowth of plant tissue, to dwarfing. Not all diseases are caused by organisms. From the plant's point of view, many are the result of an adverse environment. These may resemble organism-caused diseases and may be just as destructive. Conversely, some diseases resemble a plant nutrient deficiency, or vice versa . . . or your plants may be afflicted with a combination of both. Don't let it get too confusing. Read on; you can handle it.

The solar greenhouse is not a sterile environment; it's full of life at all times and sometimes it will seem as if insects and diseases appear out of thin air. Please take your time about dealing with what you think may be a disease. All too often I have come across greenhouses where the supposed cure turned out to be worse than the ''disease'' itself. As with insect and pest control, we should approach spraying only as the very last resort.

Solar greenhouses often run at high humidities, especially in winter months; and high humidities are conducive to development of disease organisms. Also, most greenhouse glazings filter out the sun's ultraviolet radiation (which has been shown to kill many disease organisms), so lower ultraviolet levels may contribute to a higher incidence of disease. To what extent is not known.

As with insect infestations, diseases often affect plants with poor health or those that are under stress. So maintaining general plant health and healthy soil is the first step in preventing disease.

Environmentally Caused Diseases

There are a number of plant maladies common in greenhouses that are solely the result of the environment. Environmentally caused symptoms usually occur on many plants of different species in a broad area of your greenhouse (such as near glazing or a cold vent), rather than affecting an individual plant. Disease organisms, however, usually affect only one plant species such as tomatoes, but not herbs, cucumbers or other plants in the immediate area.

The following chart may help you identify environmental maladies.

Symptoms of Common Environmentally Caused Diseases

Cause	Symptoms/Comments
Cold damage:	Dark green, wilted or dry leaves occurring on plants nearest glazing or vents with air leaks. Also misshapen fruit, poor fruit set and blossom drop.
Smoke:	Yellow, tan or papery blotches between the leaf veins, while veins usually stay green. All ages of leaves affected. Affects most crops, but lettuce is somewhat resistant. Check any heaters for down-drafting (not good for people either).
Nitrogen oxides:	Same symptoms as smoke damage, along with growth suppression. Common with greenhouses located near manufacturing plants, refineries, combustion of fossil fuels, and busy highways.
Ammonia:	When high amounts are in the air, leaves may have splotchy, cooked appearance ranging from brown to red. Damage may also appear as tan and white spots on cabbage family plants, and leaves may drop off. Some people believe small amounts of ammonia may actually help plants, but there is debate.
Pesticides:	Variable symptoms. The herbicide 2,4-D causes unusual leaf and stem curling. Many pesticides cause burn spots on leaves. Pesticides should be used only as a last resort. When used, please read the label for safety precautions and for a list of crops that the pesticide is cleared for. Even strong soap may cause some leaf damage. Spray drift may also enter the greenhouse through an outside vent in summer.
Nutrient deficiencies:	A little fertilizer is good, more is often disaster. If you suspect you overfertilized, look for burnt leaf tips. Read *Getting to the Roots* for guidance. Also see discussion of blossom end rot in tomatoes later in this chapter.
Wind damage:	Brown, papery leaf spots, wilting, stunted growth. Occurs on plants nearest vents, fans and windows.
Finger blight:	Dead green areas on the leaves due to too much handling. Occurs most often on unusual plants or scented herbs and other plants located near a walkway. Also, smokers transmit tobacco mosaic virus to tomatoes by touching the leaves.
Ethylene:	Growth reduction; leaf buds and flowers may fall off; also leaf deformities. Ethylene comes from leaks of L.P. or natural gas, methane gas, automobile exhaust and combustion of fossil fuels.
Sun scald:	Areas of round or angular browning caused by water droplets acting as magnifying glasses in greenhouses with glass glazing. Also may occur in greenhouses with aluminum foil on walls where light was focused on the plant surface.

Lack of light: Wherever there is shading, look for plants with stems becoming elongated and spindly. This can be helped by the addition of a light colored mulch over the soil and by painting white everything that is *not* thermal mass, plants or soil. Try hanging white sheets over thermal mass in summer.

Organism Caused Diseases

Micro-organisms, both disease causing and beneficial, have very complex biologies. To even begin to understand the ecology involved is a great task. Identifying the disease symptom is essential to proceeding with the proper steps of control.

Diseases are caused primarily by three organisms: bacteria, fungus and virus. Many species of each group cause disease, and symptoms of one type will sometimes mimic another. Depending on the microbe, they may survive and move through the air, water, soil, plant debris or be carried by insects. In these same environments, however, there are also predator or parasitizing beneficial microbes that attack the disease-causing microbes. That is why a sterile environment doesn't always offer the best control. In fact, the more we encourage high microbial populations, especially in the soil, the less we see disease organisms taking hold. Much like beneficial insects, the harmful microbe populations are controlled by beneficial microbe populations. In a soil culture this means adding organic matter to increase microbe populations (See *Getting to the Roots*). This may be why I've found plants grown hydroponically somewhat more susceptible to disease problems.

Before we look at specific diseases and organisms, let's first look at the options we have to control disease.

Prevention of Disease

The adage, "an ounce of prevention is worth a pound of cure," also applies in the greenhouse. Here are some guidelines:

1. Maintain plant health. Avoid overcrowding and provide a healthy growing environment with proper levels of ventilation, humidity, water, light, nutrition, etc. This also involves maintaining soil health.

2. Sanitation. Keep your greenhouse clean. Remove diseased plants. Keep the hose nozzle off the ground. Clean pots with hot water and soap before replanting in them and keep dead leaves, etc., off the soil surface.

3. Start young seedlings in clean containers using storebought potting soil, or sterilize your own seedling mixture (see discussion later in this chapter).

4. Compost from greenhouse plants should be used *only* in an outside garden. Outside garden plants may be composted for greenhouse use. Running two compost piles in this parallel system helps to break disease cycles because outside and inside diseases are often different.

5. Try to avoid taking on other people's plants, especially sickly looking ones.

6. Air circulation—Keep the air moving. Diseases, like insects, love stagnant air (see the insect control section earlier in this chapter).

7. Crop Rotation. This helps to break disease cycles. Keep a map of your planting layout to be sure you are rotating. Avoid following crops with their relatives (which often occurs within the large cabbage family or the tomato family). See *Crop Layout* for crop family lists.

8. Interplanting. This will greatly slow a disease, as well as insect infestation. Again, see *Crop Layout*.

Environmental Management

The environment can often be slightly altered to help control your disease problems. The action you take depends upon the specific disease. Here are a few examples:

Powdery Mildew—unlike most mildews, this fungus disease can't spread when there is water on the leaves, but it does spread with high humidities. It may be a fine line between the two.

Early Blight—this disease, like many other fungus diseases, spreads rapidly with water on the leaves.

Seed and seedling diseases—they are more of a problem with salty soils, fertilizer applications, planting in old soil, low light conditions and overcrowding.

High humidities—this will increase the incidence of many diseases (see *Greenhouse Environment*).

Resistant Varieties

Disease resistant plant varieties are much more common than insect resistance. Don't be mislead; seed companies use the term "resistant" much too freely. Usually they will be only *more* tolerant than other varieties. Resistant varieties may still become infested with the disease to which they are supposedly resistant. But the increased tolerance to a disease is still worth it. Read catalogs for descriptions of resistant varieties. If none is available, do your own varieties testing to discover more tolerant types. Whenever you see the word "resistant," replace it in your mind with "tolerant." (See *Selecting Solar Greenhouse Crops* and *Varieties*.)

Spraying

As with spraying for insect control, spraying for disease control is a last resort. Refer to the insect section for spraying techniques and methods. There are some homemade preparations that may be of minor help.

Homemade Sprays

Milk has been shown to prevent tomato seedlings from picking up mosaic virus. Dried skim milk is often added to pesticides because it helps the spray stick to the plant better (see tomato disorders later in this chapter).

Acetic Acid (Vinegar) is an old method to help prevent seedling diseases in the soil. A ¾ quart, .8% solution per 1 square foot of planting tray is the recommended dose. Let it sit 5-6 days before sowing seeds. This may be an alternative to purchasing sterilized planting soil or sterilizing soil yourself for seedlings.

Baking Soda sprayed on leaves may be of some help in controlling powdery mildew. Mix 4 tablespoons of baking soda to 1 gallon of water. Spray every 5-7 days.

Synthetic Sprays

A wide choice of fungicide sprays rated for food crops exist. But it should be a very rare case where you need to use a fungicide. It might be better to forget that crop for the season. If you do want to spray, ask your county agricultural extension agent for the *safest* food-rated fungicide. Follow all directions and safety precautions outlined in the insect spray section of this book.

Dusts for Disease Control

Many fungicides as well as pesticides are available in both spray and dust formulations. The two that are most commonly used in the greenhouse are sulfur and Thiram®.

Sulfur is an age-old fungicide used primarily for mildew control. It will also kill mites (both good and bad mites). On occasion I've used sulfur against powdery mildew with success. If used in moderation it is safe. However, high quantities of sulfur may burn leaves, particularly squash, cucumbers and houseplants. Always try a test dose on a leaf.

Thiram® is a synthetic chemical used to protect seeds from seedling diseases. It's frequently used in place of clean or sterilized soil for starting seedlings; for home gardeners it's really a lazy substitute. Thiram® dust in the air is harmful to breathe or get on your skin, so use extreme caution. First try all other controls for seedling diseases (see Damping Off later in this chapter).

Soil Sterilization

Soil sterilization, also known as pasteurization, is the heating of the soil to 180°F (65°C) for 30 minutes to kill any pests and diseases in it. It must be done before each planting because pests and diseases are quickly reestablished.

Sterilization is a common practice for commercial growers who are set up with steam heaters or electric soil sterilization units. But for the small greenhouse owner it is usually more trouble than it's worth. Can you imagine how hard it would be to rig up your greenhouse to sterilize all your soil every 4-6 months? Instead, small greenhouse owners should practice techniques to promote soil health and disease prevention. The only exception would be to sterilize the soil in which you start seedlings for later transplanting. Small amounts may be done in the oven. If you try this in your oven, preheat for 30 minutes and wrap the soil in aluminum foil. However, it's even easier to buy a sack of commercially made potting soil for seedling starts. It has been sterilized, it's usually a good mix and it's relatively cheap.

Another method of sterilizing soil is to use the sun. Place 1 gallon of soil in a clear plastic bag and set it in the sun for a week (longer if cloudy). Be sure the soil feels warm inside or it won't work. Turn the bag every other day. It may be hard to find a warm sunny spot in the winter.

If your soil is high in decomposed compost, the sterilization process may cause an increase in soluble salts, which may be detrimental to plant growth. If this is a potential problem, read the salts section in *Getting to the Roots*.

Disease Organisms

Viruses

Viruses are very small—ultramicroscopic—and very unusual life forms. They don't even have cell walls. Symptoms of virus infections include mosaics (yellow mottling or spotting), angular yellowed or brown areas, many yellow spots, and occasional leaf curling.

Viruses are commonly transmitted by insects such as aphids. But people can also spread the disease, as in the case of tobacco mosaic on tomatoes, spread by tobacco-smokers' fingers. Controlling viruses usually involves growing resistant varieties, being careful when handling plants, eliminating insects that transmit the disease, and using disease-free seeds or cuttings for propagation.

Bacteria

Many people think of bacteria when they think of disease, but only a small percentage cause disease. Many, in fact, are beneficial and essential to our lives. Bacteria enter plants through leaf wounds, places damaged by insects, or through natural microscopic openings in plant leaves. Bacteria need relatively warm temperatures to live.

Symptoms of harmful bacteria include both circular and angular leaf spots. At first, leaf spots often appear to be some shade of green in color, then gradually they turn yellow, brown or black. Other symptoms include bacterial rots where the plant tissue disintegrates, and is often slimy and smelly. Control involves disposing of plants that are infected and practicing greenhouse sanitation such as keeping the soil surface clean and removing any dead parts of plants from both the plants and the soil. Often bacterial problems are associated with high humidities and overwatering in a warm greenhouse.

Fungi

Fungi cause the great majority of plant diseases, but there are also very beneficial species that control some diseases. Fungi generally reproduce by spores which spread in the air, soil and plant debris. Fungi characteristically have complex life cycles which have many different stages.

The symptoms of fungus diseases include leaf spots, wilting, rots, mildews, rusts and blights (a rapid withering or decay of tissue without rotting). They are controlled with good sanitation, resistant varieties, environmental management, and lastly, spraying fungicides.

In general, fungus diseases are very difficult to identify unless you work with them on a daily basis. They are famous for mimicking each other or deviating from the textbook symptoms. If you have a particularly major problem and need a positive identification get it diagnosed by a plant pathologist at your nearest agricultural university or experimental station. Mailing instructions are at the end of this chapter.

Because most people grow tomatoes in their greenhouse, here's a rundown of tomato disorders, followed by a list of greenhouse vegetable diseases, and how to control them:

Common Greenhouse Tomato Disorders

Disease Name: **Blossom End Rot**

Description: First, water-soaked spots appear at the blossom end of fruits. Later the spots increase in size and become sunken, flat, brown and leathery round areas.

Cause: Environmental—low moisture, stress, low calcium levels in soil; vertical training intensifies the symptoms. Non-infectious.

Control: Mulch the soil. Use bone meal for extra calcium in the soil. Spray a 1% solution of calcium chloride on the leaves for immediate results.
Resistant varieties: Texto, Tropic, Manapal, Floradel.

Disease Name: **Catfacing**

Description: Deformed marks, lines on fruit. Odd shaped fruit.

Cause: Insect damage, growth disturbances, and cold temperatures. Non-infectious.

Control: Provide even growing conditions. The variety "Walter" is listed as resistant.

Disease Name: **Fruit Cracking**

Description: Cracks in skin of tomato fruit.

Cause: Widely fluctuating temperatures. Non-infectious.

Control: Maintain foliage covering fruits to avoid direct radiation on fruit's skin. Moderate temperatures. Resistant varieties include: Jumbo, Pink Forcing TMV, Floradel, Manapal, Early Cascade, Pink Delight Hybrid.

Disease Name: **Grey Mold (Botrytis cineria)**

Description: Fruits rotting during and after harvest. Some molding on stems.

Cause: Fungus.

Control: Promote good air circulation. Lower humidity, raise temperature (if possible), remove all infected stems or fruits. Keep area clear of debris.

Disease Name: **Leaf Mold (Cladosporium fulvum)**

Description: Whitish spots on upper surface of older leaves. They may enlarge and turn yellow. The underside has a velvet, olive-brown coating. Spores spread by air and watering. Sometimes carried on seed.

Cause: Fungus.

Control: Improve air circulation. Lower humidity. Grow resistant varieties: Floradel, Marion, Marglobe, Globelle, Vetamold, Tuckcross 533.

Disease Name: **Fusiarium (Fusiarium oxysporum)**

Description: Usually at first all leaves on one side of the stem become yellow and wilt. Later all leaves wilt and die. There are two main races, Fusiarium 1 and Fusiarium 2.

Cause: Fungus.

Control: Best control is resistant varieties and healthy soil.
                    These varieties are resistant: Marglobe, Floradel, Manalucie, Tropic, Tuckcross 533.

Disease Name: **Verticillium (Verticillium hydromycosis)**

Description: Yellowing of older, lower leaves which later turn brown and die; wilting of the tips of plants during the day; may recover at night. Defoliation is common. Branches droop. Leaves are dull in appearance and fruits are small. Brownish discolored vascular system within stem.

Cause: Fungus.

Control: Promote a healthy soil life. Use resistant varieties: Floradel, Marglobe, Tropic, Bonus.

Disease Name: **Early Blight (Alternaria solani)**

Description: Tan-colored spots appear on leaves and sometimes stems. Spots enlarge to ¼''-½''. Close inspection shows concentric rings inside of spots. Whole leaf may yellow and defoliate. Fruit may show dark brown spots.

Cause: Fungus.

Control: Keep humidity down, avoid water on leaves. Control insects better, they spread Early Blight. Use tolerant varieties: Floradel, Manapal, Calypso, Early Cascade.

Disease Name: **Grey Wall**

Description: Grey-brown streaks on fruit; blotchy ripening.

Cause: Low light intensities, low temperatures, high nitrogen levels, low potassium levels, high soil moisture levels, sometimes caused by mosaic virus, but usually non-infectious.

Control: Keep soil potassium level high. Try to increase temperature above 60°F (15°C). Use resistant varieties such as Tropic, Floradel and Walter.

Disease Name: **Tobacco Mosaic Virus (Marmor tabaci)**

Description: *Plants infected early*—Stunted growth, light green and dark green mottled areas or mosaic pattern. Few blossoms set. Inferior quality fruit.

Plants affected after blooming stage—Light green and dark green mottled areas. Yellow netting appearance on leaves. Uneven fruit ripening, sometimes yellow streaks on fruit.

Cause: Virus. Lives in Solanoceae family such as tobacco, tomato, eggplant and pepper.

Control: Avoid use of tobacco in any form while handling tomato plants. Don't allow smoking. Don't let strangers touch plants. Wash hands before handling tomato plants. Wash after touching infected plants.
Pull up all infected plants. Control insects. Prune infected plants last. Clean pruning knife with disinfectant between use on plants if infection is suspected. Pour milk into soil of suspected infection area. Milk that would otherwise be discarded can sometimes be obtained from school lunch programs. Grow resistant varieties: Tropic, Jumbo, Tuckcross 533.

Common Greenhouse Vegetable Diseases

Name: **Mildews, powdery** and **downy**

Description: White to greyish leaf surface growth with a powdery appearance. Downy mildew has a grey appearance, unlike powdery mildew which is white. They severely reduce yield.

Cause: Fungus.

Control: Use resistant varieties; sulfur applications (be careful of leaf burn); baking soda spray. Powdery mildew is inhibited by wet leaves. Downy mildew thrives when leaves are wet. Both love high humidity. Disease growth is slower in dry air.

Name: **Leaf Rot**

Description: Top portion of leaves have wet, brownish rot. Often found on heading lettuce, cabbage, chinese cabbage. More serious in shady locations.

Cause: Usually bacteria.

Control: Try to minimize splashing soil while watering or the problem will spread. Overwatering, high humidities and poor air circulation aggravate this problem. Also try different varieties or, in the case of lettuce, switch to leaf rather than heading varieties.

Name: **Root Rot**

Description: Plants wilt constantly, roots rot.

Cause: Fungus and bacteria.

Control: Often caused by overwatering, which is the unfortunate urge when people see a wilting plant. Try replanting in new soil with a higher percentage of sand. Water only when soil needs it (see *Greenhouse Environment*).

Name: **Leaf Spot**

Description: Leaf is covered with spots ranging from pinpoints to larger-sized. Leaf spots are caused by a variety of insect pests, diseases and the environment. You may have to use outside help to positively identify.

Cause: Usually bacteria, fungus and insects.

Control: Based on identification. For leaf spots on tomato plants see discussion of tomato diseases earlier in this chapter.

Name: **Sooty Mold**

Description: Black, sticky, dirty, dusty-like growth usually on lower leaves.

Cause: Insect drippings triggering fungus mold.

Control: Control sucking insects—see Aphids section of this chapter.

Damping Off (seedling diseases)

Description: Damping off is a general term describing many different seedling diseases. The symptoms include: 1) stem rotting near the soil surface and the seedling falls over; 2) seed decays in soil before or after germination; 3) root rots after plant is germinated and growing. Plant first appears stunted, then dies. Roots often turn a rust color at rotted point.

Cause: Usually fungi.

Control: Control the environment. Certain environments tend to increase the incidence of damping off. In order to know how to control the damping off of seedlings, we must first understand the environment that fosters it.

Environments Affecting the Promotion of Damping Off Diseases

1. Overwatering—of course you should never let your seedlings dry out, but overwatering and maintaining soggy soil will increase damping off. Keep the soil moist, but not dripping wet.
2. Fertilization—the higher the level of nitrogen in the soil, the softer the plant growth will be. The softer the growth, the more susceptible the plant will be to seedling diseases.
3. Light—seedlings grown in ample light are more resistant to seedling diseases. If your seedlings are showing signs of a light deficiency (elongated, lanky growth; light green leaves), they will also be more susceptible to damping off diseases.
4. Soil salinity—if your soil test shows a high concentration of salts in the soil or an unusually high pH (about 7.5 or more) you'll see more damping off.

5. Temperature—seeds germinate best at temperatures between $65°$-$80°$F ($18°$ - $27°$C) depending on the specific requirements of each crop. When seeds are grown at higher or lower temperatures than what's optimum for each crop, they'll be more susceptible to damping off.

6. Poorly aerated soil—a great place for damping off diseases to grow. Add extra amounts of sand and decomposed organic matter such as peat moss to increase the aeration of your germinating soil. Too much organic matter or peat moss, however, may tend to make the soil hold too much water. (See *Plant Propagation*.)

7. Old, infested soil—using soil that previously had seedlings or greenhouse plants grown in it will increase the incidence of damping off diseases. Such soil tends to be infested with the damping off disease organisms. Virgin soils, or soils that have not been used for growing for at least 1 year usually have less of a problem. To successfully use older soil for seedlings, try sterilizing it first. Store-bought potting soils are already sterilized and work great for starting seedlings.

8. Depth of planting—planting seeds too deep delays the plant's emergence and keeps the seedlings more susceptible to damping off diseases. A seed should be planted at a depth that's 2 times its width.

9. Age of seed—older seed tends to be weaker, and as a result, they may have more problems with damping off. Use new seeds if damping off is a problem. Store seeds in cold, dark, dry places in dry, air tight containers.

10. Crowded seedlings—thickly planted seedlings compete for light, water and nutrients. This creates a stress situation for the seedlings, which in turn makes it easier for them to be attacked by damping off diseases. Give each seed plenty of room to grow so that it would be some time before the adjacent seedling leaves touch each other. Also, when starting plants in flats or cut milk cartons, etc., it is better to plant the seedlings in rows rather than to broadcast or scatter them about in the container.

When all else fails you need to get a . . .

POSITIVE DISEASE I.D.

I know it's rough to figure out exactly what your problem is. This is just a brief list from hundreds of possibilities. For positive identification mail a sample of your problem to your nearest state agricultural university. Your county agricultural extension agent should have the address. Here's how to prepare the sample:

1. Clip a few diseased leaves, stems or roots and place them in a plastic bag containing a moist paper towel.

2. Seal the bag and place it in a crush-proof box for mailing.

3. Enclose all the information about the plant and disease you possibly can think of, including: plant variety and its age, soil type, location in the solar greenhouse, fertilizer or sprays applied, etc.

4. Enclose a self-addressed stamped envelope for their reply. *Mail as soon as possible.*

Weeds

Weeds are really any plants that are growing out of place. Their beginnings may include tomato or other vegetable seeds that survived composting, manures containing weed seeds, and runners from mint plants or dill seeds that'll take over the beds. For control I recommend pulling out weeds and not using herbicides. Herbicides will wipe out your vegetables along with the weeds, besides possibly being poisonous to us humans. You may also mulch your growing beds, as well as avoiding manures with weed seeds.

Further Reading

If you want to do your own disease identification in greater depth, I recommend the *Plant Disease Handbook* by Cynthia Westcott, published by Van Nostrand Reinhold Company. It's a large, extensive book that is easy to understand once you grasp its basic vocabulary. She has listed every plant disease you could ever imagine, and then some.

EPILOGUE: THE FUTURE

The future ... that twilight zone which has no memory ... always approaching but never arriving. Being a former science fiction nut, I can't help but speculate a bit. If any of you are a time-traveling visitor from the future, I invite you to get in touch with me and correct my speculations.

In the near future, I see more community-type solar greenhouses, much like the one I have been directing. I believe every neighborhood can use something similar to the Cheyenne, Wyoming, project. Community greenhouses can be adapted easily to the needs of different neighborhoods, and even to the different cultures, ages and abilities of the people involved. Many universities offer degrees and study programs in horticultural therapy, and the solar greenhouse offers an ideal environment for year-round gardening therapy for those with varying disabilities—besides providing food, heat and employment.

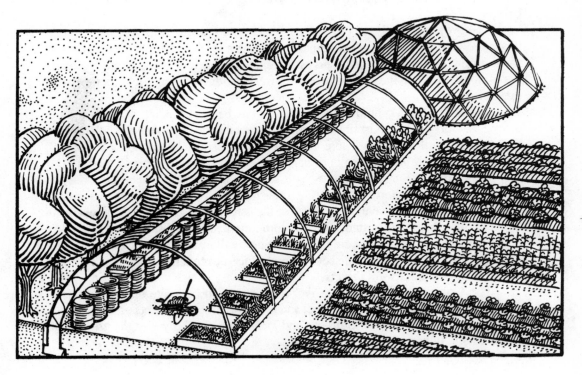

Profile of a Community Solar Greenhouse: The Cheyenne Experience

The Cheyenne Community Solar Greenhouse planted its first crop in January, 1978. It is sponsored by Community Action of Laramie County, Inc. (CALC) and received initial funds from the Community Services Administration under a Community Food and Nutrition Program grant. The Cheyenne Greenhouse is a prototype, the first of its kind in the country. Most of the greenhouse construction occurred in 1977 and was supervised by two carpenter-foremen. A large part of the labor was volunteered by senior citizens, local skilled workers, and handicapped workers. Many of the construction materials were donated, recycled or obtained at lower costs. It was truly a community effort.

The Cheyenne Greenhouse is a three-sectioned, 5,000 square foot, 100% passively heated structure. Solar heat is collected and stored in more than 200 55-gallon drums containing water and painted black. The glazings are fiberglass on the exterior and polyethylene on the interior (both are greenhouse grade). The north, east and west walls, as well as the roof, are heavily insulated. The north wall is slightly earth bermed. The passive system performs so well that the greenhouse has never had to rely on back-up heating—even during record cold winters. Cheyenne ranks fourth highest in the nation for yearly average wind speed.

One section of the greenhouse is commercial. Bedding plants, vegetable seedlings, cut flowers, potted plants and growing accessories are sold to the public out of a small store area. Volunteers provide most of the labor. All profits supplement the greenhouse operating budget, covering 20% - 30% of the total operating budget.

The project initially served low income senior citizens who volunteered their labor to do daily greenhouse maintenance. In return for their efforts, they took home fresh produce. The greenhouse serves more than 100 senior citizens either directly (as a labor force) or indirectly (receiving fresh produce through low income food programs).

Currently, the Community Greenhouse has been expanded to involve youth offenders working off court fines, and handicapped people who receive job training and horticultural therapy. There is an excellent social interaction between all involved, which is uncommon in a society where young and old rarely mix.

Being the nation's first large scale solar greenhouse, it's been necessary to develop several new horticultural techniques for the different environments created within the large solar greenhouse. Because the safety of pesticides is questionable in a greenhouse that is in constant use by community people, the staff has developed a poisonless system of pest control. The use of new cultural techniques and the release of many different beneficial insects have produced excellent results in controlling the populations of harmful insects.

The Community Greenhouse is a solar demonstration site that thousands of people visit yearly to actually see, feel and learn the simple concepts of passive solar energy. The school system, churches and local clubs regularly visit the greenhouse for tours and talks on its many programs.

Surrounding the greenhouse are twenty-four 10' x 30' community gardens where low income people without land can grow their own foods. Other outside gardens, which are managed cooperatively, also surround the greenhouse. In 1980 the greenhouse and outside gardens together produced more than 20,000 lbs. of fresh produce.

Recently we began to move into new areas. A beekeeping demonstration project was initiated to train low income people in honey production. The beehives are at the greenhouse site and the bees provide pollination for the outdoor community gardens. A cold frame season extender project, using low-cost conventional structures and easy-to-build geodesic domes, is demonstrating ways to add 5 months to Cheyenne's short, cold growing season. The greenhouse also sponsors an annual farmers' market at a local park where regional gardeners sell their fresh produce directly to the community. The market has been very successful, with as many as 3,000 participants in one morning of sales.

Now being planned is the nation's first community root cellar where individual gardeners and the greenhouse can store their excess produce for later distribution to food programs. (Root crops are the best producers in Cheyenne's short growing season). A root cellar requires no outside energy to function and is an ideal way to store many crops.

CALC and the Cheyenne Community Solar Greenhouse believe the community solar greenhouse concept can be successfully applied to many other communities with similar, excellent results. They have a prepared slide show and audio tape presentation to help other communities plan such a project.

As food prices rise and people become more interested in home food production for economic and quality reasons, the solar greenhouse will become the keystone of a family food operation. Along with it will come some nice lifestyle changes, as any present greenhouse owner can vouch for.

The yield of crops grown in the solar greenhouse could be greatly increased if there were a concerted effort to breed plants that are better adapted to the solar greenhouse environment. Overall yields can potentially increase by 30-40 percent. The problem is to convince seed companies and government and university breeding programs that this is a worthwhile investment.

Another way to increase solar greenhouse yields is to utilize permaculture crops as outlined in *Crops*. This also requires a concerted effort, as well as getting people to eat new and different foods. In the near future—and we're now beginning to see it—the solar greenhouse will greatly affect our outside environment as people in large numbers propagate vegetables and flowers and even trees for their outside gardens. Plants that are already well established when they're transplanted outside, produce higher yields in a shorter period of time.

As people develop closer relationships with their greenhouse ecology, a logical step may be to attach homes onto large greenhouses rather than to attach a small greenhouse to a single home. Living space will then begin to spill into the greenhouse, with possible greenhouse kitchens, living rooms and bedrooms. To choose to live in a home attached to a large greenhouse, the inhabitants would have to commit themselves to change. More than one home might be attached to a large greenhouse, with gardening done either communally or on separate plots. Areas could be set aside for permaculture, wild gardens, annual gardens, fish production, hot tubs, and livestock. By somehow incorporating livestock grazing inside a large greenhouse, the livestock would have a much better feed-to-food conversion ratio, because they would not be burning as many calories to keep warm in winter—and they'd also provide added CO_2 for plants.

The culture of fish in water tanks already has been practiced successfully by a number of individuals and groups. The management of fish production is as complex as vegetables, if not more so. Fish have detailed biological requirements which must be met. The fish generally feed on algae, as well as nutrients added to the water. In turn, they provide an efficient source of protein (fish meat) in the greenhouse. For more information on fish culture, see references at the end of this section.

Another possible idea for future greenhouses is algae production for *human* consumption—a very direct food conversion. As mentioned in the permaculture section of *Crops*, a suitable algae for greenhouse production would have to be either developed or found. There may be a problem with toxic algae species contaminating edible types, but the overall culture and management may be simpler than fish culture. It could become an excellent source of protein for people, or fertilizer for plants. At the 1981 Great Lakes Solar Greenhouse Conference in Kalamazoo, Michigan, I chaired a discussion group on the topic of Futuristic Concepts. During that discussion a wild idea evolved of utilizing edible, phosphorescent algae that commonly live (and glow) in the oceans, not only as a greenhouse food source, but as a supplementary light source. They would be cultured in clear tanks, where they could light up the greenhouse (or at least portions of it) all night long, absolutely free. This idea would take a lot of research and possibly selective algae breeding—which would be quite complex and time consuming. I know it sounds kind of crazy, but who knows?

The future will also provide us with some interesting new glazing materials. They will have amazing abilities to handle and manage both light and heat. They may be permeable to certain gases such as CO_2 or water vapor, and possibly they will be of very high strength. Such a tough, versatile glazing could greatly alter both the horticulture of greenhouse plants and overall greenhouse design. Large areas could then be covered with much less structure. A "greenhouse" could even someday cover many acres of farm or city, creating a controlled environment for large scale agriculture or urban pursuits. And soon we will probably begin to see new phase-change materials which are relatively cheap, take up much less space than thermal mass and very efficiently store the sun's heat.

Hopefully in the near future both large and small solar greenhouses will be available in low cost, kit versions. It may mean less of the beautiful custom designs, but it may enable more people to afford greenhouses or to afford larger greenhouses onto which they can attach their homes. The larger ones will probably be of either geodesic or quonset designs. They'll include some north wall insulation, double glazing, foundation insulation, thermal storage and possibly night insulation. Besides the advantage of lower cost, they'll go up in days rather than in weeks or months.

As we work more with the concept of biological, solar heated shelters, many of these concepts will someday be put into use in space. Orbiting communities in space is now an idea that's taken seriously by many people. A self-contained food producing system will be a key to the idea becoming a reality. It will be exciting to watch it evolve. Hopefully we will preserve a respect for biology, nature and human happiness throughout the evolution.

In the future, it's important to ensure that the benefits of solar greenhouse food and heat production be available to all classes of society. The changes brought so far have been wonderful. The solar greenhouse is here to stay, and will continue to provide for our physical needs, as well as add to our mental well being and creativity. It will constantly help us renew our connection to the earth, the heavens and to our own family and friends.

References for the Future

Seaweed in Agriculture and Horticulture prepared by W. A. Stephenson. Published by Bargyla and Gylver Rateaver, Puma Valley, CA 92061.

Fish Farming in Your Solar Greenhouse by William Head and Joe Splane. Published by Amity Foundation, P.O. Box 7066, Eugene, OR 97401.

Co Evolution Quarterly, P. O. Box 428, Sausalito, CA 94965. This journal will keep you stimulated and up to date about tomorrow as well as today.

We Grow Things, an audio slide show. This is an oral and visual history of the Cheyenne Community Solar Greenhouse. It makes a great organizing tool for interested groups. Available from Community Action of Laramie county, 1603 Central Ave., Cheyenne, WY 82001.

Seedpeople Associates, a consulting cooperative of specialists in the many fields of community based agriculture including: community greenhouses and outside gardens, greenhouse design and operation, biological pest controls, horticultural therapy, perma-culture, turtle management, small scale commercial agriculture, lectures and workshops. Contact Seedpeople, Shane Smith, c/o John Muir Publications, Box 613, Santa Fe, NM 87501.

The Journal of the New Alchemists by the New Alchemy Institute, P.O. Box 432, Woods Hole, MA 02543.

Tomorrow is Our Permanent Address by John Todd and Nancy Jack Todd, published by Harper and Row, 1980.

Appendix A

─── Seed Catalogs ───

Abundant Life Seed Foundation
P.O. Box 772
Port Townsend, WA 98368

A non-profit group that sells primarily to the north Pacific coast area. Beautiful catalog—their seeds are adapted to the winter solar greenhouse.

Bruinsma Seed Co.
6346 Avon Beldon Rd.
North Ridgeville, OH 44039

This address is the distributor for a European seed company that is much like Rijk Zwaan. Their selection is smaller, but they carry some good varieties for greenhouses. The price is a bit expensive however.

Burpee Seed Co.
Warminster, PA 18991

Wide selection of vegetables. A few greenhouse crops. Owned by ITT.

Cameron Seeds
4141 Springhill Road
Bozeman, MT 59715

They have tried to offer seeds that are adapted to the solar greenhouse, cold frames, and short season areas. Sometimes I get the feeling that they haven't tried some of the things they are offering. In the near future, with more experience I see them becoming an important source of seeds. Catalog is $1.00.

Carobil Farms
Church Rd., Rt. 1
Brunswick, ME 04011

Specializing in popular, rare and scented geraniums.

Casa Yerba
Star Rt 2, Box 21
Days Creek, OR 97429

Herbs, unusual and rare seeds.

William Dam Seeds Limited
Highway #8
P.O. West Flamboro
Ontario, LOR 2K0 Canada

Untreated vegetable, flower and herb seed. Interesting European strains.

Dean Foster Nurseries
Hartford, MI 49057

Specializing in strawberries. They have some day-neutral varieties for the greenhouse.

J.A. Demonchaux Co.
827 N. Kansas
Topeka, KS 66608

Selection of French vegetables.

Epicure Seeds
Box 69
Avon, NY 14414

Selection of European vegetable seeds.

Exotica Seed Co.
1742 Laurel Canyon Rd.
Los Angeles, CA 90046

Sub-tropical and tropical plants.

Continued . . .

Appendix A *(Cont'd)*

H. G. Hastings Co.
P.O. Box 4274
Atlanta, GA 30302

Good for bolt resistant greens.

Herbst Brothers Seedsmen
1000 N. Main St.
Brewster, NY 10509

Excellent choice of disease tolerant varieties (see tomatoes). Also European cucumbers.

Horticultural Enterprises
P.O. Box 34082
Dallas, TX 75234

Best selection of different peppers and chilis. Also Mexican vegetables and herbs.

J. L. Hudson Seedsman
P.O. Box 1058
Redwood City, CA 94064

Rare and unusual seeds; vegetables, imported varieties, medicinal and dye herbs.

Hurvous Tropical Seeds
P.O. Box 10387
Honolulu, Oahu, HI 96816

Tropical seeds.

Le Jardin Du Gourmet
Box 51
West Danville, VT 05873

Imported vegetable seeds, shallots, herbs.

Johnny's Selected Seeds
Albion, ME 04910

"Organically" grown seeds, short season varieties for the north.

Kilgore Seed Co.
1400 W. First St.
Sanford, FL 32771

Vegetables, herbs, botanical pesticides, nice information on planting by the moon.

Kitazawa Seed Co.
356 W. Taylor St.
San Jose, CA 95110

Wide selection of oriental vegetables.

Lowdens Better Plants and Seeds
Box 10
Ancaster, Ontario L9G 3L3
Canada

Northern adaptive hardy tomatoes and raspberries.

Mountain Seed & Nursery
Route 1, Box 271
Moscow, ID 83843

Varieties for short season areas.

Nichols Garden Nursery
1190 N. Pacific Hwy
Albany, OR 97321

This is one of my favorite catalogs. They have excellent choices for the greenhouse as well as oriental, gourmet and odd vegetables. Their herb selection is one of the best. Read it cover to cover.

Continued . . .

Appendix A *(Cont'd)*

Porter & Son Seedsmen
1510 E. Washington St.
Stephenville, TX 76401

Good heat tolerant tomatoes and disease resistant melons.

Redwood City Seed Co.
P.O. Box 361
Redwood City, CA 94064

Tropicals.

Seed Savers Exchange
Kent Whealy
RFD 2
Princeton, MO 64673

This is a catalog where anyone can trade, look for, or sell old heirloom, unusual, rare or local seed varieties. It is also full of information and news concerning seeds. They have already saved many varieties headed for extinction. Send $5.00 donation to get catalog.

Stark Bros. Nurseries
Louisiana, MO 63353

Popular temperate zone fruit. They have fig trees.

Stokes Seeds Inc.
Box 548
Buffalo, NY 14240

One of the best for the solar greenhouse. Wide choice of everything. Many varieties are specifically for greenhouse culture. Good sections on tomato, cucumber, lettuce and flowers.

Thompson & Morgan
P.O. Box 100
Farmingdale, NJ 07727

Somewhat expensive but interesting selection. Many European varieties. Take the claims with a grain of salt. Has many good vegetable varieties that can't be found anywhere else.

Otis Twilley Seed Co.
P.O. Box 65
Trevose, PA 19047

Good selection for greenhouse. Many disease tolerant varieties.

K. Van Bourgondien & Sons
245 Farmingdale Rd.
Babylon, NY 11702

Specializes in bulbs and ornamentals, also some interesting tropicals.

Rijk Zwaan
Zaadteelt en Zaadhandel B.V.
De Lier, Holland

These folks are far ahead of us in growing food under glass. They have a number of different crops developed for under-glass production.

Appendix B

Garden Planning and Planting Guide
Nutritional Value of Selected Vegetables

Nutritional group	Vegetable	Vitamin content A (I.U.)	C (mg.)	Food energy (calories)
Group I	Parsley (raw)	8,500	172	44
High in Vitamins A and C	Spinach	8,100	28	23
	Collards	7,800	76	33
	Kale	7,400	62	28
	Turnip Greens	6,300	69	20
	Mustard Greens	5,800	48	23
	Cantaloupes	3,400	33	30
	Broccoli	2,500	90	26
Group II	Carrots (raw)	11,000	8	42
High in Vitamin A	Carrots (cooked)	10,500	6	31
	Sweet potatoes	8,100	22	141
	Swiss Chard	5,400	16	18
	Winter Squash	4,200	13	63
	Green Onions	2,000	32	36
Group III	Peppers (mature green)	420	128	22
High in Vitamin C	Brussels Sprouts	520	87	36
	Cauliflower	60	55	22
	Kohlrabi	20	43	24
	Cabbage	130	33	20
	Chinese Cabbage	150	25	14
	Asparagus	900	26	20
	Rutabagas	550	26	35
	Radishes (raw)	322	26	17
	Tomatoes (ripe, raw)	900	23	22
	Tomatoes (ripe, cooked)	1,000	24	26
Group IV	Green Beans	540	12	25
Other Green Vegetables	Celery	240	9	17
	Lettuce (leaf)	1,900	18	18
	Lettuce (head)	330	6	13
	Okra	490	20	29
	Peas (garden)	540	20	71

Appendix B *(Cont'd)*

Garden Planning and Planting Guide
┌──Nutritional Value of Selected Vegetables──┐

Nutritional group	Vegetable	Vitamin content A (I.U.)	C (mg.)	Food energy (calories)
Group V	Lima Beans	280	17	111
Starchy Vegetables	Sweet Corn (yellow)	400	9	91
	Onions (dry)	40	10	38
	Peas (field, southern)	350	17	108
	Potatoes (baked in skin)	Trace	20	93
Group VI	Beets	20	6	32
Other Vegetables	Cucumbers	250	11	15
(plant from this group	Eggplants	10	3	19
for variety in flavor,	Pumpkins	1,600	9	26
color, texture, etc.)	Rhubarb	80	6	141
	Summer Squash	440	11	15
	Turnips (roots)	Trace	22	23

Figures are for amounts of vitamins and calories per 100-gram sample for cooked vegetables (unless normally eaten raw). Vitamin A is expressed in International Units (I. U.) per 100-gram sample; Vitamin C is expressed in milligrams per 100-gram sample; and Food Energy is expressed in Bilogram calories per 100-gram sample.

100 grams is equal to about ½ cup.

Active adults require daily about 5,000 I.U. of vitamin A for men and 4,000 for women; 45 mg. of vitamin C (men and women); and 2,700 calories for men and 2,000 for women.

Vitamin C values are generally higher if the vegetable is eaten raw. An example is cabbage: 33 mg. cooked; 47 mg. raw.

From USDA Yearbook of Agriculture 1977.

Appendix C

──NOAA Weather Radio Stations as of 1981──

Alabama
Anniston
Birmingham
Demopolis
Dozier
Florence
Huntsville
Louisville
Mobile
Montgomery
Tuscaloosa

Alaska
Anchorage
Cordova
Fairbanks
Homer
Juneau
Ketchikan
Kodiak
Nome
Petersburg
Seward
Sitka
Valdez
Wrangell
Yakutat

Arizona
Flagstaff
Phoenix
Tucson
Yuma (P)

Arkansas
Ash Flat
Fayetteville
Fort Smith
Gurdon
Jonesboro
Little Rock
Star City
Texarkana

California
Bakersfield (P)
Barstow
Coachella (P)
Eureka
Fresno
Los Angeles
Merced
Monterey
Point Arena
Redding (P)
Sacramento
San Diego
San Francisco
San Luis Obispo
Santa Barbara

Colorado
Alamosa (P)
Colorado Springs
Denver
Grand Junction

Greeley
Longmont
Pueblo
Sterling

Connecticut
Hartford
Meriden
New London

Delaware
Lewes

Dist. of Columbia
Washington

Florida
Daytona Beach
Fort Myers
Gainesville
Jacksonville
Key West
Melbourne
Miami
Orlando
Panama City
Pensacola
Tallahassee
Tampa
West Palm Beach
Clewiston

Georgia
Athens
Atlanta
Augusta
Chatsworth
Columbus
Macon
Pelham
Savannah
Waycross

Hawaii
Hilo
Honolulu
Kokee
Mt. Haleakala
Waimanalo (R)

Idaho
Boise
Lewiston (P)
Pocatello
Twin Falls

Illinois
Champaign
Chicago
Marion
Moline
Peoria
Rockford
Springfield

Indiana
Evansville
Fort Wayne

Indianapolis
Lafayette
South Bend
Terre Haute

Iowa
Cedar Rapids
Des Moines
Dubuque (P)
Fort Dodge
Sioux City
Waterloo

Kansas
Chanute
Colby
Concordia
Dodge City
Ellsworth
Topeka
Wichita

Kentucky
Ashland
Bowling Green
Covington
Elizabethtown (R)
Hazard
Lexington
Louisville
Mayfield
Pikeville (R)
Somerset

Louisiana
Alexandria
Baton Rouge
Buras
Lafayette
Lake Charles
Morgan City
New Orleans
Monroe
Shreveport

Maine
Ellsworth
Portland

Maryland
Baltimore
Hagerstown
Salisbury

Massachusetts
Boston
Hyannis
Worcester

Michigan
Alpena
Detroit
Flint
Grand Rapids
Houghton
Onondaga
Sault Ste Marie
Traverse City
Marquette

Minnesota
Duluth
Int'l Falls
Mankato
Minneapolis
Rochester
Saint Cloud (P)
Thief River Falls
Willmar (P)

Mississippi
Ackerman
Booneville
Bude
Columbia (R)
Gulfport
Hattiesburg
Inverness
Jackson
Meridian
Oxford

Missouri
Camdenton
Columbia
Hannibal
Joplin/Carthage
Kansas City
St. Joseph
St. Louis
Sikeston
Springfield

Montana
Billings
Butte
Glasgow
Great Falls
Havre (P)
Helena
Kalispell
Miles City
Missoula

Nebraska
Bassett
Grand Island
Holdrege
Lincoln
Merriman
Norfolk
North Platte
Omaha
Scottsbluff

Nevada
Elko
Ely
Las Vegas
Reno
Winnemucca

New Hampshire
Concord

New Jersey
Atlantic City

New Mexico
Albuquerque
Clovis
Des Moines
Farmington
Hobbs
Las Cruces
Ruidoso
Santa Fe

New York
Albany
Binghamton
Buffalo
Elmira
Kingston
Rochester
Syracuse
New York City

North Carolina
Asheville
Cape Hatteras
Charlotte
Fayetteville
New Berne
Raleigh/Durham
Rocky Mount
Wilmington
Winston-Salem

North Dakota
Bismarck
Dickinson
Fargo
Jamestown
Minot
Petersburg
Williston

Ohio
Akron
Caldwell
Cleveland
Columbus
Dayton
Lima
Sandusky
Toledo

Oklahoma
Clinton
Enid
Lawton
McAlester
Oklahoma City
Tulsa

Oregon
Astoria
Brookings
Coos Bay
Eugene
Klamath Falls
Medford
Newport
Pendleton

Appendix C *(Cont'd)*

—NOAA Weather Radio Stations as of 1981—

Oregon *(con't)*
Portland
Redmond
Roseburg
Salem

Pennsylvania
Allentown
Clearfield
Erie
Harrisburg
Johnstown
Philadelphia
Pittsburgh
Wilkes-Barre
Williamsport (P)
State College

Puerto Rico
Maricao
San Juan

Rhode Island
Providence

South Carolina
Beaufort
Charleston
Columbia
Florence
Greenville
Myrtle Beach
Sumter (R)

South Dakota
Aberdeen
Huron
Pierre
Rapid City
Sioux Falls

Tennessee
Bristol
Chattanooga
Cookville
Jackson
Knoxville
Memphis

Nashville
Shelbyville
Waverly

Texas
Abilene
Amarillo
Austin
Beaumont (P)
Big Spring
Brownsville
Bryan
Corpus Christi
Dallas
Del Rio (P)
El Paso
Fort Worth
Galveston
Houston
Laredo
Lufkin
Lubbock
Midland
Paris

Pharr
San Angelo
San Antonio
Sherman
Tyler
Victoria
Waco
Wichita Falls

Utah
Logan
Milford
Roosevelt
Salt Lake City

Vermont
Burlington
Windsor

Virginia
Heathsville
Lynchburg
Norfolk
Richmond
Roanoke

Washington
Neah Bay
Seattle
Spokane
Wenatchee
Yakima

West Virginia
Charleston
Clarksburg

Wisconsin
Green Bay
La Crosse (P)
Madison
Menomonie
Milwaukee
Wausau

Wyoming
Casper
Cheyenne
Lander
Rawlins
Rock Springs
Sheridan (P)

Notes: (1) Stations marked (R) are low powered experimental repeater stations serving a very limited local area. (2) Stations marked (P) operate less than 24 hours/day. However, hours are extended when possible during severe weather. (3) Occasionally the frequency of an existing or planned station must be changed because of unexpected radio frequency interference with adjacent NOAA Weather Radio stations and/or with other government or commercial operators within the same area. (4) The list of operating stations is updated periodically. For a current list please write: NOAA, National Weather Service, 8060 13th St., Silver Spring, MD, 20910, Attn: W112.

Appendix D

Average Percentage of Possible Sunshine
For Selected Locations

The average monthly percentage of sunshine available in cities throughout the United States.

LOCATION	JAN	FEB	MAR	APR	MAY	JUN	JUL	AUG	SEP	OCT	NOV	DEC	ANN
ALA. BIRMINGHAM	43	49	56	63	66	67	62	65	66	67	58	44	59
MONTGOMERY	51	53	61	69	73	72	66	69	69	71	64	48	64
ALASKA, ANCHORAGE	39	46	56	58	50	51	45	39	35	32	33	29	45
FAIRBANKS	34	50	61	68	55	53	45	35	31	28	38	29	44
JUNEAU	30	32	39	37	34	35	28	30	25	18	21	18	30
NOME	44	46	48	53	51	48	32	26	34	35	36	30	41
ARIZ. PHOENIX	76	79	83	88	93	94	84	84	89	88	84	77	85
YUMA	83	87	91	94	97	98	92	91	93	93	90	83	91
ARK. LITTLE ROCK	44	53	57	62	67	72	71	73	71	74	62	47	62
CALIF. EUREKA	40	44	50	53	54	56	51	46	52	48	42	39	49
FRESNO	46	63	72	83	89	94	97	97	93	87	73	47	78
LOS ANGELES	70	69	70	67	68	69	80	81	80	76	79	72	73
RED BLUFF	50	60	65	75	79	86	95	94	89	77	64	50	75
SACRAMENTO	44	57	67	76	82	90	96	95	92	82	65	44	77
SAN DIEGO	68	67	68	66	60	60	67	70	70	70	76	71	68
SAN FRANCISCO	53	57	63	69	70	75	68	63	70	70	62	54	66
COLO. DENVER	67	67	65	63	61	69	68	68	71	71	67	65	67
GRAND JUNCTION	58	62	64	67	71	79	76	72	77	74	67	58	69
CONN. HARTFORD	46	55	56	54	57	60	62	60	57	55	46	46	56
D.C. WASHINGTON	46	53	56	57	61	64	64	62	62	61	54	47	58
FLA. APALACHICOLA	59	62	62	71	77	70	64	63	62	74	66	53	65
JACKSONVILLE	58	59	66	71	71	63	62	63	58	58	61	53	62
KEY WEST	68	75	78	78	76	70	69	71	65	65	69	66	71
MIAMI BEACH	66	72	73	73	68	62	65	67	62	62	65	65	67
TAMPA	63	67	71	74	75	66	61	64	64	67	67	64	68
GA. ATLANTA	48	53	57	65	68	68	62	63	65	67	60	47	60
HAWAII. HILO	48	42	41	34	31	41	44	38	42	41	34	36	39
HONOLULU	62	64	60	62	64	66	67	70	70	68	63	60	65
LIHUE	48	48	48	46	51	60	58	59	67	58	51	49	54
IDAHO. BOISE	40	48	59	67	68	75	89	86	81	66	46	37	66
POCATELLO	37	47	58	64	66	72	82	81	78	66	48	36	64
ILL. CAIRO	46	53	59	65	71	77	82	79	75	73	56	46	65
CHICAGO	44	49	53	56	63	69	73	70	65	61	47	41	59
SPRINGFIELD	47	51	54	58	64	69	76	72	73	64	53	45	60
IND. EVANSVILLE	42	49	55	61	67	73	78	76	73	67	52	42	64
FT. WAYNE	38	44	51	55	62	69	74	69	64	58	41	38	57
INDIANAPOLIS	41	47	49	55	62	68	74	70	68	64	48	39	59
IOWA. DES MOINES	56	56	56	59	62	66	75	70	64	64	53	48	62
DUBUQUE	48	52	52	58	60	63	73	67	61	59	44	40	57
SIOUX CITY	55	58	58	59	63	67	75	72	67	65	53	50	63
KANS. CONCORDIA	60	60	62	63	65	73	79	76	72	70	64	58	67
DODGE CITY	67	66	68	68	68	74	78	78	76	75	70	67	71
WICHITA	61	63	64	64	66	73	80	77	73	69	67	59	69
KY. LOUISVILLE	41	47	52	57	64	68	72	69	68	64	51	39	59
LA. NEW ORLEANS	49	50	57	63	66	64	58	60	64	70	60	46	59
SHREVEPORT	48	54	58	60	69	78	79	80	79	77	65	60	69
MAINE. EASTPORT	45	51	52	52	51	53	55	57	54	50	37	40	50
MASS. BOSTON	47	56	57	56	59	62	64	63	61	58	48	48	57
MICH. ALPENA	29	43	52	56	56	60	64	70	64	52	44	24	51
DETROIT	34	42	48	52	58	65	69	66	61	54	35	29	53
GRAND RAPIDS	26	37	48	54	60	66	72	67	58	50	31	22	49
MARQUETTE	31	40	47	52	53	56	63	57	47	38	24	24	47
S. STE. MARIE	28	44	50	54	54	59	63	58	45	36	21	22	47
MINN. DULUTH	47	55	60	58	58	60	68	63	53	47	36	40	55
MINNEAPOLIS	49	54	55	57	60	64	72	69	60	54	40	40	56
MISS. VICKSBURG	46	50	57	64	69	73	69	72	74	71	60	45	64
MO. KANSAS CITY	55	57	59	60	64	70	76	73	70	67	59	52	65
ST. LOUIS	48	49	56	59	64	68	72	68	67	65	54	44	61
SPRINGFIELD	48	54	57	60	53	69	77	72	71	65	54	48	63
MONT. HAVRE	49	58	61	63	63	65	78	75	64	57	48	46	62
HELENA	46	55	58	59	59	63	77	74	63	57	48	43	60
KALISPELL	28	40	49	57	58	60	77	73	61	50	28	20	53
NEBR. LINCOLN	57	59	60	60	63	69	71	67	66	59	55	56	64
NORTH PLATTE	63	63	64	62	64	72	78	74	72	70	62	58	68
NEV. ELY	61	64	68	65	67	79	79	81	81	73	67	62	72
LAS VEGAS	74	77	78	81	85	91	84	86	92	84	83	75	82
RENO	59	64	69	75	77	82	90	89	86	76	68	56	76
WINNEMUCCA	52	60	64	70	76	83	90	90	86	75	62	53	74
N.H. CONCORD	48	53	55	53	51	56	57	58	55	50	43	43	52
N.J. ATLANTIC CITY	51	57	58	59	62	65	67	66	65	54	58	52	60
N. MEX. ALBUQUERQUE	70	72	72	76	79	84	76	75	81	80	79	70	76
ROSWELL	69	72	75	77	76	80	76	75	74	74	74	69	74
N.Y. ALBANY	43	51	53	53	57	62	63	61	58	54	39	38	53
BINGHAMTON	31	39	41	44	50	56	54	51	47	43	29	26	44
BUFFALO	32	41	49	51	59	67	70	67	60	51	31	28	53
CANTON	37	47	50	48	54	61	63	61	54	45	30	31	49
NEW YORK	49	56	57	59	62	65	66	64	64	61	53	50	59
SYRACUSE	31	38	45	50	58	64	67	63	56	47	29	26	50
N.C. ASHEVILLE	48	53	56	61	64	63	59	59	62	64	59	48	58
RALEIGH	50	56	59	64	67	65	62	62	63	64	62	52	61
N. DAK. BISMARCK	52	58	56	57	58	61	73	69	62	59	49	48	59
DEVILS LAKE	53	60	59	60	59	62	71	67	59	56	44	45	58
FARGO	47	55	56	58	62	63	73	69	60	57	39	46	59
WILLISTON	51	59	60	63	66	66	78	75	65	60	48	48	63
OHIO, CINCINNATI	41	46	52	56	62	69	72	68	68	60	46	39	57
CLEVELAND	29	36	45	52	61	67	71	68	62	54	32	25	50
COLUMBUS	36	44	49	54	63	68	71	68	66	60	44	35	55
OKLA. OKLAHOMA CITY	57	60	63	64	65	74	78	78	74	68	64	57	68
OREG. BAKER	41	49	56	61	63	67	83	81	74	62	46	37	60
PORTLAND	27	34	41	49	52	55	70	65	55	42	28	23	48
ROSEBURG	24	32	40	51	57	59	79	77	68	42	28	18	51
PA. HARRISBURG	43	52	55	57	61	65	68	63	62	58	47	43	57
PHILADELPHIA	45	56	57	58	61	62	64	61	62	61	53	49	57
PITTSBURG	32	39	45	50	57	62	64	61	62	54	39	30	51
R.I. BLOCK ISLAND	45	54	57	56	60	62	62	60	59	59	50	44	56
S.C. CHARLESTON	58	60	65	72	73	70	66	66	67	68	68	57	66
COLUMBIA	53	57	62	68	69	68	63	65	64	68	64	51	63
S. DAK. HURON	55	62	60	62	63	68	76	72	66	61	52	49	63
RAPID CITY	58	62	63	62	61	66	73	73	69	66	58	54	64
TENN. KNOXVILLE	42	49	53	59	64	66	64	59	64	64	53	41	57
MEMPHIS	44	51	57	64	68	74	73	74	70	69	58	45	64
NASHVILLE	42	47	54	60	65	69	69	68	65	65	55	42	59
TEX. ABILENE	64	68	73	66	73	81	78	78	73	71	72	66	73
AMARILLO	71	71	75	75	75	82	81	81	79	76	76	70	76
AUSTIN	46	50	57	60	62	72	76	79	70	70	57	49	63
BROWNSVILLE	44	49	51	57	65	73	78	74	67	70	54	44	61
DEL RIO	53	55	61	63	60	66	75	80	69	66	58	52	63
EL PASO	74	77	81	85	87	87	78	78	80	82	80	73	80
FT. WORTH	56	57	65	66	67	75	78	74	70	70	63	58	68
GALVESTON	50	50	55	61	69	76	72	71	70	74	62	49	63
SAN ANTONIO	48	51	56	58	60	69	74	75	69	67	55	49	62
UTAH, SALT LAKE CITY	48	53	61	63	73	78	82	82	84	73	53	44	66
VT. BURLINGTON	34	43	48	47	53	59	62	59	51	43	25	24	46
VA. NORFOLK	50	57	60	63	67	66	66	66	63	64	60	50	61
RICHMOND	49	55	59	63	67	66	65	62	63	64	58	50	61
WASH. NORTH HEAD	28	37	42	48	48	48	50	46	48	41	31	27	41
SEATTLE	27	34	42	48	53	48	62	56	53	36	28	24	45
SPOKANE	26	41	53	63	64	68	82	79	68	53	28	22	58
TATOOSH ISLAND	26	36	39	45	47	46	48	44	47	38	26	23	40
WALLA WALLA	24	35	51	63	67	72	86	84	72	59	33	20	60
YAKIMA	34	49	62	70	72	74	86	86	74	61	38	29	65
W. VA. ELKINS	33	37	42	47	55	55	56	53	55	51	41	33	48
PARKERSBURG	30	36	42	49	56	60	63	60	60	53	37	29	48
WIS. GREEN BAY	44	51	55	56	58	64	70	65	58	52	40	40	55
MADISON	44	49	52	53	58	64	71	68	62	58	43	38	56
MILWAUKEE	44	48	53	56	60	65	73	67	62	56	44	39	57
WYO. CHEYENNE	65	66	64	61	59	68	70	68	69	60	65	63	66
LANDER	66	70	71	66	65	74	76	75	72	67	61	62	69
SHERIDAN	56	61	62	61	61	67	76	74	67	60	53	52	64
YELLOWSTONE PARK	39	51	55	57	56	63	73	71	65	57	45	38	56
P.R. SAN JUAN	64	69	71	66	59	62	65	67	61	63	65	65	65

Index

If you would like another copy or copies of *The Bountiful Solar Greenhouse* by Shane Smith, please fill out the form below and send it and your check or money order to:

John Muir Publications
P.O. Box 613-BG
Santa Fe, NM 87501

Ship to: _____

    Address _____

        City _____ State _____ Zip _____

_____

Please send _____ copies of *The Bountiful
Solar Greenhouse* @ $8.00 each.   Total _____
Postage ($1.50 for first copy, .50 for each additional
copy)   Total _____

Add 34¢ per copy for tax if you live in
Sunny New Mexico   Total _____

        Total Enclosed _____

7 4 3
6 8 1

7 4 3
6 8 1
$ 15.⁰⁰

62 miles
15 mpg

4 | 6 2
4
22
20

15